TALES OF TWO CITIES

TALES OF TWO CITIES

CHRISTIANITY AND POLITICS

Edited by
Stephen Clark

INTER-VARSITY PRESS
38 De Montfort Street, Leicester LE1 7GP, England
Email: ivp@ivp-editorial.co.uk
Website: www.ivpbooks.com

First published 2005

British Library Cataloguing-in-Publication Data
A catalogue record for this book is available from the British Library.

ISBN–10: 1–84474–096–X
ISBN–13: 978–1–84474–096–3

Set in Monotype Garamond 11/13pt
Typeset in Great Britain by Servis Filmsetting Ltd, Manchester
Printed and bound in Great Britain by Ashford Colour Press Ltd,
Gosport, Hampshire

*Inter-Varsity Press is the publishing division of the Universities and Colleges Christian
Fellowship (formerly the Inter-Varsity Fellowship), a student movement linking Christian
Unions in universities and colleges throughout Great Britain, and a member movement of the
International Fellowship of Evangelical Students. For more information about local and
national activities write to UCCF, 38 De Montfort Street, Leicester LE1 7GP, email us at
email@uccf.org.uk, or visit the UCCF website at www.uccf.org.uk.*

CONTENTS

CONTRIBUTORS

Stephen Clark is minister of Freeschool Court Evangelical Church, Bridgend, and was chairman of the Affinity Theological Study Conference, at which the papers forming chapters 1 to 6 in this volume were presented. He studied law and worked as a solicitor before entering the Christian ministry.

David Field is Lecturer in Christian Doctrine and Ethics, Oak Hill Theological College, London.

Paul Helm is emeritus professor, University of London.

David McKay is Professor of Systematic Theology, Ethics and Apologetics, Reformed Theological College, Belfast, and minister of Cregagh Road Reformed Presbyterian Church.

David W. Smith is Lecturer in Urban Mission and World Christianity, International Christian College, Glasgow.

Jonathan Stephen is Director of Affinity.

Gordon Wenham was Senior Professor of Old Testament, University of Gloucestershire, Cheltenham. He has written commentaries on Genesis, Leviticus and Numbers, and a study of Old Testament ethics entitled *Story as Torah*.

Steve Wilmshurst is Director of Training, Kensington Baptist Church, Bristol and Chairman of the Affinity Theological Team.

INTRODUCTION

Jonathan Stephen

Ever since Augustine's monumental exposition of 'The City of God'[1] and its evil antithesis, there have been countless attempts to plot the relationship between the Two Cities. Of perennial concern to writers and preachers have been the status and conduct of Christians caught up in the unavoidable tension resulting from the competing claims of such diametrically opposed realms. While they wait for 'the Holy City, the new Jerusalem'[2] to be finally revealed, how in practice are believers to live out their lives in this fallen world?

In particular, is the world of politics something in which the citizens of heaven should play no active part? Or is it, rather, the sacred duty of the church to bring its enlightening influence to bear on the public affairs of a godless world?[3] How might we nuance a way forward, in a manner which honours the biblical data? Is it remotely possible, after so many centuries of scholarly

---

1. The Bishop of Hippo wrote his great classic in response to the sacking of Rome (AD 410). This profoundly traumatic event was seen by many as a judgment on the Empire's adoption of Christianity. The consequent demise of the Christian faith was widely predicted. There are many fascinating parallels which can be drawn between Augustine's age and ours.

2. Revelation 21:2.

3. It is, perhaps, interesting to note that the word 'politics' derives from *polis*, the Greek word for 'city', while the Greek word *ekklesia*, normally translated 'church', originally referred to the ruling assembly of the *polis*.

debate and disagreement, to reach conclusions with which all
Bible-centred Christians might concur?

Such questions are no longer of mere academic interest.
Christians in the West are increasingly troubled about the nature of
the society in which they live. Waking up from the long sleep of
privatized faith and culturally disengaged pietism has proved to be
a painful process on a number of fronts. For many, having to
watch the systematic dismantling of the remains of Christendom
has been particularly hard to bear. As never before, and with
mounting desperation, Christians are being mobilized to underpin
the crumbling foundations of a society founded and developed on
Christian beliefs and values. And yet, at the same time, others are
much more sanguine. Their attitude to the juggernaut of global-
ized, secular pluralism seems to be 'Bring it on!' Let the stark
distinction between the kingdoms of light and darkness be clearly
seen! Let everyone know that Christ's kingdom is not of this
world![4]

Many thoughtful believers, however, are not satisfied with either
of these alternatives. They are urgently looking for a more convincing explanation of how the Two Cities should relate at this
point and for a more definite understanding of the ultimate goal in
view. Fortunately, between the common – but opposite – reactions
mentioned above, there is plenty of space to do some serious biblical thinking and, thankfully, that is what is beginning to occur.
Inevitably, and rightly, some very old questions are being
unearthed, dusted down and asked all over again. Time-honoured
answers are being critically examined for what they are worth.
Then, of course, several new and significant approaches to the
Bible's teaching on socio-economic and political systems have also
emerged in recent years.

This mixture of old and new is reflected in this symposium.
The distinguished contributors represent a variety of viewpoints.
Those hoping for a grand unified theory will be disappointed –
although the vigorous debates which followed the presentation of
the original papers offered some glimmerings of synthesis! The

---

4. John 18:36.

principal value of the following chapters lies in the combination of biblical and scholarly integrity which they all display. None should therefore be dismissed lightly. Each deserves careful and prayerful consideration. Another feature shared by all the contributors is their commitment to serving the churches. Too many theologians operate as loose cannon, without any sense of accountability. These, at least, have resolved to use their gifts for the building up of God's people. We honour them for that, and thank them for their contributions to this symposium.

These chapters were first presented as papers at a three-day, residential Theological Study Conference organized by Affinity. For those unfamiliar with this recent initiative, a few words of explanation may not be out of place. Affinity is a network of approximately 1,200 churches, located throughout Great Britain and Ireland. It was launched in 2004 in order to promote Bible-centred, Christ-centred, gospel-centred Christianity. We live at a time when majority 'evangelicalism' is no longer defined by what the Bible says but rather by whatever 'evangelicals' choose to believe. Perhaps as a result, there has proved to be a strong desire amongst those who see the necessity of maintaining and proclaiming the objective truths of the gospel for the kind of encouragement Affinity provides.

We aim to act as a catalyst, promoting the exchange of resources between essentially like-minded churches while actively seeking to dismantle the 'glass walls' which can so easily isolate Bible-centred church groupings from one another. Affinity facilitates the formation and development of regional and local church partnerships and is especially concerned to support the planting and recommissioning of congregations who want to bring the gospel to bear on their culture without losing their doctrinal edge.

On behalf of the churches, Affinity is also involved in researching and analysing current thinking and societal trends in the light of Scripture. Part of that brief means keeping its constituency informed of the moral and ethical implications of impending parliamentary legislation. When deemed necessary, we issue statements and make appropriate representation to government departments and the media.

An Affinity theological team is committed to advancing and

deepening an understanding and acceptance of biblical Christianity. Inevitably, it finds itself monitoring the ever-increasing number of challenges to orthodox doctrine which appear to be sheltering under the umbrella of evangelicalism. The effect of the postmodern mindset with which many contemporary theologians approach the biblical data is revealed in the sense of insecurity and uncertainty it eventually produces within the churches. As we cannot be satisfied with the false peace which comes from denying the existence of the propositional truth claims of the Bible, we must therefore work all the harder to clarify, defend and proclaim what the text really says.

Affinity produces a theological journal, *Foundations*, and also *Table Talk*, an occasional theological briefing for church leaders. It also organizes conferences; which brings us back to the subject in hand. One interesting feature of this particular conference was the fact that, although the attendees were mostly experienced pastors and teachers, many admitted to having found themselves being swayed by the argument first one way, then another. Most acknowledged that their thinking on this vital and topical area had been greatly stimulated and developed. As a result, we are confident that this volume will be a significant help not only to those who simply wish to keep abreast of the debate but also to those who are determined to contribute constructively to it.

Finally, I must issue a word of sincere gratitude to Affinity Administrator Ian Herring and to Barbara Homrighausen, our Conference Coordinator. Without their sterling efforts the event simply would not have taken place. Stephen Clark also deserves special mention. Not only did he devise, organize and chair the conference, he has also contributed the last chapter in the book. It forms a fitting conclusion, but makes no claim to be the final word.

Jonathan Stephen
Director, Affinity
www.affinity.org.uk

1. BIBLICAL ETHICS IN A MULTICULTURAL SOCIETY

Gordon Wenham

Introduction

When I read the agenda for this paper in the conference brochure, I was taken aback. It seemed as though the conference organizers hoped I would tackle some of the knottiest and most controversial areas of Old Testament history and ethics in a single paper: from ethnic cleansing in the time of Joshua to divorce in the time of Ezra. These are the typical problems thrown up in undergraduate theology degrees where the historical-critical method is the regnant paradigm. This paradigm holds that by examining the origins of customs and ideas one will arrive at an understanding of their significance. Thus, to understand Christian baptism one must explore its roots in the Jewish rites of purification that preceded it; or to understand the Old Testament's attitude to interracial marriage one must appreciate the social situation in the Judges period. Now, I am not going to argue that such historical information is irrelevant; it is in fact extremely valuable, but it is not sufficient. More important is to discover why these topics are included in Holy Scripture. It is more important to think canonically than historically, if we wish to grasp the biblical approach to the issues this paper is asked to address.

The second false trail that is often associated with the historical-critical paradigm is the developmental or evolutionary model of religion, sometimes called progressive revelation. This holds in its crudest Marcionite form that the god of the Old Testament was a god of wrath, quite different from the New Testament god of love. In more recent centuries more sophisticated versions of this have been put forward. Religion develops from animism to polytheism to monolatry to monotheism. And this outlook has left its mark on many studies of biblical theology and ethics. There is a general feeling that within the Old Testament later ideas are superior, and of course that the New Testament is superior to the Old Testament. The highly respected New Testament scholar Richard Hayes wrote: 'If irreconcilable tensions exist between the moral vision of the New Testament and that of particular Old Testament texts, the New Testament vision trumps the Old Testament.'[1] And countless churches, even in the evangelical tradition, adhere to this implicit Marcionism by rarely reading from – let alone preaching on – the Old Testament.

But this approach to Scripture is of course ruled out by the New Testament itself, with its constant quotation from, allusion to and discussion of the Old Testament. In particular, the evolutionary model was rejected by our Lord himself when he referred the Pharisees back to Genesis 1 and 2 to establish God's principles for marriage. And it is his approach to Scripture which I think provides the most important justification for what is known as the canonical approach to the Bible, an approach that is now being increasingly recognized in academic scholarship as a valid and important method of biblical study. It is of course the way the universal church has always supposed Scripture ought to be read. The historical-critical method is, in the perspective of two millennia of church history, just a two-century-long aberration.

---

1. Richard B. Hays, *The Moral Vision of the New Testament* (Edinburgh: T. & T. Clark, 1997), p. 336.

The canonical approach to Scripture insists on two points. First, it is the final form of the text that is authoritative, not some historically reconstructed original message. Thus, in reading the book of Amos, our job is not to assess which sayings are authentic and reach back behind the text to the prophet himself, but to accept the portrait of Amos as depicted in the book itself. Indeed, the reader's focus should not be on the message of Amos in itself, but rather on the message of the *book* of Amos. In the Gospels, the central task of the theologian is not to discover the 'historical Jesus', but to discover what the evangelists are saying through writing biographies of Jesus.

This interest in the final canonical message of the texts of Scripture has been helped by another turn in biblical scholarship. Instead of, as in the recent past, asking about the genesis of texts, the identity and circumstances of the authors, and similar issues, many scholars now insist that the focus of attention must be on the texts themselves: the literary devices used in prose and poetry, the conventions of ancient writers, how texts are constructed and what they are trying to communicate. Old Testament narrative interpretation has been greatly enriched in the last two decades by this approach, and useful contributions have been made to the study of the Psalms and Prophets by a more literary approach.

While both literary and canonical approaches to Scripture concur in their insistence on the primacy of the final form of the text, they diverge in their approach to the relationship between the different books of the Bible. Whereas the literary approach tends to view the different books as discrete entities, whose relationship to one another is incidental and unimportant for interpretative purposes, the canonical approach sees the relationship between the different books as fundamental. 'All Scripture is breathed out by God and profitable for teaching, for reproof' (2 Tim. 3:16).[2] This means that every part of Scripture has its part to play and 'it is not lawful for the Church to . . . expound one place of Scripture, that it be repugnant to another.'[3] In this regard canonical

---

2. Scripture quotations in this chapter are from the English Standard Version.

3. Article 20 of the Thirty-nine Articles of Religion.

criticism is calling us back to the principles of interpretation that were normative in the Church (and in the synagogue) until the nineteenth century. And it is to these principles of literary and canonical criticism that I shall be appealing, as I seek to elucidate what the Old Testament has to say about the relationship of its teaching to a society in which, although the large majority profess to be Christians, only a small minority actually appear to practise their faith actively.

The significance of Genesis 1 – 11

The opening chapters of Genesis are of the utmost importance for our discussion, for three reasons. First, because, as literary critics point out, the opening of a work often discloses the standpoint of the author, his attitude to the events he subsequently relates and so on.[4] Second, because these chapters are universal in their perspective: they are telling the story of all humanity, not just the descendants of Abraham, the chosen people. Adam, and for that matter Noah too, are presented as the fathers of all mankind, so their experiences are decisive for the whole human race, not just for the Jews or for the Church. Third, these chapters are fundamental to Christian theology, because both Jesus and Paul appeal to them to establish Christian doctrines of marriage (Matt. 19:3–12), sin and the fall (Rom. 5), while the book of Revelation uses the imagery of Eden to describe the heavenly Jerusalem (Rev. 21 – 22). It is therefore both a literary and theological imperative to read these chapters with great care, for they may disclose to us both the fundamental assumptions of the human author of Genesis and also our divine creator's intentions for all mankind.

---

4. 'Information and attitudes presented at an early stage of the text tend to encourage the reader to interpret everything in their light.' Shelomith Rimmon-Kenan, *Narrative Fiction: Contemporary Poetics* (London: Routledge, 1983), p. 120.

The ethical teaching of Genesis 1 – 2

It does not require much sophistication to see some very obvious points that Genesis 1 is making about man.[5] Man's creation is clearly the high point of the six-day process. God's works on the preceding five days are described in most detail where they have most impact on human existence: for example, plants on day three, sun and moon on day four. On day six, when man is created in God's image, God pronounces his work not just 'good', as on the preceding days, but 'very good'. It is as if the narrator were saying: man was not made for the world, but the world was made for man.

However the concept of the divine image in man rules out the idea, sometimes ascribed to Genesis, that mankind is licensed to exploit the earth ruthlessly. Rather, he is told to 'Be fruitful and multiply and fill the earth and subdue it and have dominion over the fish of the sea and over the birds of the heavens and over every living thing that moves on the earth' (1:28). Commentators now agree that the idea of the image of God is borrowed from royal ideology: neighbours of ancient Israel held that their kings were in the image of God; that is, kings were the representatives of God on earth. Genesis democratizes this notion by stating that every human being is in God's image and represents him to the rest of creation. But if every human being is a divinely appointed monarch, he or she also has the obligations of a monarch towards subjects: to manage them for their own good, not for the monarch's private benefit. (For a statement of royal duties vis-à-vis subjects, see Psalm 72.) So here Genesis is implying that all mankind has a duty of care towards the rest of creation. We must act as God's representatives in managing the earth.

But how is man to fulfil this divine mandate? Genesis 1:27 tells us:

> In the image of God he created him;
> male and female he created them.

---

5. For a fuller exegesis of points made here see G. J. Wenham, *Genesis 1– 15* (Waco: Word Books, 1987).

It goes on to tell of the first command given to the human race: 'Be fruitful and multiply'. For Genesis 1 the differentiation between the sexes is fundamental, and its purpose is clear: procreation. Genesis 2 reinforces this message in the story of Eve's creation. God doubtless could have cloned another Adam out of Adam's rib, but he chose to make just one Eve. Between them these opening chapters of Genesis make clear that God's design for all mankind is heterosexual monogamy. But it is not childless monogamy: his command is 'be fruitful and multiply'. Traditional Jews take this command seriously, but Western society, including the churches, has been so brainwashed by the 'family planning' lobby and sheer selfishness that the birth rate has collapsed, with potentially catastrophic consequences.[6]

Genesis 1:29–30 sets out another universal principle, which the affluent West tends to overlook. In the pre-fall world man and beast were vegetarian:

> And God said, 'Behold, I have given you every plant yielding seed . . . You shall have them for food. And to every beast of the earth and to every bird . . . everything that has the breath of life, I have given every green plant for food.'

But it is not just vegetarianism that characterized the original creation, but lack of violence. The lion did not eat the lamb, and man did not kill his brother man or the animals. All lived in perfect harmony. The prophets look forward to a day when this state of affairs will be restored.

> The wolf shall dwell with the lamb,
>   and the leopard shall lie down with the young goat,

6. See Meic Pearse, *Why the Rest Hate the West* (London: SPCK, 2003). On present trends, the indigenous population of Europe will fall by nearly three-quarters by the end of the century. The pension crisis is the first sign of the problem. Caring for an ageing population is another issue: we are scouring the developing world for health workers, causing hospitals in Africa and the Philippines to close for lack of nurses.

and the calf and the lion and the fattened calf together;
   and a little child shall lead them.
The cow and the bear shall graze;
   their young shall lie down together;
   and the lion shall eat straw like the ox.
The nursing child shall play over the hole of the cobra,
   and the weaned child shall put his hand on the adder's den.
They shall not hurt or destroy
   in all my holy mountain;
for the earth shall be full of the knowledge of the Lord
   as the waters cover the sea.
(Isaiah 11:6–9)

Commentators debate whether Isaiah is speaking symbolically or literally: do the animals, as often in Scripture, symbolize different nations? Taken this way, Isaiah is predicting an era of universal human peace under 'the root of Jesse'. My inclination is to see it as both literal and symbolic, for, as we shall see, Genesis sees strife between man and beast as a significant problem, which must be checked and will one day be cured.

Though, as we shall see soon, absolute vegetarianism is rescinded after the flood, there is no doubt that ancient Israel ate very little meat. Domestic animals were too valuable to kill except at big festivals, or when special guests were entertained (e.g. Gen. 18:1–8), and the food laws of Leviticus limited the types of game that could be hunted for food. They certainly would have been astonished at the amount of meat we consume and shocked by the methods by which it is produced and by the amount of grain that is used in meat production.[7]

The vegetarianism of Genesis 1 is one aspect of the universal harmony and peace that it describes. Another is the Sabbath.

---

7. Compassion in World Farming exposes the shocking inhumanity of much of today's livestock industry. It is calculated that it takes about ten tons of corn to produce one ton of beef. The need for pasture drives deforestation, and the cattle also produce the greenhouse gas methane.

Though the climax of the creation story is the creation of human beings, its goal is rest on the Sabbath. 2:2–3 tells how God rested on the seventh day.

> And on the seventh day God finished his work that he had done, and he rested on the seventh day from all his work that he had done. So God blessed the seventh day and made it holy, because on it God rested from all his work that he had done in creation.

Genesis describes a Sabbath when God rested: the clear implication is that man, made in his image, should do the same, a point made explicitly in the Ten Commandments:

> Remember the Sabbath day, to keep it holy . . . For in six days the Lord made heaven and earth, the sea, and all that is in them, and rested the seventh day. Therefore the Lord blessed the Sabbath day and made it holy.
> (Exodus 20:8, 11)

Often it is argued that because the Sabbath is regarded as a sign of God's covenant with Israel, it does not apply to other nations. But this is incompatible with Genesis, which implies that the Sabbath should be observed by all who are created in God's image. To suppose that Gentiles were not expected to observe the Sabbath is also contradicted by Isaiah 56:6, which envisages foreigners joining themselves to the Lord and keeping his Sabbath.

Genesis 1 therefore sets out quite clearly a divine blueprint for the ideal human society. It is a society where human beings, as God's representatives manage the world benevolently for the good of the rest of creation. It is a society which values heterosexual marriage and the children that are born into it. It is a society characterized by non-violence, where humans are at peace with their fellow humans and with the animals. Animals are not killed by humans, and they do not attack humans or each other. Finally, it is a society which rests on the seventh day.

Historical critics might well recognize that Genesis is making these ethical points, but they would tend to see them as merely the aspirations of some Israelites at a particular point in their history.[8] But this is to diminish – indeed to miss – the claim this opening chapter is making. It is speaking about God's perfect creation before its disruption by sin. It is talking about God's intentions for all humanity. Although the call of Abraham and the establishment of Israel as a nation could be seen as one step towards realizing these intentions,[9] it must not be forgotten that the Bible is claiming that these principles apply to all peoples and all nations, for they are all made in God's image and descended from Adam.

The story of the fall in Genesis 2 – 3 reinforces these points. Adam is created and put in charge of the garden, 'to work it and keep it' (2:16). The garden is filled with all sorts of trees that are 'good for food'. The animals are seen as potential companions for Adam, not a threat or to be killed. Eve is created to be 'a helper fit for him': indeed, their relationship is held up as a model for every marriage.

> Therefore a man shall leave his father and his mother and hold fast to his wife, and they shall become one flesh.
> (Genesis 2:24)

Harmony reigns: between God and man, Adam and Eve, man and the beasts. The whole story suggests an atmosphere of openness ('naked and not ashamed') and tranquillity (The Lord God walking in the garden in the cool of the day). While not exactly a perpetual Sabbath, as Adam had to work and keep the garden, he seems originally to have been free of the battle with nature that characterized the post-fall scene:

> Cursed is the ground because of you;
>   in pain you shall eat of it all the days of your life;
> thorns and thistles it shall bring forth for you;
>   and you shall eat the plants of the field.

---

8. Typically the exilic or post-exilic era, as Genesis 1 is assigned to the Priestly source.

9. D. J. A. Clines, *The Theme of the Pentateuch* (Sheffield: JSOT Press, 1978), p. 29.

By the sweat of your face
   you shall eat bread,
till you return to the ground,
   for out of it you were taken;
for you are dust,
   and to dust you shall return.
(Genesis 3:17–19)

The fall and the flood (Genesis 3 – 9)

The effects of the fall on the human situation hardly need repeat-
ing, but I should just like to focus on the avalanche of violence it
initiated. It is alluded to in Genesis 3:15:

I will put enmity between you and the woman,
   and between your offspring and her offspring;
he shall bruise your head,
   and you shall bruise his heel.

This is of course the first messianic prophecy, the protevan-
gelium. But if in the long term it predicts the triumph of the
woman's offspring over the serpent's, in the short term it
envisages a bitter struggle between humans and animals, the
serpent representing the animal kingdom. Though modern urban
dwellers tend to forget this struggle, except when they are struck
low by a bug or a virus, Israelite peasants were ever aware of the
threat to their existence posed by everything from lions to locusts.
They witnessed the violence of nature at first hand: something we
miss until we see a wildlife programme, or a cat killing a bird.

Genesis traces the growth of violence among man and beast in
chapters 4 – 6. First there is Cain, who commits the worst kind of
murder imaginable, fratricide; brothers are supposed to protect
each other, not kill each other. Cain's great-great-grandson is even
more vicious, boasting to his wives:

I have killed a man for wounding me,
   a young man for striking me.

> If Cain's revenge is sevenfold,
>> then Lamech's is seventy-sevenfold.
>
> (Genesis 4:23–24)

But, according to 6:11, this savagery was not confined to Lamech: 'For the earth was filled with violence', a remark repeated by God himself in verse 13. Regrettably, not only humans were infected with violence, but 'all flesh', a phrase which in this context includes both people and beasts. It was not only pervasive corruption of the human heart that was to blame for the flood (6:5), but the epidemic of violence that affected all creatures on earth. It was this that prompted the decree of total destruction in the flood.

The flood is portrayed as reversing creation: the earth returns to the situation described in 1:2, with water covering the whole face of the globe. But gradually, as the water falls, a sort of new creation occurs: the land and the trees appear; the birds start flying over them; the animals and humans walk on dry land; and Noah is told, like Adam before him, 'Be fruitful and multiply'.[10] Like Adam before him, he is seen as the father of the whole human race, so what happens to him affects all mankind.

However, the root problem still exists: the sinfulness of the human heart God observed before the flood.

> The LORD saw that the wickedness of man was great in the earth, and
> that every intention of the thoughts of his heart was only evil
> continually. And the Lord was sorry that he had made man on the earth,
> and it grieved him to his heart. So the Lord said, 'I will blot out man
> whom I have created.'
>
> (Genesis 6:5–7)

But immediately after the flood, although Noah is described as 'righteous, blameless in his generation', God notes that the intrinsic problem of human sin is still there. 'And when the LORD smelled the pleasing aroma, the LORD said in his heart, "I will never again curse the ground because of man, for the intention of

---

10. Not once, as Adam was, but three times (8:17; 9:1, 7).

man's heart is evil from his youth"' (Gen. 8:21). Clearly the sacrifices offered by Noah have changed God's attitude to man's sinfulness, but what is to stop violence breaking out again and filling the earth?

This issue is directly addressed in Genesis 9. We have seen that Noah is depicted as a second Adam, that the retreat of the flood waters is seen as an act of re-creation, and that the command to be fruitful and multiply is repeated to Noah. This echoing of Genesis 1 is especially obvious in Genesis 9:1–6. These verses need to be carefully compared with Genesis 1:28–30, as in Table 1:1.

Both passages begin by God blessing mankind and commanding procreation (1:28; 9:1). In both texts man is given dominion over the other creatures, but in the second the dominion is described as 'fear' and 'dread', doubtless reflecting the animosity of 3:15. Both continue by God providing his creatures with food; but whereas in 1:28–29 man is given just the green plants to eat, in 9:3 he is expressly allowed to eat anything, as long as the blood is not consumed. Already the changed atmosphere after the fall is being legislated. Animals may be killed, because they attack humans. Nevertheless, their lives are precious, and this must be acknowledged by not consuming the blood, 'For the life of the flesh is in the blood' (Lev. 17:11). Already there is a hint of divine compromise here: ideally man and beast should be vegetarian and non-violent, but since that is no longer the case, limited meat-eating is permitted.

But, as Genesis 4 showed, the problem is not simply inter-species violence: humans can kill humans. Cain's fratricide and Lamech's seventy-sevenfold vengeance could soon lead the world into the state that precipitated the flood. God has promised he will not send another flood, but how then is the chaos that the flood swept away to be prevented from recurring? Genesis 9:6 gives the remedy: the death penalty for murder, whether by human or beast, will stop the unrestrained reaction of future Lamechs. Unending blood feuds will be halted.

There is an inherent paradox in exacting the death penalty. It is required because human beings are made in God's image, so that an assault on a human is also an implied attack on God. In this case, then, surely the murderer should not be put to death.

Table 1:1 – Adam and Noah compared

Genesis 1:28–30, 27–28	Genesis 9:1–7
And God blessed them. And God said to them, 'Be fruitful and multiply and fill the earth and subdue it and have dominion over the fish of the sea and over the birds of the heavens and over every living thing that moves on the earth.'	And God blessed Noah and his sons and said to them, 'Be fruitful and multiply and fill the earth. The fear of you and the dread of you shall be upon every beast of the earth and upon every bird of the heavens, upon everything that creeps on the ground and all the fish of the sea. Into your hand they are delivered.
[29] And God said, 'Behold, I have given you every plant yielding seed that is on the face of all the earth, and every tree with seed in its fruit. You shall have them for food. And to every beast of the earth and to every bird of the heavens and to everything that creeps on the earth, everything that has the breath of life, I have given every green plant for food.' And it was so.	[3] Every moving thing that lives shall be food for you. And as I gave you the green plants, I give you everything. But you shall not eat flesh with its life, that is, its blood.
	[5] And for your lifeblood I will require a reckoning: from every beast I will require it and from man. From his fellow man I will require a reckoning for the life of man.
Genesis 1:27–28 So God created man in his own image, in the image of God he created him; male and female he created them.	[6] Whoever sheds the blood of man, by man shall his blood be shed, for God made man in his own image.
[28] And God blessed them. And God said to them, 'Be fruitful and multiply and fill the earth and subdue it.'	[7] And you, be fruitful and multiply, teem on the earth and multiply in it.'

However, if the survival of the human race is at stake, which is what the flood story teaches is the effect of unrestrained violence, then the logic of 9:6 is that it is necessary to execute the murderer. God's command to be fruitful and multiply is then reaffirmed in 9:7; the Creator does not want mankind to destroy itself through uncontrolled violence. Thus the fundamental goal of the preservation of the human race is to be achieved by eliminating those who wantonly take human life.

The gap between law and ethics in the Bible[11]

This illustrates a very important point about many laws in the Bible: they do not set out the ideal types of behaviour; rather, they set limits for conduct, which if transgressed must be punished. Deuteronomy 6:5 insists that 'You shall love the LORD your God with all your heart and with all your soul and with all your might.' No penalties are prescribed if you love God half-heartedly, but if your brother starts to encourage you to worship other gods, 'you shall kill him' (Deut. 13:9). Likewise, 'You shall love your neighbour as yourself' is the ultimate goal of interpersonal relationships, but a lukewarm affection is not punished. The law starts to operate when lack of love turns to theft, adultery or murder. In other words, the law sets a floor for behaviour in society; it does not define the ultimate ceiling to which all should aspire.

This understanding of the role of law is beautifully expounded by Jesus in his debate with the Pharisees about divorce.[12]

> And Pharisees came up to him and tested him by asking, 'Is it lawful to divorce one's wife for any cause?' He answered, 'Have you not read that

---

11. For a fuller discussion of this point see G. J. Wenham, 'The Gap between Law and Ethics in the Bible', *Journal of Jewish Studies* 48 (1997), pp. 17–29.

12. For a fuller discussion of this episode see G. J. Wenham, 'Does the New Testament Approve Remarriage after Divorce?' *Southern Baptist Journal of Theology* 6 (2002), pp. 30–45; and M. Strauss (ed.), *Remarriage after Divorce: Three Views* (Grand Rapids: Zondervan, 2005 forthcoming).

he who created them from the beginning "made them male and female",
and said, "Therefore a man shall leave his father and his mother and
hold fast to his wife, and they shall become one flesh"? So they are no
longer two but one flesh. What therefore God has joined together, let
not man separate.'
(Matthew 19:3–6)

Whereas the Pharisees read the Mosaic provision for divorce
as justifying it, Jesus appeals to Genesis 1:27 and 2:24 to show
that God intended lifelong monogamy. This is the Creator's
purpose in constituting mankind in two sexes. Jesus goes on to
argue that the provision of divorce was a concession caused by
human sin: 'He said to them, "Because of your hardness of heart
Moses allowed you to divorce your wives, but from the beginning
it was not so"' (Matt. 19:8). That Moses allowed divorce does
not mean God approves it, only that he tolerates it. Many of the
regulations in the law must be taken the same way. Laws on
bigamy, warfare, slavery, mortgaging land and property, pledges,
moneylending and so on do not mean that the situations that give
rise to these issues are inherently good or that the solutions proposed in the law are ideal. In a sinless world these problems
would not arise. The laws could be said to make the best of a bad
situation.

This is clearly the drift of the laws on war in Deuteronomy. The
book as a whole looks forward to a time 'when you go over the
Jordan and live in the land that the LORD your God is giving you to
inherit, and when he gives you rest from all your enemies around,
so that you live in safety' (Deut. 12:10). The blessings of chapter
28 and the blessing of Moses hold out a prospect of peace:

So Israel lived in safety,
    Jacob lived alone,
in a land of grain and wine,
    whose heavens drop down dew.
(Deuteronomy 33:28)

To appreciate the point of the laws on war, we need to examine
not only the context in the whole book, but also their immediate

context. We should note that the laws on war are part of a section of the book, Deuteronomy 19 – 21, devoted to expounding the sixth commandment, 'You shall not murder'. Chapter 19 is concerned that the accidental manslayer should not be executed, but have a chance to escape to a city of refuge. Chapter 21 is devoted to expounding a rite to atone for the death of someone by an unknown hand. Clearly the book of Deuteronomy is just as averse to wanton killing as Genesis, and this predisposition governs its approach to war in chapter 20.

First, it prescribes that certain people should be exempt from call-up: men who have just built new houses, planted vineyards or married recently. It would be wrong for these men to die in battle without having enjoyed these God-given blessings. But second, the fearful and fainthearted are excused from going to war too, for a more pragmatic reason: 'lest he make the heart of his fellows melt like his own'(Deut. 20:8).

Then come the laws on war itself, which insist that all enemies[13] must be offered terms of peace. If the enemy surrender without a fight, they can be used for forced labour (20:11). However, if the enemy do not surrender, the punishment is severe. If the city is outside the land of Canaan, all males in the city must be killed, leaving only the women, children and livestock to live. But if the city is within the land, 'you shall save alive nothing that breathes' (20:16). Though one may be shocked by this policy, it must be seen as part of a book dedicated to achieving peace and minimizing the loss of human life. Perhaps it was hoped that such a threat was more likely to induce surrender with no losses on either side. What is clear is that, though Deuteronomy does not like war and looks forward to an age when Israel will live in peace, it accepts that war will sometimes be necessary and it makes proposals about how it should be conducted humanely. Like Genesis 9 prescribing the death penalty for murderers, the prosecution of war is seen in Deuteronomy as sometimes necessary to avoid worse evils and encourage peace.

---

13. This is Lohfink's view in *Theological Dictionary of the Old Testament,* vol. 5, p. 197.

Some corollaries of the gap between law and ethics

This gap that we have identified in the Pentateuch between the minimum standards that the law enforces and the ethical ideals of the Lawgiver and Author has some interesting corollaries. First, it suggests that the God of Scripture is more tolerant than often portrayed: he may urge us to love him with all our hearts, but he does not punish us till we start to worship other gods or encourage others to apostatize too. He may decree that husbands should make their wife's welfare their first priority (Gen. 2:24), but he does not insist on punishment till adultery is committed.

Second, it suggests that often the Old Testament is disparaged unfairly when people compare its laws – its minimum standards – with the New Testament ethical ideals. Really, the ideals of the Old Testament (you shall love the Lord your God with all your heart, Deut. 6:5; and your neighbour as yourself, Lev. 19:18) should be compared with the ideals of the New Testament (Mark 12:29–31). If this is done, it becomes very much more difficult to see a difference between the ethical stances of the testaments.

Third, we must ask whether our ethical situation as the church under the New Covenant is so different theologically from that of Israel under the Old Covenant. Clearly our society is very different technologically and sociologically from the Old or New Testament societies, but that is not what I mean. The Old Testament looks forward to a messianic age in which God will reign over the hearts of all, both within Israel and without. 'Out of Zion will go the law' and 'all nations shall flow to it' (Isa. 2:2–3).

> 'But this is the covenant that I will make with the house of Israel
>   after those days,' declares the LORD:
> 'I will put my law within them,
>   and I will write it on their hearts.
> And I will be their God,
>   and they shall be my people.
> And no longer shall each one teach his neighbor
>   and each his brother, saying, "Know the LORD,"
> for they shall all know me,

from the least of them to the greatest'
   declares the Lord.
(Jeremiah 31:33–34)

But the prophets were as conscious as the rest of the Old Testament that Israel's behaviour fell far short of this ideal. And surely the same is true of the church of the New Covenant. We know the kingdom has been inaugurated: 'the kingdom of God is at hand' (Mark 1:15), but it has not been consummated. We still pray 'Thy kingdom come!' 'Maranatha: Come Lord Jesus!' We know Christ's teaching, but are we any nearer to loving God with all our heart and our neighbours as ourselves than the people of the Old Covenant? We still need law to curb the excesses of society, and from time to time to keep order in the church. The Old Testament presents a vision of God's ideals and also practical laws to keep society from straying too far from these ideals. I suggest we need such a blend of idealism and realism today.

Ideals and reality in the historical books of the Old Testament

This distinction between ideals and reality must also be borne in mind in reading the historical books of the Bible. It is a fairly obvious point that not everything described in Scripture is meant to be emulated. It is equally obvious, however, that this principle is often forgotten by commentators and preachers. The great commentator Gunkel thinks Genesis approves of Abraham saying Sarah was his sister and admires Jacob's pretending to be Esau to obtain Isaac's blessing. Recently I have heard an argument that Judges justifies suicide bomb attacks like 9/11 because Samson killed 7,000 Philistines by pulling down their temple on top of himself!

Instinctively, as Christian readers of the Bible, we reject such interpretations of these stories, but are we justified in so doing? The historical-critical method does not help us much. Sometimes it eliminates problems, by declaring that the troublesome event never occurred. But this is to throw the baby out with the bath water.

It solves the moral difficulty by creating a different problem, the unreliability of Scripture. We may feel relieved that Joshua did not massacre the Canaanites or that Samson did not set light to the fields of the Philistines or whatever. But what happens to the theology of the Old Testament if the flood or the plagues did not happen? It would take too long to follow up these historical/theological issues. The literary and canonical approach to Scripture points us in another direction.

The question we should be asking of events described in Scripture is not: did they happen? But why has the author included an account of these events in his narrative? He may not be telling a story as an example to follow but as a warning about what ought not to be done. But this is where the problem begins: how do we distinguish the author's perspective from our own gut reactions? It is here that the insights of literary criticism have proved so valuable. The works of writers like Alter, Licht and Sternberg have transformed the method of reading biblical narratives.[14] They have taught us to look for the perspective of the implied author and to try to recapture his perspective on the stories he tells. There have been fine studies of particular books of the Bible, which help us to read these works as canonical wholes. Already above, in commenting on some episodes in Genesis, I have drawn on some literary-critical insights. By and large, in Genesis it is fairly clear where Genesis is offering models to emulate and dangers to avoid, but the book of Judges is a different story.

Judges presents us with a series of heroes who deliver Israel in a variety of spectacular ways from their oppressors. Samson's feats are well known, but Ehud's assassination of King Eglon, Gideon's night attack on the Midianites, and Jael's despatch of Sisera are some of the most dramatic tales in Scripture. In that these successes

---

14. R. Alter, *The Art of Biblical Narrative* (New York: Basic Books, 1981);
J. Licht, *Storytelling in the Bible* (Jerusalem: Magnes Press, 1978);
M. Sternberg, *The Poetics of Biblical Narrative* (Bloomington: Indiana University Press, 1985). I have attempted to apply their insights to ethical readings of the Old Testament in G. J. Wenham, *Story as Torah: Reading the Old Testament Ethically* (Edinburgh: T. & T. Clark, 2000).

all follow the Israelites crying out to God in prayer and him raising up these heroes, it is tempting to suppose that the text is endorsing their actions without reservation. But in the context of Judges as a whole this cannot be the case: the book begins with most of the tribes failing to capture the land assigned to them and it ends with a civil war in which one tribe is almost wiped out. In other words, the book of Judges is portraying a relentless decline of the nation, from the relative faithfulness that characterized Joshua's day to the godlessness of the later era. The heroic deeds of the individual judges are sparks of light in a world that spiritually is getting ever darker. This means that the editor can hardly be viewing the particular episodes as illustrations of unalloyed virtue. Rather it is showing that the bravery of the judges is by itself insufficient to rescue the nation. Thus their own lifestyles and the tactics they employ need careful evaluation by the author's own standpoint, lest we mistakenly conclude that the recounting of the judges' deeds necessarily implies the author's approval.[15]

Similar considerations must inform our evaluation of actions in other books. We must read the stories with the author's eyes. Thus it seems likely that, contrary to many commentators, the author of 1 Kings 1 – 12 is not portraying Solomon as a king who had a glorious early reign, but in later life went off the rails. Rather, somewhat like Judges, it traces back his later decadence to his early years on the throne. It suggests the roots of his later polygamy, syncretism and oppressive regime may be traced back to a certain lack of principle and ruthlessness when he first came to power.[16] So too in reading the story of Ruth's marriage to Boaz or the compulsory divorces of Ezra's day, we need to recover the author's implied standpoint by asking what he is doing by recording these actions.

---

15. For further discussion of Judges see Y. Amit, *The Book of Judges: The Art of Editing* (Leiden: Brill, 1999); R. H. O'Connell, *The Rhetoric of the Book of Judges* (Leiden: Brill, 1996); D. I. Block, *Judges, Ruth* (New American Commentary) (Nashville: Broadman, 1999). For a brief discussion see Wenham, *Story as Torah*, pp. 45–71.

16. J. J. Kang, *The Persuasive Portrayal of Solomon in 1 Kings 1 – 11* (Bern: Peter Lang, 2003).

But this is not easy. The diversity of interpretation of different episodes in the Bible by different commentators shows this. It all depends on the interpreter's assumptions as to what the author's fundamental views were. Did the author approve of interracial marriage, for example? Did he differentiate between marriage between Israelites and Canaanites and between Israelites and members of other nations? Why is interracial marriage often condemned? Is it only because it may lead to apostasy, or is there some other factor? Reading Genesis may lead one to one conclusion, whereas Deuteronomy may lead to another conclusion. Each book will have to be investigated on its own merits.

But how does one discover the moral standpoint of the implied author? Sternberg in his works on biblical poetics[17] argues that the viewpoint of the implied author coincides with the stance taken in the law. I believe that this is a reasonable starting point, but, as I have argued above, there is a distinct gap between the level of behaviour required by the law and the ideals of the biblical writers.[18] Loving God with all one's heart is the goal, but it is only worshipping other gods or encouraging others to do so that was a punishable offence in Israel. The law certainly allows for polygamy and regulates it, but Genesis implies that God wants monogamy (only one Eve was created) and that polygamy (e.g. Lamech and Jacob) is fraught with problems. Thus the stance from which Genesis relates the past is not the law, but the high ethical ideals which are most prominent in the opening and closing chapters of the book.

The value of the law

So far, I have argued that the narrative works of the Old Testament are written from an ethical perspective that is more

---

17. See above, note 14.

18. See my article 'The Gap between Law and Ethics in the Bible', *Journal of Jewish Studies* 48 (1997), pp. 17–29, and *Story as Torah* for a fuller exposition of this argument.

demanding than its legal collections, or more precisely from the case law that makes up the bulk of these collections. The law permits polygamy, but the narratives disapprove of it. The law allows limited retaliation; the narratives encourage reconciliation. It would therefore be easy to jump to the conclusion that all that is needed is the higher morality of the narrators and we can dispense with the compromise-ridden standards of the case law. But this is not the view of the Bible itself. Our exegesis of Genesis 9:1–7 showed that it regarded the punishments of the law as necessary, if regrettable, in our fallen world. Unless the violent are punished, the earth may be swamped in violence as it was before the flood. There are many other offences that, left unpunished, will enrage the victim and lead to violence. The law thus has a vital role in the management of sinful humanity, to stop sin getting totally out of hand.

We therefore need to have a closer look at the functioning of law in the Old Testament. It does, I think, show how, even in imperfect and sinful societies like ancient Israel or modern Britain, the law can prevent society from falling through the floor of acceptable behaviour, even if it can never raise it to the heights which imitators of God should aspire to. We shall begin by taking another look at Genesis 9, before drawing out some other principles that could give modern legislators or at least Christian lobbyists some goals to move toward.

Genesis 9:6 – 'Whoever sheds the blood of man, by man shall his blood be shed, for God made man in his own image' – is the first example of case law in the Bible, of which there are numerous examples in Exodus to Deuteronomy. In case law an offence is defined, and the punishment prescribed: for example, in Exodus 21:26, 'When a man strikes the eye of his slave, male or female, and destroys it, he shall let the slave go free because of his eye.' Case law does not set out ideal behaviour; rather it deals with situations where someone has been wronged and needs a just response. In the case of Genesis 9 people should never be murdered, but if that does happen the appropriate response is the execution of the murderer. This is an application of the principle of talion: 'But if there is harm, then you shall pay life for life, eye for eye, tooth for tooth, hand for hand, foot for foot, burn for burn, wound for wound, stripe for stripe' (Exod. 21:23–25; cf. Lev. 24:19–21; Deut. 19:21). Many people belittle this *lex talionis*, dismissing it as barbaric. It was, though, a principle that most ancient oriental law worked with. It is the do-as-you-would-be-done-by principle. It expresses the principle of fair and appropriate punishment, neither too lenient nor too harsh.

However, talion was often not applied literally, as the following law shows. A slave who had his tooth knocked out was compensated by being given his freedom. In most cases the talion principle formed the basis for negotiation between the parties. Exodus 21:28 deals with an ox which gores someone to death. If it was known to be dangerous, the owner as well as the ox was liable to be executed. But the owner may negotiate a ransom, in which case 'he shall give for the redemption of his life whatever may be laid upon him' (Exod. 21:30). It would seem likely that many offences for which the law prescribes talionic penalties could involve paying compensation instead. The victim or his family could say: 'You will die, lose your eye, or whatever, unless you pay so much.' Proverbs 6:20–31 warns a young man of the perils of adultery and warns him not to count on the injured party, who could demand the death penalty, being bought off.

> For jealousy makes a man furious,
> > and he will not spare when he takes revenge.
> He will accept no compensation;
> > he will refuse though you multiply gifts.
> (Proverbs 6:34–35)

The basic principle of talion is justice; the offender must suffer in the same way as his victim or potential victim: 'then you shall do to him as he had meant to do to his brother. So you shall purge the evil from your midst' (Deut. 19:19). It is regarded as a universal principle applicable to immigrants as well as native Israelites: 'You shall have the same rule for the sojourner and for the native, for I am the LORD your God' (Lev. 24:22).

Another important function of the law is to protect the weak and vulnerable. This is a recurrent refrain in Exodus and Deuteronomy, while Leviticus 25 devotes a long discussion to mitigating the effects of debt on the poor. Some quotes will illustrate the point.

> You shall not wrong a sojourner or oppress him, for you were sojourners in the land of Egypt. You shall not mistreat any widow or fatherless child. If you do mistreat them, and they cry out to me, I will surely hear their cry, and my wrath will burn, and I will kill you with the sword, and your wives shall become widows and your children fatherless.
> (Exodus 22:21–24)

> You shall not pervert the justice due to your poor in his lawsuit.
> (Exodus 23:6)

> If among you, one of your brothers should become poor, in any of your towns within your land that the Lord your God is giving you, you shall not harden your heart or shut your hand against your poor brother, but you shall open your hand to him and lend him sufficient for his need, whatever it may be.
> (Deuteronomy 15:7–8)

One way of alleviating the plight of the poor was to give them a job. Most Israelites were peasants owning their own small plot of land. Drought could lead to famine and debt. In this situation wealthier landowners were encouraged to take on individuals, or even whole families, for a limited period: this is what is called 'slavery' in the Old Testament. It was akin to being employed as opposed to being self-employed. It was viewed as an act of charity to save people from starvation by this means. The Egyptians say to Joseph: 'You have saved our lives; may it please my lord, we will be servants to Pharaoh' (Gen. 47:25). Exodus 21:1–6 and Deuteronomy 15:12–17 envisage a slave being so contented with his lot that he might refuse to leave his employer after six years, when he would be entitled to his freedom.

Justice and protection of the poor are two major recurrent concerns of the law. Can one say what the law indicates were the gravest offences in Israel? Clearly the Ten Commandments express the quintessence of biblical religious and ethical concerns. The accounts of their promulgation in Israel indicate their prime importance, while Deuteronomy 12 – 26 may well be construed as a commentary on the different commandments.[19]

A comparison of the case law in Exodus to Deuteronomy dealing with each commandment is instructive. Any transgression of the first seven commandments is liable to the death penalty, even if in some situations this might be commuted, whereas the eighth and ninth (theft and false witness) do not attract such a heavy condemnation. This suggests that the commandments are arranged roughly in order of their gravity.[20]

This conclusion is supported by another approach, most clearly enunciated in Leviticus. Certain actions made people unclean: that is, unfit to approach God in worship. These ranged from menstruation and skin disease to homicide and idolatry. The lightest forms of uncleanness, such as marital intercourse, could be dealt with by washing and waiting a day. Intermediate uncleanness required the offering of sacrifice. But the gravest types of uncleanness polluted the land and ultimately led to expulsion from the promised land. The Canaanites were expelled from the land because of their devotion to other gods, their sexual misbehaviour and homicide. Leviticus warns Israel that they will suffer the same fate if they behave in this way (18:24–30; 20:1–5; Num. 35:30–34).

Old Testament law as a paradigm

Over the centuries there have been very different approaches to appropriating OT law. On the one hand there is the rejectionist view, which is represented by Luther and dispensationalism, which regards the law as outdated because it belongs to the Old Covenant not the New, or that it serves merely to awaken our conscience to make us aware of our need for the gospel. At the

---

19. Cf. J. G. McConville, *Deuteronomy* (Leicester: Apollos, 2002).

20. See B. N. Kaye and G. J. Wenham, *Law, Morality and the Bible*, (Leicester: IVP, 1978), p. 29.

other extreme is the fundamentalist approach of theonomy, which believes that modern law should not simply reflect and apply the Ten Commandments, but that the penalties of the case law should be implemented today. In between these two extremes comes the paradigmatic approach of C. J. H. Wright,[21] who has argued in a number of books and articles that the OT law gives a model of law that is good for any society. It gives us clues to the values that society should promote, particularly in its relationship to God, to the land, and to family life. Some of the rules, like those about gleaning fields, are quite irrelevant in a high-tech agriculture, but they point to a concern for the poor that every society ought to make a priority.

It seems to me that this paradigmatic approach to the law is the most helpful of the various options put forward hitherto. It allows us to penetrate to the concerns and values of a traditional society and ask ourselves how far short our own society falls in promoting these concerns.[22] Indeed, in some tribal and peasant societies many of the OT laws could still be directly relevant. Deuteronomy does indeed assert that other peoples will admire Israel's legal system:

> Keep them and do them, for that will be your wisdom and your understanding in the sight of the peoples, who, when they hear all these statutes, will say, 'Surely this great nation is a wise and understanding people.' For what great nation is there that has a god so near to it as the Lord our God is to us, whenever we call upon him? And what great nation is there, that has statutes and rules so righteous as all this law that I set before you today?
> (Deuteronomy 4:6–8)

---

21. *Living as the People of God* (Leicester: IVP, 1983); *God's People in God's Land* (Grand Rapids: Eerdmans, 1990); *Walking in the Ways of the Lord* (Leicester: Apollos, 1995); *Old Testament Ethics for the People of God* (Leicester: Apollos, 2004).

22. The work of the Jubilee Centre and the associated Relationships Foundation and Keep Sunday Special Campaign has been informed by the paradigmatic approach.

Historians suggest that one of the reasons for the growth in Judaism in the first centuries BC and AD was its legal system, as well as its monotheism.[23] Gentiles were attracted by the sexual morality, the care for women and slaves, and the institution of the Sabbath.

It is all very well to assert that the Old Testament law is paradigmatic, but how do we transpose its ideas into Western multicultural society? Of course, some principles are transparently as relevant today as ever they were. The OT insists on evidence being well corroborated and punishes perjury severely:

A single witness shall not suffice against a person for any crime or for any wrong in connection with any offense that he has committed. Only on the evidence of two witnesses or of three witnesses shall a charge be established. If a malicious witness arises to accuse a person of wrongdoing, then both parties to the dispute shall appear before the Lord, before the priests and the judges who are in office in those days. The judges shall inquire diligently, and if the witness is a false witness and has accused his brother falsely, then you shall do to him as he had meant to do to his brother. So you shall purge the evil from your midst. (Deuteronomy 19:15–19)

We may find it more difficult to see the point of laws insisting on erecting a parapet around one's roof (Deut. 22:8) or forbidding reaping up to the edge of one's field (Lev. 19:9–10). However, a look at the motive clauses attached to these commands may help us to find a modern application ('that you may not bring the guilt of blood upon your house, if anyone should fall from it'; 'You shall leave them for the poor and for the sojourner'). Clearly the first is designed for a culture where people used their flat roofs for living purposes and for sleeping on in summer. A parapet would prevent people falling to their death. But this general principle of preventing accidental death and injury motivates health and safety regulations today. Leaving the edges of fields unharvested helped the poor of ancient Israel,

---

23. S. W. Baron, *A Social and Religious History of the Jews*[2] I (New York: Columbia UP, 1951), pp. 164–211.

because they lived in the countryside. The modern poor do not live there, but this ancient law should challenge modern society to support the poor appropriately.

What can we learn from all the laws demanding the death penalty for everything from adultery to Sabbath breaking? In what sense are they paradigmatic? These severe penalties give us an insight into the biblical scale of moral values. The Bible considers these sins very serious: they threaten to destroy society and therefore cannot be tolerated. That the death penalty could be imposed, even if in some cases, as I have already discussed, it could be commuted by the payment of compensation to the injured party, also witnesses to the rarity of these offences in ancient Israel. If all Sabbath breakers and adulterers in Britain were executed, there would be few of us left! Clearly, what our society considers a tolerable floor of behaviour is much lower than that of ancient Israel.

But this is where I believe that the idea of the law being a compromise between the moral ideals of the Old Testament and the free-for-all situation that prevailed before the flood can help us. Every society tends to recognize a gap between the ideal behaviour that every citizen should live by and the laws which punish those who fall too short of these ideals. The Old Testament tells us both what its ideals are and what its minimum requirements are. The minimum requirements are set out in the case law and represent a compromise with the ideals of loving God and neighbour, which ought to characterize everyone's behaviour. The Old Testament had its minimum standards, which imply that the era in which they were promulgated set a high moral tone. Unfortunately, modern society sets its minimum standards much lower, tolerating deeds that ancient Israel would have regarded as beyond the pale. But if we see Old Testament laws as a compromise between what God really wanted, total love and loyalty, and what required punishment, we can have a model for our situation. We must establish the ideals of behaviour that we think God has laid down for every human being, and push for laws that encourage people not to flout these ideals. We shall be forced to accept compromise because sinful individuals will never want to implement God's principles fully in their own lives, however much they would like society to be more law-abiding and respectful of each other's rights.

What Christians need to understand is the ideals that we ought constantly to have before our eyes, so that legislation does not get too far out of kilter with God's purposes. So we need to clarify what moral principles are indeed universal and apply not just to Israel but to all mankind. A strong case has been made for seeing the Ten Commandments as being universally applicable.[24] In that the Commandments are part of Israel's paradigmatic law I find this plausible. However, the opening chapters of Genesis also set out 'the primal divine intentions for man'. In the commands given to Adam and reiterated to Noah, slightly altered, we are presented with a vision of how man ought to live. From Genesis 1 – 9 we inferred five major principles that should govern human society: monogamous marriage that is both heterosexual and fertile; protection of human life (capital punishment for murder to prevent worse violence); benevolent human management of the rest of creation, a preference for vegetarianism; and the observance of the Sabbath. The overlap of these principles with the ethical demands of the Ten Commandments is obvious. In that these principles are depicted as applying to the whole human race, we should not feel inhibited in pressing them on multicultural Britain; indeed, on any nation.

Laws on immigrants

Ancient Israel was also a multicultural society with immigrants, 'sojourners' from neighbouring lands. Though these sojourners were not expected to conform in every respect to Israel's laws and customs, it is quite often mentioned that a particular law applies to them as well as to native Israelites.

In the law the immigrant is seen as very vulnerable. Sojourners are mentioned alongside the poor Israelites, slaves, widows and orphans as specially deserving of support, not least because the Israelites were sojourners in Israel. Leviticus 19:33–34 sums up the attitude to the sojourner.

---

24. E.g. P. G. Kuntz, *The Ten Commandments: Mosaic Paradigms for a Well-Ordered Society* (Grand Rapids: Eerdmans, 2004).

When a stranger sojourns with you in your land, you shall not do him
wrong. You shall treat the stranger who sojourns with you as the native
among you, and you shall love him as yourself, for you were strangers in
the land of Egypt: I am the LORD your God.

In this spirit of welcome, the sojourner is allowed to offer
sacrifice and participate in the major festivals (Lev. 22:18; Num.
15:15–27: Deut. 16:11, 14) (the Passover only if he is circumcised
[Exod. 12:49]). The only specifically Israelite religious rules sojourners must observe are no leaven at Passover; no working on
the Day of Atonement; and no sacrificing of children to Moloch
(Exod. 12:19; Lev. 16:29; 20:2). But it does appear that they must
observe the rules that reflect God's intentions for all humanity that
we have noted in Genesis 1 – 9.

Sojourners must adhere to the creation principles of sexuality.
After the prohibitions of incest, adultery, homosexuality and
bestiality in Leviticus 18, it is specifically noted that these rules apply
to sojourners as well as native Israelites (18:26). Sojourners are
subject to the laws on homicide, and to the death penalty if guilty,
but they are also given the opportunity to flee to the cities of refuge
in cases of accidental killing (Lev. 24:22; Num. 35:15). They must
also refrain from consuming blood, which I suggested reflected the
pro-vegetarian ideal (Lev. 17:10, 13; cf. Gen. 9:4). Finally, they must
observe the Sabbath (Exod. 20:10; 23:12; Deut. 5:14). The inclusion
of this rule in the Ten Commandments highlights its importance.

Conclusion

This chapter has concentrated on the Pentateuch for two reasons.
First, because the opening chapters of Genesis depict God's ideals
for mankind, set out in Genesis 1 – 2, and then how he made
arrangements that reflected those ideals for fallen humanity. Laws,
such as capital punishment, were instituted to limit violence and
prevent society reverting to the chaos of pre-flood times. This
model, which sees law as a necessity in a fallen world, is I think
endorsed by our Lord's comment that 'because of the hardness of
your heart Moses allowed you to divorce'.

Second, I focused on the Pentateuch in order to examine the laws. Though specifically given to the redeemed people of God, they are paradigmatic for all peoples; indeed, it is hoped other nations will try to imitate them. I have argued that these laws represent a pragmatic compromise with the creation ideals set out in Genesis 1 – 2; they represent a floor of behaviour which the Old Testament hoped Israel would not fall below. It was of course the contention of the prophets that Israel had not even lived up to the basic requirements of the law, let alone the ideal of loving God and one's neighbour wholeheartedly.

But this pragmatic compromise of the law for ancient Israel gives us a model to imitate today. We should work for legislation in society that reflects the Bible's ideals about sexuality, the sanctity of life, the environment, and the Sabbath. Like Moses of ancient Israel, we shall be forced to make compromises because of the hardness of the human heart, but we should not abandon the vision of Genesis 1 and 2, which express 'the primal divine intentions for man'.[25] These patterns of human life, whether it be marriage or the Sabbath, the sanctity of life or the protection of the environment, are still most attractive to people, whatever modern libertarians assert, and we should not give up commending them to our political leaders.

© Gordon Wenham, 2005

---

25. Clines, *Theme of the Pentateuch*, p. 29.

2. WAS JESUS POLITICAL?

Steve Wilmshurst

Introduction

It has long been the case that interpreters cast the message of Jesus into categories they are comfortable with. The option of understanding him in political terms has thus been an appealing one to those who are at home in the political world. I well remember the BBC radio discussion programme where Malcolm Muggeridge responded to Arthur Scargill – then approaching the height of his powers as a socialist icon – with the riposte 'Arthur, you make Jesus sound like the Honourable Member for Galilee South!' The task of this chapter is to examine how far, if at all, it is meaningful to understand Jesus' message in such terms. The point is not merely academic. We seek to understand so that we may obey his claims, wherever and whenever we encounter them.

I shall argue that Jesus' mission and message display an unmistakably political dimension. The claims Jesus makes in the Gospels are the claims of the kingdom. It is an uncompromising message of unconditional loyalty; and its political implications are best understood in terms of the collision of power structures. In a world where the authority of Rome was equally uncompromising in its claims, such collision was not only inevitable but highly visible. To understand Jesus' political claims, therefore, we will need to understand clearly what is meant by the kingdom. And to appreciate how the message was first heard, we must appreciate his political context.

'Political' is a term we need to pin down at the outset. To say that someone is 'political' can have a derogatory sense, as in the expression 'playing politics', which means that someone is manipulating an issue for personal or party advantage rather than engaging with it on its merits. It can also have a very restricted sense, as when specifically attached to *party* politics or the details of the 'science and art of government' (the words are from the Concise Oxford Dictionary). Clearly we can exclude such meanings from this discussion. Jesus was *not* the Honourable Member for Galilee South! He was not standing for political office or trying to manoeuvre his way into Jewish power structures such as the Sanhedrin. In that sense he is non-political. But 'political' has also been used in the specific case of Jesus to mean, in effect, 'revolutionary'. The question would then become 'Was Jesus a political *agitator*?' Some claim that he was. However, we shall use 'political' in its most usual sense, to mean 'relating to public, state or civil affairs' and, in particular, public matters over against individual, or private, ethics.

At this stage it is important to point out one way in which our own era is unusual – even bizarre. The idea of separating out the categories 'political' and 'religious' is unique to Western modernity. It was the Enlightenment that began the process of privatizing religion, removing it from the public sphere to the point where any claim to influence, let alone to determine public policy, is anathematized. Today in the UK, one's religious orientation is reduced to an item on a list of categories such as race, gender and disability – categories which must be seen to affect nothing, to attract no discrimination. In other words, its existence or otherwise carries no weight. In the last few years, Western commentators have been surprised as well as dismayed to discover that there exist ambitious and vigorous alternative points of view –

surprised, almost as if they had first sprung into being in
September 2001. The truth is that throughout most of the world
and most of history, politics and religion have always been like two
sides of the same coin. That is not to suggest that they are the
same thing, but it *is* to point out that the notion of privatized,
inward religion divorced from political realities makes little sense
to most human societies. This was certainly the case in first
century Palestine. There could be no religion without politics.

In a sense, then, a positive answer to the initial question is
inevitable. The question recasts itself as 'How directly does Jesus'
ministry address public affairs?' or, to put it another way, 'What
claims does the kingdom of God make on earthly authorities?'
A huge range of answers has been offered to questions like these.
I will make no attempt at a historical survey or a discussion of
how the early church related to the State (though I shall hint at
how certain New Testament themes began to be developed); and
I will not even begin to address the realm of political theology in
a systematic way. Oliver O'Donovan's masterly, though demanding, *The Desire of the Nations* is recommended as an introduction.[1]
We shall begin with a sketch of the different views of Jesus on
offer today.

The Jesus of history: Quests and interpretations

Why spend time examining the current field of play? Partly
to remind us that serious and intelligent people who have reviewed
the evidence about Jesus are still coming to widely different
conclusions. The field of 'historical Jesus research' is very
active today; and many questions we may think of as closed

---

1. Political theology aims to 'open up "commonplace politics" to the activity
   of God' (O'Donovan, *The Desire of the Nations*, p. 2). It is the attempt by
   theologians to define political ends, allowing theology to speak to politics.
   O'Donovan's discussion of the idea of Christendom is one of the most
   interesting parts of the book but goes well beyond the scope of the
   present chapter.

are seen quite differently by many scholars. But the exercise is worthwhile also because, although we may not like the alternative answers, considering them can help to sharpen our own and will sometimes lead us to refine them.

First, an interpretation some way off the academic mainstream. A good example of a very 'political' Jesus was that portrayed by John Howard Yoder, the prominent American Mennonite.[2] Yoder describes Jesus as a model political activist. He understands Luke 4:16–21 as a literal declaration of that year as a Jubilee year: a one-off, to include the redistribution of capital, prefiguring the 're-establishment of all things'.[3] In Gethsemane Jesus' struggle is with the temptation which has constantly pursued him: to adopt worldly, violent methods of conquest. To call on twelve legions of angels (Matt. 26:53) would be to launch the holy war, but this is precisely what Jesus refuses to do. Ultimately his non-violent way is such a subversive threat that Pilate can afford to free a run-of-the-mill revolutionary like Barabbas in his place. For Yoder, Jesus' disavowal of violence is central.

Meanwhile, many different positions have been thrown up by the 'Quest for the Historical Jesus'. The expression describes scholars' attempts to understand Jesus as a figure of history, without looking through the lens of the early church or later dogmas. Often the Quest has served negatively to separate the 'Jesus of history' from the 'Christ of faith'. It is a term usually associated with the nineteenth and early twentieth centuries and especially the highly influential writing of Albert Schweitzer, who named, chronicled and redirected the Quest. Schweitzer believed that Jesus' message foretold the *imminent* intervention of God and the end of the world; and that Jesus was wrong. Politics is an irrelevant category for such a viewpoint. The Quest was written off by the influential Bultmann as pointless. What mattered to him was the personal, spiritual response to the demands of God, not the supposed historicity of the Jesus narratives; but the Quest was

---

2. Yoder, *The Politics of Jesus*.

3. Yoder, *The Politics of Jesus*, p. 76.

revived after the Second World War by Käsemann (the 'New' or 'Second Quest').

More recently, what is known in some quarters as the 'Third Quest' has taken shape.[4] This movement is characterized by its determination to investigate Jesus' ministry firmly within its own context. Recognizing that the Enlightenment has inflicted on us an artificial separation between politics and theology, the Third Quest aims to hear Jesus as his own time would have heard him; and thereby to understand his message, which is seen to have a strongly *eschatological* shape. That is to say, Jesus saw himself as representing the climactic moment in God's dealings with Israel and, through them, the world. Tom Wright identifies himself firmly with this movement. The 'Third Quest' itself covers a wide spectrum of views and is often willing to see Jesus as highly political.

Following more in the path of the 'New Quest' is the Jesus Seminar, which is the source of many recent, radical attacks on the historicity of the Bible's accounts of Christ. It began in 1985 under the auspices of the Westar Institute in Santa Rosa, California, and is composed of liberal Christians, atheists and Jews.[5] Describing its mission as 'to evaluate the historical significance of every shred of evidence about Jesus from antiquity', it meets regularly to agree statements about the words and actions of Christ. These it aims to promulgate not only to academics but also to the public. It is best known for voting (using a system of colour-coded beads) on the genuineness of the words of Jesus as presented in the Gospels (the Gospel of Thomas being included on the same level as the canonical Gospels, which the Seminar refuses to privilege). The conclusion was that only fifteen of his 'supposed' sayings can confidently be attributed to

---

4. The field of current scholarship, at least as far as the 'Third Quest' and the Jesus Seminar are concerned, is very helpfully described by Tom Wright in *Jesus and the Victory of God*, which is the key work among his large output on this and related topics.

5. The Jesus Seminar and the Westar Institute both have websites which very clearly set out their agenda: see the Bibliography for details.

him. The group openly displays its anti-supernaturalistic bias. The introduction to *The Five Gospels*, which explains the Seminar's project, presents its mission as a heroic quest conducted in the face of the obscurantism and dogmatic blindness of the religious establishment.

From within this group spring many of the recent additions to history's long list of differing interpretations of Jesus' identity. An example of interest is Jesus as the wandering Cynic philosopher, one of those men who could have been seen across the Roman world and perhaps even in Galilee in Jesus' day. Surviving by begging, they were distinguished by their untidy appearance and ragged woollen cloaks. They rejected contemporary society and its values and wisdom; and sought to subvert it both by their words and by their sometimes outrageous actions. It is not hard to see this reconstruction as a reading back of recent Western anti-heroes into the first century; it is *very* hard to see such a character being regarded as a serious threat by the authorities, let alone becoming the origin of a movement which turned the world upside down. In any case, anyone committed to the truthfulness of Scripture will not need to spend very long considering such an account (or any of the others produced by the Jesus Seminar). But just here is the relevance for our purpose: our own understanding of Jesus' ministry has to account *both* for the fury of the Jewish authorities, to the point where they actively sought his death, *and* for their ability to persuade the Romans to execute him. Too 'other-worldly' an approach will fail to do this.

It is at this point that some evangelical interpretation of Jesus' mission falls short. In answer to the question posed by the title of this chapter, some will argue as follows. Jesus in his ministry is trying to disentangle his true kingdom from the political expectations of the Jews, which are for freedom from Rome, national supremacy and the like. In contrast, Jesus constantly presents the kingdom of God as entirely spiritual, 'not of this world', and therefore completely non-political. And the logical conclusion of such an argument would be that the kingdom does not interact with human power structures at all, except secondarily through private, 'personal' morality. Here, for example, is

Gerhaardus Vos: 'From all political bearings our Lord's teaching on the Kingdom was wholly disassociated'.[6]

Vos is not alone in understanding Jesus' words in John 18:36 ('My kingdom is not of this world') as supporting this viewpoint. Much of the New Testament evidence can certainly be read that way; we may often have done so. But there is a strong element in Jesus' message which resists this view, as we shall see when we consider the evidence of the Gospels in greater detail. The New Testament presents us with a kingdom that constantly collides with other, earthly kingdoms. It is in those collisions that we can find the earthly-level explanation for his execution and that the political implications of Jesus' ministry emerge clearly.

The context of Jesus: Powers and parties

'When the fullness of time had come, God sent forth his Son' (Gal. 4:4, ESV). Jesus was born not at an arbitrary time, but at the *right* time, the time precisely of God's choice. Jesus' context, the background against which we view his earthly life, was different from other times and in particular from our own. The pitfall we have to avoid is that of absolutizing Jesus' words and actions before we have considered how they would have been perceived and – literally – what *sense* they would have made, in the setting of first century Palestine. This is not to suggest we should leave Jesus' ministry in the first century; rather it is to improve our prospects of properly grasping his mission and especially its political implications. Our route here will be to give an overview of the contemporary situation and aspirations of Israel, especially the power structures to which its people were subject. Then we will look more closely at the sects and parties which made up the Judaism of Jesus' day: the specific affiliations that were on offer.

---

6. Vos, *The Kingdom and the Church*, p. 42. Some more recent treatments of Christ's mission have a similar emphasis – see, for example, Gruenler's 'Atonement in the Synoptic Gospels and Acts' in Hill and James (eds.), *The Glory of the Atonement*.

We need to begin by summarizing (and here we can only summarize) the Old Testament foundations of the contemporary Jewish hope. Israel's sense of identity, shared by every division of Judaism, was in being the uniquely chosen, Covenant people of the one true God, who as an expression of his favour had given them the special privilege of possessing the Law. The exile experience had clarified this identity: the problem of idolatry was no more and Torah was at the heart of national life. But in no sense did they feel that this was the end of the story or that God intended things to remain as they were. The earnest hope of the Jews was that the God who had chosen and formed the nation, who had brought them out of Egypt, given them kings, Temple and prophets and sustained a remnant through the exile, still had purposes to fulfil. The prophecies of the later chapters of Isaiah especially taught them to expect the coming of a new age when God's rule, already expressed through the institutions of Jewish national life, would be made visible and effectual among all nations. The date of the 'Day of the Lord' which would inaugurate the new age was, of course, unspecified; but it would come. The common interpretation of the prophetic message was that God would break into history; vindicate and establish his own people in their rightful, pre-eminent place; banish idolatry and other sinful, Gentile practices wherever they were found; and make Jerusalem the focal point of his kingdom on earth.

As a sub-theme within this great, political-religious hope we find the concept of Messiah. The word means simply 'anointed one' and in Old Testament times could be applied literally to kings and priests and symbolically to prophets as well. In the context of future national expectations it denoted an individual whom God would appoint as his agent to bring about deliverance. However, Jewish hopes did not *centre* on such a figure; they were more concerned with the new age and its characteristics. It is best to say that the idea of Messiah was available in the first century as a category within which a coming deliverer could be understood.

The hopes derived from the prophets of ancient times, however, were overlaid with the traumas of more recent history. It was understood in Jesus' time that authentic, authoritative prophecy had ceased centuries before – even before the arrival of

Alexander's armies in the late fourth century BC. The subsequent rule of the Seleucids had been brought to an end in the 160s and 150s BC by the Maccabean revolt. Never were religion and politics more closely intertwined than in this time, when the fight for national self-determination was launched at an altar and guerrilla tactics included forced circumcision; and when the question of whether it was legitimate to fight on the Sabbath became a key facet of military tactics. Under the Hasmonean kingdom which had succeeded the revolt, the Jews enjoyed a brief though troubled period of independence. True political independence lasted from 142 to 63 BC (with a short interruption around 130 when Syrian control was reasserted). The nation was riven by internal disputes over issues such as the validity of the Hasmoneans' high priest-hood, Hellenization and the personal qualities of the kings. However, in 63 the Romans under Pompey entered Jerusalem and the region was placed under the supervision of the province of Syria. The dream of independence was over, at least for the fore-seeable future. At the time of Jesus' ministry, the very last living memory of Jewish self-rule was fading away.

Jesus' direct interactions were with Jews in Palestine, so we will not consider the position of the Jewish diaspora here. However, we should note that as well as Jews moving out into the wider world, the wider world had also come to Palestine in the form of Hellenizing influences. For nearly 200 years, until soon after the Maccabean revolt, the land had been under the control of Alexander and his successors. Resistance to or acceptance of the culture they had sought to impose, sometimes by force, had been a source of division among Jews ever since. The origins of the Pharisees, Sadducees and Essenes may well lie in these divisions. Nor did Hellenization cease with the end of Seleucid rule. In add-ition to this influence, the Jews had to tolerate the presence of the Samaritans, whose origins are hard to pinpoint but for whom their antipathy is very clear in the New Testament. To a large extent, then, and not for the first or last time in history, Judaism felt itself to be under threat culturally as well as politically at the time of Jesus.

Herod the Great (37–4 BC) and his successors were client kings who had to comply with Rome's demands. As long as they main-tained security and supplied the requisite tax revenues, they were free to organize the internal administration and politics as they pleased. Herod himself was unpopular with the Jews in spite of his lavish rebuilding of the temple. When Herod died, the kingdom was divided and at the time of Jesus' ministry his son Herod Antipas still ruled Galilee and Perea (Luke 23:7). Matthew and probably Zacchaeus worked for Antipas, not for the Romans.[7] However, Judea, along with Samaria and Idumea, was by this time ruled directly by the Romans through prefects (later known as procurators), of whom Pontius Pilate was one. Pilate's overlord was the emperor Tiberius Caesar, whose head would have appeared on the silver denarius handed to Jesus with the question over tax in Matthew 22:19. Although Judea saw no major upheavals during the reign of Tiberius (and no legions were based there, the nearest being in Syria), it was nevertheless a troublesome posting. Pilate would make sure to be present in Jerusalem at the time of the Passover, when the commemoration of that earlier liberation would stir the longings of the great crowds for God's anticipated deliverance. Pilate clashed on several occasions with the Jews: a case of Roman political demands confronting Jewish religious sensibilities. In this world, politics and religion were inseparable.

The Roman occupation restricted, but did not eliminate, the ability of the Jews to organize themselves and in part to govern their own affairs. The Sanhedrin comprised leading priests, lay aristocracy and experts in the Law. Its exact functions during the period before AD 70 are unclear, but it was certainly connected closely with the temple and wielded religious, judicial and political power. The temple itself dominated Jerusalem physically, occupying a quarter of its area; according to Josephus it appeared like a 'mountain of snow' as one approached the city. Scholars conventionally describe the whole post-exilic period as 'Second Temple', but in spite of the continuity with the one described in Ezra, Herod's was a different and far grander building. The temple was very wealthy at this time, supported by the half-shekel tax (Matt. 17:24). It dominated the nation's religious life. It was, of course, the place of

---

7. Zacchaeus' job would have been to assess taxes payable on goods passing from Perea, across the Jordan, into Judea.

sacrifice and pilgrimage. This meant that it was also a centre of power. The priestly clique who ran the temple controlled the great annual festivals as well as the system of sacrifices, both the regular 'national' ones and those brought by individuals. The attitude of different groups to the integrity – even the validity – of the temple ceremonies and authorities was a key part of their religious and political outlook. The Samaritans represent an extreme example of rejection, maintaining the rightfulness of worship on Mount Gerizim even though their rival temple there had been destroyed.[8]

So, in the light of the glorious expectations of God's intervention and yet in the darkness of the current realities, how did the Jews of Jesus' time understand their own position? What was the 'state of mind' of his first hearers? Certainly, it was largely one of frustration at their powerlessness; but there is some disagreement over how exactly that was expressed. There is an influential view, strongly articulated by Wright, that the Jews believed they were still in exile, and that this theme is basic to Jewish self-understanding in the first century. The exile had never ended and the magnificent prophecies of the later chapters of Isaiah had never been fulfilled. The fact that Israel was not free, that the supreme authority was a Roman prefect rather than the Davidic king, and crucially that the Lord had not intervened in the expected way to bring in his eschatological reign – all these pointed to the continuation of exile, the penalty for Israel's repeated failure to keep the covenant.

In response to this view, several points can be made. The first is to agree that the return-from-exile prophecies had *not* been completely fulfilled in the returns under Zerubbabel and Ezra. Both Jews of the first century and Christians today freely acknowledge this: we look to the ingathering to Christ of the peoples of the world as the fulfilment of passages such as Isaiah 49 and 55. But does this mean that the exile still continued? The view should

----

8. Jesus' conversation with the Samaritan woman in John 4 declares both the correctness of Jerusalem as the location of the temple and the end of the era when it mattered. The woman's interjection about where to worship was far from being a 'red herring', as is often claimed; it went to the heart of Jewish–Samaritan divisions.

at least be qualified. Against Wright, we should point out firstly that the Jews of Palestine were *in the land*. The Covenant curses for disobedience dwelt heavily on displacement from the land (stated most climactically in Deut. 29:28 but also through the previous chapter). It was not strictly their *own* land, yet they enjoyed a measure of independence, especially in religious observances. The Romans had made a number of concessions such as avoiding the display of standards bearing the imperial image in Jerusalem. Moreover there *had* been a time, within the past century, when true political independence had prevailed.

A second point concerns the temple, which was not only overwhelming in appearance but which operated freely (again with Roman consent) and represented a focus of pride for the Jewish nation (Mark 13:1). True, *some* Jews regarded Herod's Temple as tainted because it had been built by an impostor; many others, however, proved their acceptance of it by freely contributing to its maintenance and turning out in droves for the festivals. Third, we should note that the Old Testament at a number of points regards the exile as strictly limited in duration. As well as Jeremiah 25:11 and 29:10 and Daniel 9:2, this is the clear implication of the final verses of 2 Chronicles, which effectively define the end-point of the exile in the proclamation of Cyrus. At least in the usual historical sense, the exile had ended over five centuries before Christ was born. Finally we must note John 8:33, where one group of Jews is heard to say, 'We have never been slaves to anyone. How do you say that we shall become free?' While this flies in the face of history, it does at least testify to a sense in which the Jews believed they were free at that time – perhaps, as O'Donovan suggests, demonstrating how a culture of obedience to the Law had effectively created a sense of autonomy.[9]

---

9. See O'Donovan, *The Desire of the Nations*, p. 100. Wright's scheme goes as far as equating 'forgiveness of sins' with 'return from exile' (*Jesus and the Victory of God*, p. 268). But if Jesus so clearly saw his mission as bringing an end to the exile, he would certainly have spoken explicitly in those terms. I think Wright has allowed the category of exile to become too controlling and the emphasis on *national* salvation too strong.

However, what is certainly the case is that the apparent failure of God to intervene in the way foretold by the prophets was felt as a cause of massive national disappointment. Some Jews at least did conclude that they might as well still be in exile. The apocalyptic writings of the intertestamental period bear witness to a sense of near-despair. These writings are inspired by the sense that Israel is no longer an idolatrous nation – she faithfully observes the Torah – yet Yahweh has abandoned her. Prophecy is no more: the Gentiles flourish while God's people are oppressed. They express the familiar theme: God will, at last, break in and establish the anticipated world order, ruling the nations through Israel, which will have a rebuilt and uncompromised temple and a pure and wholehearted dedication to observing the Torah.[10] It is against this background that we can understand the disciples' plea to the departing Jesus: 'Lord, are you *at this time* going to restore the kingdom to Israel?' (Acts 1:6). It goes without saying that this compound of despair and enduring hope seamlessly integrated religion and politics.

Having surveyed what the Jews mostly shared in common, we now need to ask what groups competed for the allegiance of ordinary people, and how did Jesus relate to them? For Judaism was far from unified. Many sayings and events in the Gospels come into clearer focus when we understand a little about the different sects and their political positions.

Of the three major Jewish sects identified by Josephus, two are mentioned frequently in the Gospels and one appears not at all. The word 'Pharisee' denotes 'separated', though how far they thought of themselves as a select group is not certain. Mostly laity rather than priests, they observed the Torah strictly and in addition

---

10. There is much debate whether or not the apocalypses reflect a break from the prophets' stance that God would bring these things about *within* history. On this view (favoured, for example, by Ladd) apocalyptic literature is inspired by the sense that 'history has got us nowhere' – the only hope is that God will break in from the outside. Others see greater continuity between the prophets and apocalypticists. What does seem clear is that apocalyptic is language adopted by the oppressed.

followed a large body of oral traditions which interpreted and expanded the original laws, especially around the cherished issue of table fellowship (Mark 7:3, 5). This oral tradition had attained the same authoritative status as Torah (Gal. 1:14; Phil. 3:5–6), and to some extent this combination was beginning to assume as much importance as the temple cult, paving the way for it to become the accepted *alternative* to the temple when the latter was destroyed. As far as politics is concerned, they were quite prepared to criticize the ruling authorities, but their primary concern was to maintain their own purity and to urge it on others. Although they had no official status, Josephus names them as the most influential of the sects: his quoted number of around 6,000 actually refers only to those involved in a specific incident and their total numbers must have been greater.

The fact that Jesus criticizes the Pharisees so frequently and so sternly does not imply a great distance from them. On the contrary, his own teaching about the Law, about resurrection and about judgment are far closer to the Pharisees' understanding than to any other group in Judaism. He had friendly relations with a number of Pharisees (Luke 7:36ff; 11:37; 13:31; 14:1). We do not need to think that all Pharisees were hypocrites or that all were opposed to Jesus. We will return to his differences with them a little later.

The Sadducees have left few historical traces outside the New Testament. None of their own literature survives. Theologically they were very conservative – they did not accept the idea of resurrection – although there is little evidence for the traditional belief that they regarded only the Pentateuch as canonical Scripture. Their importance for now lies in their holding political power in Jerusalem. The High Priests and other high-ranking officials were Sadducees: they were quite willing to cooperate with the Roman authorities in order to preserve the status quo and with it their own position. The Sadducees would cooperate with the Pharisees when it suited their purpose, but it was not hard for an expert like Paul to exploit their divisions (Acts 23:6–8)!

The Essenes are usually associated with the Qumran community, who (probably) wrote the Dead Sea Scrolls. In fact, Josephus says that the Essenes were widely distributed in Judea and there may well have been a community within Jerusalem itself: a 'gate of the Essenes' is recorded. The Essenes were a strict grouping devoted to the study of the Law: entry required a probationary period. The Qumran sect seems to have represented a strict branch of the Essenes who had withdrawn into ascetic seclusion as an act of protest against the corruption of the Jerusalem establishment. Qumran was a disciplined and highly regulated community which looked back to its founding by the unnamed 'Teacher of Righteousness'. Here we do find evidence of an explicit Messianic hope, for the Scrolls look forward to the coming of (at least) two Messiahs – one priestly, one military/kingly.

The Essenes in general rejected the temple and its ruling group. In view of the Sadducees' accommodation with Rome, this attitude is hardly surprising. We might suppose that the Essene community of Qumran forms an exception to the rule that religion and politics were everywhere entangled. Not so: the withdrawal to Qumran was very much a political statement, a condemnation of the Jewish ruling establishment as corrupt and condemned by God.

A fourth group we need to identify here are the Zealots. At the time of Jesus they were not yet a defined political grouping – they took the lead in the Jewish revolt from AD 66 onwards – but the term could be used more generally of those involved in or sympathetic to revolutionary activity (as with the disciple Simon, Luke 6:15). Acts 5:36–39 and 21:38 show that Jesus' movement would readily be understood in such terms. Their presence reminds us that violent revolution was an obvious and definitely available option for anyone who was serious about changing the status quo. Yoder is certainly right to say that Jesus' steadfast refusal to get involved in such actions was a highly political stance to take. Indeed, since *all* these groups represent political as much as religious positions, Jesus' failure to align himself with any of them is politically significant.

Such, then, is the background against which Jesus' message was first heard. It was in the days of Tiberius, of Pilate and the Herods, of fervent unfulfilled national hopes, of warring factions covering the full range of responses to occupation, that John the Baptist came preaching repentance and Jesus brought the message of the kingdom.

At this point a further question arises: how far should historical context *dictate* the way we understand that message? Given that Jesus was a first-century Jew speaking to first-century Jews in first-century Palestine, are we bound to insist that the terms and categories we find in his message, especially the language of the kingdom of God, can have been used *only* in ways which his first hearers would have thoroughly understood? The fact that Jesus never actually *defines* the kingdom of God – and no-one is recorded as having asked him to do so – strongly implies that much of the meaning, at least, was taken for granted.[11] Jesus' audiences may have misunderstood much, but there *was* an existing conceptual framework into which his words could be slotted. This framework often gives an important guide to our understanding of Jesus' intended meaning. However, it is possible to impose it too rigidly. Wright insists on making it a methodological principle that we may ascribe to Jesus' sayings only meanings which would be thoroughly accessible to a first-century Palestinian audience, implying that we cannot expect to find too much originality![12] But this is surely to bind Jesus too far into his context. We can reasonably ask whether there would have been so much misunderstanding if all that he said fitted so neatly into the existing categories.

The mission of Jesus

It is now time to make the closer acquaintance of the Gospel accounts. It is an instructive exercise simply to read through the Gospels on the lookout for political overtones – something that evangelicals are not accustomed to doing. It at once becomes clear that a great deal of what Jesus said and did can be understood in political terms. We have already seen that the hope of Israel had strong political content. O'Donovan puts it neatly when he remarks that 'almost the whole vocabulary of salvation

---

11. See Ladd, *Jesus and the Kingdom*, p. 41.

12. The same approach is found in Jeremias' very influential treatment of Jesus' parables.

in the New Testament has a political pre-history of some kind'.[13] The word 'shepherd' is a good example. Does Jesus fill this language entirely with new, non-political meaning? We shall see.

In this section, then, we shall work through Jesus' life and ministry in three stages: his birth and early life; his public ministry; and the events surrounding his death and resurrection. We shall pay attention not only to Jesus' own words and deeds in their context but also to the immediate reactions of others; and we shall also keep an eye on the geography of his mission, a factor often overlooked. And although we shall look at all four Gospels, understanding the likelihood that they were written for different theological purposes and with different audiences in view, we shall honour the unity of Scripture by bearing in mind that all represent the same Jesus.

Birth and early life

The opening of Matthew clearly presents Jesus as the fulfilment of Israel's hopes. The genealogy in chapter 1 represents Jewish national history in three stages of equal length, with Jesus as the culmination. He is the rightful successor to Abraham the nation's elect founder, David the prototypical king and Zerubbabel the restorer from exile. His name is to be Jesus, the Saviour of his people – a term which immediately evokes political salvation, yet such expectation is immediately qualified (corrected?) 'from their sins' (Matt. 1:21).

The visit of the Magi to Jerusalem represents the first clash between Jesus (though he is absent!) and earthly rulers. The visitors style the new arrival 'King of the Jews', a term which must have induced near-apoplexy in Herod the Great, for it was the title that he claimed and spent his entire reign struggling to have acknowledged as rightful. The scribes quote Micah 5:2, 4, with its promise of a 'ruler' and 'shepherd', both political terms. And Herod's request to the Magi is couched in religious language but is clearly political in intent: the power of an earthly ruler is at stake. His failure to secure his visitors' compliance costs the babies of

---

13. O'Donovan, *The Desire of the Nations*, p. 22.

Bethlehem their lives. He may have been wrong about the nature of the challenge, but he was right to see that the new King would pose a threat to power like his own. Was Jesus political? Herod the Great certainly thought so!

The Gospel writer is clear that Jesus' subsequent sojourn in Egypt represents more than a convenient bolt-hole. The fulfilment quotation from Hosea 11:1 ('Out of Egypt I called my son') is puzzling only until we understand that Jesus is seen as personifying the new Israel. It is significant that Joseph returns with his family, not simply to 'Israel', but to 'the *land* of Israel' (Matt. 2:20, 21). This is clearly a re-enactment of the exodus. The new Joshua has arrived in the land. Of course, this is a theological interpretation of events which could never have been seen that way at the time, but that does not diminish its importance as a pointer to the true nature of Jesus' mission. At the very least, Matthew has grounded it deeply in Jewish history and hopes. And we have strong hints that the new King will make earthly claims as well as heavenly ones.

Luke is the other Gospel which gives an account of Jesus' human origins. His story begins at the very heart of Jewish religious life – the Jerusalem temple,[14] where Zechariah is found experiencing his once-in-a-lifetime opportunity to offer incense in the Holy Place. He and his wife represent the faithful Jews who are fully committed to the Law (Luke 1:5–6). In spite of the fact that the temple is widely regarded as compromised, the Lord arranges that the first announcement of his new work should be made there. There will be continuity with what has gone before as well as discontinuity.

This continuity is stressed too in the annunciation to Mary. The One to be born will reign on David's throne: he will receive the promise made to David of a never-ending kingdom (2 Sam. 7:16; Luke 1:31–33). Although the nature of this kingdom is not here specified, Gabriel's words would be heard clearly as announcing the arrival of the new age, the longed-for eschatological kingdom.

---

14. Herod's temple was still under construction at this point (indeed, work was still in progress at the time of Jesus' ministry), but the work was carefully arranged so as not to obstruct the regular rituals.

And while we may instinctively attempt to spiritualize Mary's song to Elizabeth, when we read it in context it is very political. Not only will humility be exalted above pride (categories we feel comfortable with?), but *rulers* will be deposed, the *hungry* (i.e. poor) fed and the *rich* turned away (Luke 1:51–53).[15] Was Jesus political? His mother thought so! The outpouring of God's mercy on 'those who fear him' (including the faithful poor such as Mary and Elizabeth) will bring about a definite change in the social order. To put it another way, the mission of Jesus, the Saviour, implies as an essential outcome precisely the kind of social justice called for by Amos and the other prophets – and, of course, in the Law itself. Whatever earthly rulers may demand, God will bring this about among the people of the kingdom.

Luke's account of Jesus' early life contains expressions whose meaning can be grasped only as it is filled in later in the story. Zechariah's song at the end of chapter 1 contains both apparently political ('salvation from our enemies', v. 71) and explicitly spiritual elements ('forgiveness of their sins', v. 77). The two are closely related, for it was understood that forgiveness would bring about national restoration. Hindsight will show that restoration did not come in quite the expected way, but that does not mean the hope was empty. Simeon foretells 'the falling and rising of many in Israel' (Luke 2:34). The full meaning is veiled, beyond the clear statement that the fortunes of the Jews will depend on the way they respond to God's revelation in Jesus.

Public ministry

When Jesus begins his public ministry, he does so by crossing the Jordan and entering the land – for the place where John was baptizing is 'on the other side of the Jordan' (John 1:28, 10:40), as is the wilderness of temptation. Again, there is a sense of re-enacting Israel's history: this is the beginning of the kingdom's conquest. His first move takes him to Galilee in fulfilment of Isaiah 9 (Matt. 4:12–17), quoting the opening of a prophetic oracle which looks

---

15. It seems best to read the series of aorists in these verses as prophetic, looking forward to what God will accomplish 'from now on' (v. 48).

forward to the coming Davidic kingdom and liberty from oppression. Why does Matthew choose to highlight Galilee as 'the area of Zebulun and Naphtali' even though this description is anachronistic? Surely it is to emphasize the *continuity* of Jesus' mission with the ancient hopes of Israel. The kingdom is coming at last – and, sure enough, this is exactly how Jesus now begins to preach (v. 17). If Jesus means something totally new and different by 'kingdom', it would make no sense to quote from Isaiah here. In words echoed by Mark 1:15, Jesus calls for repentance as the appropriate response. The kingdom's arrival is good news for the repentant; judgment is implied (and later pronounced) for the unrepentant.

Another link to Isaiah is made in Luke 4, where we read of Jesus' visit to the synagogue in Nazareth. Here he claims to be fulfilling Isaiah's vision of an eschatological Jubilee year. Jubilee was a highly political institution. Properly observed, it would severely limit the concentration of power and wealth into a few hands. Isaiah's vision expands the concept from a time-bound cycle into a description of a new regime which truly reflects God's justice and where his faithful people receive the full measure of his blessing. And Jesus announces the inauguration of this new age 'today'. Read in its context, this must imply the dawning of a new day where God's justice will be seen at work, where wrongs will be righted: specifically, the injustices which lead to oppression and captivity. Just as with the song of Mary, we need to understand these words in a way consistent with their fulfilment 'today', not in some still future golden age. Does it not strain credulity to believe that Jesus intended to empty them entirely of their most obvious meaning: relationships between men and women here on earth?

We cannot discuss every aspect of Jesus' teaching on the kingdom of God.[16] We will dwell on the features relating to power structures and allegiances. Running through the crucial thirteenth chapter of Matthew, with its seven parables of the kingdom, are certain common themes. One is the *progress* of the kingdom from

---

16. 'Kingdom of God' and 'kingdom of heaven' can be taken as synonyms, the different usage determined largely by the different audiences for which the Gospels were intended.

small to great, from hiddenness to visibility and prominence. In its early (seedling) stages, the kingdom's impact will be limited and hard to discern. But as it grows it becomes both obvious and effective, bearing distinctive and identifiable fruit. Another theme is the extended *coexistence* of the kingdom with the world outside it. Only at the end of the age will it be completely clear who belongs to which realm. For our purposes, both these themes can be regarded as sub-themes of another: the kingdom is an *objective reality*. It is not a state of mind, a feeling or an inward disposition only; it exists in the real world and it has defined boundaries. People are in it or they are not in it, for it or against it; and when they truly encounter it, not only is there untold joy but their reaction is to abandon all that they have in order to become part of it. That is what the kingdom of God is 'like'. Those who, like the rich man of Matthew 19, will not abandon all will not receive joy, will not receive eternal life, and will be unable to enter the kingdom.[17]

The parable of the Good Samaritan (Luke 10) takes the expression of allegiances further. Who is a true neighbour? For the one who wants to inherit eternal life (enter the kingdom), the answer is made clear. The representatives of the temple – priest and Levite – fail to be 'neighbours'. Instead, the Samaritan acts as a 'neighbour' to the Jew in need. In addition to the more spiritual lessons with which we are so familiar, the parable makes two important political points. First, as far as the coming kingdom is concerned, the temple is a dead end. Its servants are concerned only with their ritual purity and ceremonies, which were never as important as mercy and justice anyway and which will soon be shown to be completely obsolete. The temple and its associated power structures are finished.

Second, within the kingdom, previous national and ethnic loyalties are abandoned. The Samaritan is the enemy – but not so in the kingdom. Allegiances to political entities such as nation states are

---

17. In this passage (and the parallel in Mark 10), 'receiving eternal life' and 'entering the kingdom' (as well as 'being saved') are regarded as equivalent. This justifies treating 'eternal life questions' as 'kingdom questions'.

undermined by the claims of the kingdom, where 'Love your neighbour' crosses every human boundary. The awkward response of Jesus' questioner in verse 37 suggests that he finds this too much to accept. And in the kingdom, previous models for ruling will not be followed either (Mark 10:42–44). The domination of underlings which characterizes Gentile kingdoms is to be replaced by mutual servanthood, initially modelled by the Twelve, the kingdom society in embryo. There will be ruling structures in the new society, but they will not be based on a culture of superiority or status. The kingdom will present an unprecedented alternative politics.

Jesus' forays outside Jewish territory further hint at the breakdown of ethnic barriers in the kingdom. Although his mission is stated to be primarily 'to the lost sheep of Israel' (Matt. 10:6), he speaks of having 'other sheep' (John 10:16) which will be called and joined to the sheep of Israel in a *single* flock. He begins this mission within his own ministry, as he heals the Gadarene demoniac and ministers in Tyre and Sidon and in the Decapolis (Mark 7) as well as in Samaria. The driving out of demons in several of these places represents a dramatic demonstration of the arrival of the kingdom: manifested, against Jewish expectations, *outside* the boundaries of ethnic Israel as well as inside.

Jesus' ministry is characterized by a refusal to be side-tracked by the demands of earthly rulers. Warned by Pharisees that Herod (Antipas) is pursuing him, he steadfastly continues with the work of the kingdom (Luke 13:31–33 – the word itself is not used, but Jesus describes its characteristic signs). Herod is dismissed as a 'fox', understood as an animal possessed of cunning but undeserving of respect. Jesus is on his way to die in Jerusalem, and the claims of the local ruler will not deflect him. The kingdom agenda takes priority.

Of course, allegiance to the kingdom of God goes well beyond issues of earthly loyalties. The spiritual claims of the kingdom are made clear in Luke 11, where Jesus is accused of driving out demons by the power of Beelzebub. His reply makes three key points: Satan has his own kingdom and he is hardly likely to be making war on himself (v. 18); the defeat of demons proclaims the arrival of the kingdom of God (v. 20); and Jesus' ministry divides everyone unequivocally into two camps – for or against, one kingdom or the other (v. 23).

Given that the kingdom makes such powerful claims, it is not surprising that Jesus' announcement of it aroused such strong responses: to these we now turn.[18] In Mark 2:1 – 3:6 we find Jesus' early ministry generating increasing opposition from the religious authorities, culminating in plots to kill him. Here is an example of Pharisees making common cause with those normally their opponents, described in this case as 'Herodians'. We know little of the Herodians, but the label proves them to be a political grouping defined by their support for the Herods. The threat posed by Jesus was sufficiently strong to warrant such cooperation; what, then, was the nature of the threat? The first point of conflict was Jesus' claim to forgive sins (2:1–12), taking the place of God. The second point was his breaking the oral traditions of purity (2:15–17); the third concerned fasting (2:18–22); and finally, and apparently most seriously, there was Sabbath breaking (2:23ff and 3:1–6). Two of these reasons – claiming equality with God and Sabbath breaking – are brought together in John 5:18, and the former recurs at greater length in John 10:31ff.

On the face of it, these are not political issues. However, the fact that the *Herodians* joined the Pharisees shows that they, at least, did perceive political issues to be at stake. Jesus' words and actions threatened to undermine the position of both groups. The Pharisees, as the defenders of the traditions, stood to lose their influence. More seriously, the Herodians – and the establishment in general – stood to lose their power. If forgiveness was available with a word,[19] the whole sacrificial system, on which the temple was based, would be obsolete. The Herodians were quite right to recognize the threat: these were precisely the implications of Jesus' message. Later in the Gospels (Matt. 22; Mark 12), the same alliance tackled Jesus again on the clearly political matter of taxpaying; we will return to this encounter a little later.

---

18. Jesus' confrontation with Pilate will be dealt with in the following section.

19. In Wright's words, it is like 'a private individual approaching a prisoner in jail and offering him a royal pardon, signed by himself' (*Jesus and the Victory of God*, p. 435).

The motives for the plot against Jesus are spelled out most directly in John 11:45–53. Here we see the Sanhedrin acting in concert despite the parties' differences. Caiaphas inadvertently prophesies that Jesus will die for the people – and indeed, for all 'the scattered children of God'. But before that, the group as a whole identifies the threat it faces: that the growing popularity of the Jesus movement will lead to the intervention of the Romans. They will 'take away from us both the place and the nation' (v. 48, literal rendering): a highly significant statement in several ways. 'From *us*' implies the personal interests of the leaders. 'The place' probably refers to the temple, in whose courts they were sitting.[20] The nation would be crushed and their own power base eliminated. In short, the establishment identified Jesus as a political threat who had to be removed. Once again, the issue is power. Was Jesus political? The Jewish authorities certainly thought so!

In sharp contrast to the attitude of the authorities, Jesus frequently found a willing and appreciative audience among the common people: 'the crowds'. Clearly, there were several strands in his ministry which appealed to them. One was undoubtedly the way that Jesus stood up against the Jewish authorities: Mark 12:37, only a few days before his death, is a good example. Another was the personal authority with which he spoke, so different from the endless quoting of traditions they were used to (Matt. 7:28–29). Of course, many came to witness or to receive the benefit of the miracles which were the signs of the kingdom. But there was also an explicitly political response, found especially in turbulent Galilee. After the feeding of the five thousand, John records that Jesus withdrew from the scene because he knew that the people wanted to 'seize him so as to make him king' (John 6:15, literal rendering). The miracles had raised the people's expectations of deliverance to fever pitch and they were ready for revolution.

We recall that this was not some new concept: messianic movements were in currency and the seeds, at least, of the Zealot movement had already been sown. It was an option available to

---

20. These verses also show that the Jewish authorities did have a significant
   degree of independence which they were seriously worried about losing.

Jesus and many would have expected him to take it. Against this background, elements of his teaching become clearer. The kingdom's claims are absolute, but they do not imply violent revolution even against the most corrupt or tyrannical authorities. It is the meek who will inherit God's earth, and the peacemakers who will be called his sons (Matt. 5:5, 9). Almost certainly, the 'violent men' who are taking hold of the kingdom (Matt. 11:12 – preached in Galilee in the context of John the Baptist's potential misunderstanding of the kingdom) are the people who would use it as a vehicle for violent ends.[21] This is the way of the world's revolutionaries, but it is not the way of Jesus.

He sets out his alternative way in the 'Good Shepherd' discourse of John 10, with its strong echoes of Ezekiel 34. There are the 'thieves and robbers' (v. 8) and there is the Good Shepherd. The thieves and robbers certainly include the corrupt Jewish leadership, headquartered in the temple and wielding both religious and political power. But the use of the word 'robber' (*lēstēs*) suggests that the proto-zealots are also in mind, especially given that 'shepherd' would be understood as a political term. Barabbas was a *lēstēs*. Josephus uses the term to describe revolutionaries. At least in part, Jesus' words are directed against such a perversion of the kingdom. In contrast he, the Good Shepherd, lays down his life for the sheep (v. 15). If he is to die, it will not be in some desperate battle or ambush, struggling to throw off Roman domination like a latter-day Judas Maccabaeus; it will be of his own volition. This is the Father's specific commission to him (v. 18).

Many temptations lay in Jesus' path. Satan himself laid another, offering him 'all the kingdoms of the world' (Luke 4:5) if he would turn aside to worship him. Jesus' public ministry demonstrates that his mission is, indeed, to claim the world's kingdoms. But he will

---

21. Ladd is among those who interpret this verse in terms of people joining the kingdom legitimately – a forceful advance demanding a forceful reaction (see *Jesus and the Kingdom*, pp. 155–160). But it makes little sense to think of submitting to God's rule as a forceful act, let alone a violent one. The objections raised against reading this verse in terms of Zealot violence are not strong.

not do it by succumbing to temptation: he will neither fall for
Satan's lies nor use violence. His claims have been clearly
expressed. The kingdom of God demands allegiances which both
transcend and subvert all earthly loyalties; they threaten and therefore arouse earthly power structures; their triumph is inevitable.

Death and resurrection

We now arrive at the final week before Jesus' death. Here we find
the clearest insights into the political implications of Jesus'
kingdom proclamation. The week begins with the triumphal entry
into Jerusalem. He is rightly hailed by the crowds as king of Israel,
coming in the name of the Lord. At the time this could only mean
identification as a deliverer, coming to vindicate the faithful and
establish God's kingdom in Jerusalem. The palm branches are
likely to have symbolized nationalistic hopes.

Yet Jesus rides on a donkey, not a war horse. The scene thus
evokes Zechariah 9, which concerns the coming of the king to
Zion, bringing peace over the nations rather than emphasizing
conquest. And on his way, he weeps over the city. His mission has
been mistaken: while the rulers oppose it because of the genuine
political threat it poses, most of the people misunderstand it
because they are looking for the wrong kind of salvation. Luke
19:41–44 shows that the Sanhedrin's strategy will not work. Their
rejection and condemnation of the coming king will not bring
them the peace they are looking for. It will not save them from the
wrath of Rome: rather, in God's providence, Rome will be the
instrument of judgment. Israel as a political entity will cease to
exist because she has not recognized the time or the mode of
God's return to Zion. The whole episode reflects the truth that for
all it demands of its followers, Jesus' is not primarily a political
kingdom and his is not a political salvation. However, that is not to
say that none of its demands is political.

The temple incident which immediately follows is a direct
confrontation between Jesus and the authorities. There have been
several interpretations of this incident: a protest against the financial abuses of the temple system and the attendant exploitation of
worshippers; a sign that the temple's day is over (because the sacrificial arrangements are temporarily interrupted); denunciation of

a symbol of national political resistance (the temple is a den of *lēstai*). The quotation from Jeremiah 7:11 recalls the corruption of the earlier temple, which in turn reminds the prophet's listeners of the destruction of Shiloh, itself corrupt, and accuses Israel of a complacency which is comfortable with all kinds of sin while using the temple as a national talisman.

Even more significant is the reference to a 'house of prayer for all nations', quoted from Isaiah 56:7, where the background is the calling of throngs of foreigners into the people of God. While Jesus obviously objects to the large-scale dealings in progress in the temple courts, it is unlikely in view of these references that financial corruption is his main target. Rather, the temple has come to epitomize Jewish national pride to the exclusion of those 'other sheep' whom Jesus has come to call. They are excluded *both* by the spirit of nationalism which is already simmering into rebellion and will soon explode; *and* by the focus on commercial activities which physically displace the worshippers (Gentiles were confined to the largest, outermost court where the trading would have taken place) and distract from the real business of prayer and worship.[22] Mark's bracketing of the temple incident with the cursing of the fig tree makes this interpretation near certain: the temple's true purpose has been subverted by becoming a vehicle for Jewish nationalism, which seeks a narrow ethnic triumph rather than the sort of kingdom Jesus is announcing. The nation is bearing none of the fruit which God intended and is destined for judgment.

The parable of the tenants (Matt. 21:33–46) makes the coming judgment crystal clear. Unlike the earlier parables, the message of this one is all too comprehensible (v. 45). The kingdom will be taken away and given to 'other tenants' who *will* produce fruit (vv. 41, 43). Both chief priests and Pharisees recognize themselves

---

22. It is very doubtful that Jesus' limited action would halt the sacrifices, even temporarily. They were being made in a different part of the temple, and the authorities could easily take steps to ensure that the regular, daily sacrifices at least were not interrupted. At the siege of Jerusalem they continued until the final possible moment!

as the target. Jesus' message is directed against all the leading players in Judaism, the influential and the powerful; and for that reason the parable is political as well as religious. The parable of the wedding banquet (Matt. 22:1–14) reinforces it: the kingdom banquet will be attended by the most unexpected guests; unexpected, that is, to the Jews.

Pharisees and opponents again make common cause when they tackle Jesus with an explicitly political trap – the question of paying taxes to Caesar (Matt. 22:15–22). The question is an invitation to make either a politically subversive statement, giving them grounds to betray him to Rome, or a submissive one, enabling them to discredit him with the crowds. But Jesus' response is to point to the existence of a higher authority. Caesar can have his tax: salvation does not lie in denying him that. Jesus appears rather indifferent to taxation issues! But it is a mistake to understand his attitude as thereby non-political. Only people with a long heritage of a democracy, with its checks and balances, could possibly read it that way! Jesus is hinting at a limit to the role of earthly rulers: in the context of a culture where not only a Roman emperor but *any* earthly ruler was likely to claim unlimited power, that is unmistakably a political statement. Rulers should learn humility; and allegiance to God is a greater demand. The implication is that Jesus' questioners are not giving it.

For most of the Jews, the true enemy is Rome and the sign of God's kingdom will be the decisive defeat of the pagan overlords. Jesus says the true enemy is 'the prince of this world' (John 12:31, spoken to the crowd; John 16:11, to the disciples). Satan's lordship over the present, evil age is thus acknowledged, but Jesus has come to condemn him and drive him out. Therefore the methods of earthly combat are inappropriate. It is no good taking up arms against Rome or any other human enemy: even if it were successful, it would not advance the kingdom at all.

So the time comes for Jesus' arrest, trial and execution. Here the issues of power and authority are focused most sharply. At Gethsemane Jesus struggles with temptation, but surely not the one Yoder proposes. Jesus has shown not the least sign of pursuing an armed struggle; it is the horror of the approaching cross and the impending shadow of the wrath of God which fill his mind. It is rather his disciples and opponents who are thinking in such terms. Peter attacks a member of the arresting party (Matt. 26:51) and Jesus responds that while infinite military power is his to call on (twelve *legions* of angels, v. 53), this is not to be his way. 'Am I leading a rebellion?' he asks (Mark 14:48). Of course not. The real enemy is not here in the garden; the climactic battle is still a few hours off.

While the hearing before the Sanhedrin does little more than reiterate the issues already raised during Jesus' public ministry, and Jesus has nothing to say to Herod, the confrontation with Pilate is very revealing. Pilate has no interest in internal Jewish disputes unless and until they threaten uprising. He is interested in the political question: 'Are you the king of the Jews?' (Matt. 27:11). Jesus answers positively. This no longer creates so direct a clash as in the days of Herod the Great, for Judea no longer has a king, but it is nonetheless a claim to authority and as such Pilate is bound to investigate it. While all the Gospels record that Pilate concludes there is really no case to answer, only John shows us why. In private, face-to-face debate, the Emperor's representative confronts the King of Kings.[23]

The political context is important to understanding what transpires. Pilate is accustomed to fighting battles of wits and wills with the Jewish leaders and he is disposed to regard these accusations against Jesus as one more example of the genre. His priority is to prevent trouble (both within the land and between himself and Rome) while demonstrating his own supreme authority over the Jews. Before the matter is closed, he will take every opportunity to taunt them and eventually to rub their noses in it (John 19:13–15, 19–22). The dramatic confession they are forced into ('We have no king but Caesar', v. 15) decisively abandons not only Jesus to the prefect's power but also their own political and religious dreams to the dustbin of history.

---

23. I am indebted to the excellent discussion of this episode by Lincoln in 'Power, Judgement and Possession: John's Gospel in Political Perspective', chapter 9 in Bartholomew, Chaplin, Song and Wolters (eds.), *A Royal Priesthood?*

The key statement in the dialogue is Jesus': 'My kingdom is not of this world' (John 18:36), which, as we have seen, is often understood as dissociating Jesus from political claims. But Jesus does not say that the kingdom is entirely 'other-worldly' or has nothing to do with this world. In its context, the statement is about the *source* of the kingdom (and therefore Jesus' authority) and its *methods* (in particular, it does not use violence – as Pilate will clearly acknowledge, Luke 23:14). John 18:37 makes it clear, as Jesus has done throughout his ministry, that he has come to establish a kingdom that is active in the world. The truth he brings throws down a challenge to the sin and evil that currently rule here.

In the respective claims which Jesus and Pilate now make, the kingdom that comes from above is colliding with the kingdoms of this world. Jesus challenges Pilate's understanding of authority. Not unnaturally, as Rome's representative, he claims to hold the power of life and death over Jesus (John 19:10); Jesus calmly points out this situation is merely delegated from above (v. 11).[24] But this is simply the kind of power that *all* political structures claim: the power to enforce their own will by means of the sword. Jesus demands the acknowledgment of the true origin of that power. His own kingdom, however, is based not on physical might or the power of legions but on the truth (18:37). Pilate finds this incomprehensible and therefore contemptible (v. 38). To him, as to other earthly tyrants, truth is no substitute for force as the basis for a power structure. He becomes disgusted with the case and seeks to dismiss it. But, ironically, he ends up releasing Barabbas the violent rebel and crucifying the Prince of Peace. Pilate does not see Jesus as a political threat. There is therefore further irony in the Jews' forcing Pilate to treat him as one, for the day will come when his kingdom first shakes and then dominates the Roman world.

---

24. Whether Jesus is saying directly that Pilate's *power* is delegated from above or that, as commentators (such as Carson, *The Gospel According to John*, pp. 601–602) argue, the reference is to the current *train of events* being handed to Pilate by God, the point that Pilate's authority is under God's sway still stands.

When Jesus is finally crucified, among the taunts is that he will come down from the cross if he is the true King of Israel. If his claims are valid, he will not allow himself to die; and surely any true king will be vindicated by God (Matt. 27:41–43). But Jesus proves once more that he is not the kind of king they are looking for. God's vindication will come after his death, not before. And his resurrection demonstrates that violence cannot ultimately prevail against the kingdom he has brought!

Jesus concludes his earthly ministry by reiterating his unlimited authority as king (Matt. 28:18–20). This closing passage describes, without actually mentioning the word, what the kingdom is about. It is the sphere where his authority is recognized and exercised; and 'in all nations' and 'until the end of the age', like the mustard seed of Matthew 13, it will continue to grow wherever that is done.

The kingdom in focus

Having surveyed the story of Jesus' earthly life and picked out at least the relevant highlights, we can now assemble the picture of a 'political Jesus' in a more coherent way. We shall expand our view of Jesus' mission somewhat by taking in the rest of the New Testament and begin to discuss how the claims of the kingdom impact the lives of its own people and beyond.

The Jewish expectation was that once the kingdom of God came, it would arrive in a single, climactic event (though this might take some time, like the war of the 'sons of light' against the 'sons of darkness' envisaged in the *Qumran War Scroll*). The idea that the kingdom could be inaugurated but coexist with the present evil age, perhaps for many years – and in some ways hidden, at that – is new with Jesus. This novelty is probably why the idea receives special attention in parables like those of the yeast and the weeds in the field. It is this overlap of the ages which produces the ongoing collision of the kingdoms and the attendant conflict which the citizens of the kingdom of heaven experience. It is therefore crucial to understanding the political claims of the kingdom properly. The Kingdom is neither entirely 'now' nor entirely 'yet to come'. It has been inaugurated by Jesus' mission and since then it advances and grows up to the present day. But it awaits its full consummation, which can come only with Christ's return and the events depicted in the book of Revelation, which space forbids us to tackle here, when the collision of the kingdoms is finally resolved and 'The kingdom of this world has become the kingdom of our Lord and of his Christ, and he will reign for ever and ever' (Rev. 11:15).

Thus there are two possible errors here. We could confine the kingdom largely to the future. That means denying its effective presence in the world for today and minimizing its political dimension. This is the way we are pushed in the post-Enlightenment West generally, but especially now in liberal democracies where the separation of politics from religion has become an article of faith. In effect, evangelicals who want to disentangle the kingdom of heaven entirely from the messy world of earthly powers and politics are guilty of this error: they are depriving the kingdom of some of its rightful claims. The tendency of this point of view is to spiritualize away all the statements about the kingdom (such as those in the songs of Mary and Zechariah) which have an immediate, earthly application.

On the other hand, to believe that the kingdom can be brought to fulfilment *within* the present age – the dream (at its height early in the twentieth century) of certain liberal optimists and Christian socialists – is to ignore the plain teaching of Scripture, supported by our own experience that the power of sin and evil does not look like fading away for some while yet. This is to attribute *too much* to the politics of the kingdom. It is the error of the social gospel, holding that the kingdom is active in political movements and human progress even where Christ is not acknowledged. While we can agree that God's will is furthered by the advance of justice and fair government (for example), this is not the same as seeing it as evidence of the spread of the kingdom.[25] In another

---

25. Sider and Packer put it like this: 'It is important to note that absolutely none of the New Testament texts on the Kingdom of God speak of the presence of the Kingdom apart from conscious confession of Jesus Christ. In the New Testament, the Kingdom of God comes only where

sense, rather oddly, this was also the error of the Jews of Jesus' time, who expected the immediate establishment of a perfect kingdom on earth and were therefore looking for a heavily political salvation. No, we will have to live with evil until the Son of God returns. In Jesus' words, 'Let both grow together until the harvest' (Matthew 13:30).

The way we should understand the kingdom is as both a *realm* – the 'space' where the rule of God in Christ is acknowledged – and a dynamic, powerful ruling *activity* at work in the world. Only by seeing it in this way can we make sense of Jesus' words about the immediate, evident arrival of the kingdom in Matthew 12:28 and Mark 9:1.[26] God is taking the initiative to bring men and women into the kingdom ('forcefully advancing'), here and now, an emphasis not found in Judaism. These are the men and women who make up the church of Christ, a people actively generated by the kingdom of God. With all its imperfections, the church is here to live out and bear witness to the reality of the kingdom, pointing to the day when it will be brought to perfect fulfilment. It is the church which is called to be the community of the kingdom, demonstrating here and now the kingdom's world-defying values of justice and mercy – a permanent state of Jubilee (Luke 4:18–21) – and subverting the world's claims of power.

The relation of church to kingdom and the demands of the kingdom on earthly powers have been understood in different ways through Christian history; the two issues are closely linked. It lies beyond the scope of this chapter to address them adequately, but we should note that Scripture does not allow us to identify church and kingdom completely. Such a view always leads to claiming too much for the church. We are not the kingdom, but we *are* the church. This mistaken identification developed through Augustine to the Catholic Church of the Middle Ages. Augustine

---

people acknowledge Christ.' ('How Broad is Salvation in Scripture', p. 104, in Nicholls (ed.), *In Word and Deed*). For further, recent discussion of the kingdom and the social gospel, see Chester's *Good News to the Poor*, chapter 5.

26. See the helpful treatment in Ladd, *Jesus and the Kingdom*, pp. 135–142.

himself proposed the famous model of 'two cities'[27] which coexist in the world, with the Church operating in an independent political space without attempting to *control* the earthly State. The medieval Church went on to claim more and more power until, from about 800 onwards, it went so far as to make temporal powers subservient to the church, with ultimately disastrous results.[28]

In the previous section we looked at the events surrounding the crucifixion as described in the Gospels. But the cross has a political significance which emerges only in the epistles. By discussing the political implications of the cross, I do not of course wish to suggest that this is all there is to say about it. As with Jesus' public ministry, we are concentrating on a particular angle. However, as Paul unfolds the meaning of the cross, these implications become evident. In Ephesians 2:11ff. we read how the cross revolutionizes the situation of the Gentiles. Those who were far away have been brought near: the hostility which divided Jew and Gentile for so long has been abolished. This was the hostility that had driven Antiochus Epiphanes to attempt the destruction of Judaism, and Jews to regard themselves as in every way superior to their pagan neighbours. What God has created in Christ is a single new humanity. Jesus pointed to this truth in his own ministry, through the parable of the Good Samaritan and his interest in Gentiles. Among the members of the new, third race the old divisions of ethnicity or politics no longer apply. In his cross, Christ 'put to death their

---

27. See Augustine's *City of God*. He says 'The Church even now is the Kingdom of Christ, and the Kingdom of Heaven' (20.9). Elsewhere, he compares the position of the church – the 'City of God' – to that of the exiled Israelites in Babylon: 'for as long as the two cities are commingled, we also enjoy the peace of Babylon. For from Babylon the people of God are so freed that it meanwhile sojourns in its company' (15.26).

28. The whole concept of 'Christendom' and the way it arose is helpfully discussed by Greene, 'Revisiting Christendom: A Crisis of Legitimation' in Bartholomew, Chaplin, Song and Wolters (eds.), *A Royal Priesthood?* Helpful for reviewing the ways in which the relationship between kingdom and church have been (mis)understood is Berkhof's *The Kingdom of God*, pp. 124ff.

hostility' and 'preached peace' to all: *not* only peace with God, but peace with one another (vv. 14–18). Old boundaries and divisions have been abolished and replaced with a new one: the boundary line of the kingdom of God, within which Jew and Gentile may now stand on the same ground and on the same level (v. 19).

So it is that the message of Galatians 3:28 is true: 'neither Jew nor Greek, slave nor free, male nor female'. In the kingdom, no-one's status is dependent on birth, race, property or social class. 'Our commonwealth[29] is in heaven' (Phil. 3:20), but that does not mean we are passive spectators while we remain here on earth. The point of the illustration – rather obvious once we realize Philippi's status as a Roman colony which operated just as if it were on Italian soil – is that we, members on earth of the kingdom of heaven, live out the life of the kingdom for all around to see. This is in stark contrast to the earthly obsessions of the 'enemies of the cross of Christ' (3:18–19).

Romans 13:1–7, which we cannot discuss in detail here, commands us to submit to earthly governments as ordained by God. Paul specifically mentions the payment of taxes, the issue on which Jesus himself was accosted. Two points are noteworthy here. The command is to submit, not to obey unconditionally. That claim belongs only to Christ, the Lord of the kingdom. Civil government is an expression of God's common grace to restrain evil in the world. But for members of the kingdom, our true commonwealth is in heaven. So, following Jesus, our attitude to the State is neither dutiful obedience nor angry defiance.[30]

Thus the kingdom creates a people with new allegiances, refusing to bow to dictators or to ethnic divides. It is a parallel society which defies power-based values and challenges earthly rulers to abandon their pretensions: Jesus' example shows that it does this both by proclamation and by practice. Meanwhile it gets on with

---

29. In opting for the translation 'commonwealth' rather than 'citizenship' (NIV), I am following O'Brien and other commentators (see the discussion of this verse in O'Brien, *The Epistle to the Philippians*, pp. 458–463, and the references there). For our purposes the distinction is slight.

30. See O'Donovan, *The Desire of the Nations*, p. 93.

its own agenda, indifferent to the rise and fall of earthly powers and to their demands, as it grows towards the final harvest. The kingdom's political claims therefore arise as a by-product of its members' new allegiance. We are those who submit to the rule of Christ, the Good Shepherd, who fulfils the Old Testament models of prophet, priest *and* king.

Conclusion: The political claims of Jesus

It is time to summarize the results of this study. We have seen that Jesus was born into a world awash with political streams and currents. Without exception, every group with whom he interacted had a political agenda. Yet of all these parties and sects, Jesus aligned himself with none. The message he proclaimed identified the true enemy of Israel not as Rome but as sin and Satan, the real slave master. And rather than the anticipated, immediate, visible deliverance which the Jews longed for, he preached a kingdom with a different identity. This kingdom would be both continuous and discontinuous with the hopes of the past. Continuous, in that through it God would indeed save, gather and rule over his people, just as the prophets had promised. Discontinuous, in that it would be born and grow quietly, sometimes in secret; and it would coexist with the kingdom of the present evil age. The Messiah would conquer through his death. He would renounce the sword, not adopt it as his instrument. In this kingdom the Jews would not have pride of place, though they were given first refusal on the call to join it.

Was Jesus political? Clearly not in the party political sense. Nor was his agenda political, in that it did not aim primarily at changing the earthly power structures of his day. How the masses longed that it would! A simple but accurate summary of his attitude to such authorities would be 'indifference'. And yet he *was* political. The kingdom's demands are so fundamental that they cut across our adherence to every other group, national, ethnic or cultural. Old allegiances are either replaced or transformed by membership of the kingdom. In effect it therefore creates a new politics for its own people and throws down the gauntlet to the world outside.

Thus we can say that the kingdom of God which Jesus proclaimed makes two kinds of political claim: the first on its members, the second on the world at large. It summons its own members to a radically new and wholly exclusive commitment to Christ the King. This allegiance takes the place of those we previously held and makes us ultimately indifferent to the authority of others. In the church – the kingdom's alternative new society – ethnic loyalties are completely abolished: we must make sure that they are. Nationalism is an obsolete anomaly: we are not to confuse the kingdom and the national flag. Human government we accept gratefully as an institution of God, with a legitimate role to play; but we do not owe it our heart loyalty. It is not 'ours'. We do not make the mistake of investing the church as a temporal power with authority over earthly kingdoms, as the medieval Catholic Church did. Subverting the arrogance of rulers is not the same as replacing it with our own. Nor are we to duplicate worldly power structures or attitudes. Jesus renounced violence and coercion in the service of the kingdom; so must we.

The kingdom of Jesus also issues a political *challenge* to the world at large. It attacks the very foundation stones of earthly politics by calling rulers to abandon their pretensions to absolute power and to recognize the true source of such power as they do possess. Their realms are temporary and contingent. The way of the kingdom is to scatter the proud and bring oppressive rulers down from their thrones. Thus in the liberal West, the church will refuse to accept the political consensus that privatizes faith and denies any absolute truth claims. At the same time, she will seek out and protect those facing injustice and without a voice, for the way of the kingdom is to exalt the humble and lift up the downtrodden. Faced by the rule of tyrants, the united, faithful witness of believers will defy their aspiration to absolute authority over human lives, even if it costs them their own. Opposed by false religions, especially where they identify themselves with political authorities, we will insist that the claims of our King must be heard and answered within every state and ethnic group on earth.

In terms of government, the alternative values of the kingdom are also a positive invitation to think differently. The kingdom calls rulers away from tyranny and oppression towards its own Jubilee values of justice and mercy. In the shaping of Western society, this invitation received a response. We do not live under a political tyranny; the societies in which we live bear the imprint of the politics of Jesus. The principles of public servanthood and accountability which democracies hold dear are, after all, kingdom principles. But the kingdom also bears loud and clear witness to the strict limitations of political salvation. The call is for every knee to bow to King Jesus and every tongue to confess him as Lord; and the day is coming when in every state, from greatest to least, everyone will.

Bibliography

Augustine of Hippo (1871 edn), *The City of God*, Edinburgh: T. & T. Clark.

Bartholomew, C., Chaplin, J., Song, R. and Wolters, A. (eds.) (2002), *A Royal Priesthood? The Use of the Bible Ethically and Politically: A Dialogue with Oliver O'Donovan*, Carlisle: Paternoster Press.

Bauckham, R. (1989), *The Bible in Politics*, London: SPCK.

Beasley-Murray, G. R. (1986), *Jesus and the Kingdom of God*, Grand Rapids: Eerdmans.

Berkhof, L. (1951), *The Kingdom of God*, Grand Rapids: Eerdmans.

Carson, D. A. (1991), *The Gospel According to John*, Leicester: IVP.

Chester, T. (2004), *Good News to the Poor*, Leicester: IVP.

Ferguson, E. (1993), *Backgrounds of Early Christianity*, Grand Rapids: Eerdmans.

Funk, R. W., Hoover, R. W. and the Jesus Seminar (1993), *The Five Gospels: The Search for the Authentic Words of Jesus*, Santa Rosa: Polebridge Press.

Green, J. B. (1998), 'The Death of Jesus and the Ways of God', in *Interpretation* 52.1: 24–37.

Hill, C. E. and James, F. A. (eds.) (2004), *The Glory of the Atonement*, Downers Grove, IL: InterVarsity Press.

Josephus, Flavius (1943 edn), *Antiquities of the Jews*, London: Heinemann.

Josephus, Flavius (1927 edn), *The Jewish War*, New York: Putnam's.

Ladd, G. E. (1966), *Jesus and the Kingdom*, London: SPCK.

Nicholls, B. J. (ed.) (1985), *In Word and Deed*, Exeter: Paternoster Press.

O'Brien, P. T. (1991), *The Epistle to the Philippians*, Grand Rapids: Eerdmans.

O'Donovan, O. (1996), *The Desire of the Nations*, Cambridge University Press.

Vos, G. (1958 reprint), *The Kingdom and the Church*, Grand Rapids: Eerdmans.
Wright, N. T. (1992), *The New Testament and the People of God*, London: SPCK.
Wright, N. T. (1996), *Jesus and the Victory of God*, Minneapolis: Fortress Press.
Yoder, J. H. (1972), *The Politics of Jesus*, Grand Rapids: Eerdmans.

Websites relating to the Jesus Seminar:

westarinstitute.org/jesus-seminar
religion.rutgers.edu/jseminar

3. 'PUT NOT YOUR TRUST IN PRINCES'
Samuel Rutherford, the four causes and the limitation of civil government

David Field

What claim has this 'Christendom' . . . upon our interest now? . . . Its claim on us is simply that of witness. It attests, as a matter of history, the actual impact of the Christian faith on European politics, and it expounds this impact in its developed political reflections. Those who ruled in Christendom and those who thought and argued about government believed that the Gospel was true. They intended their institutions to reflect Christ's coming reign. We can criticise their understanding of the Gospel; we can criticise their applications of it; but we can no more be uninterested in their witness than an astronomer can be uninterested in what people see through telescopes. And while no testimony to Christ can safely be ignored, this one lays claim with a special seriousness; for although it is no longer our tradition, we are its *dénouement*, or perhaps its *débâcle*. It was the womb in which our late-modernity came to birth. Even our refusal of Christendom has been learned from Christendom. Its insights and errors have fashioned, sometimes by repetition and sometimes by reaction, the insights and errors which comprise the platitudes of our own era.

(Oliver O'Donovan, *The Desire of the Nations*, p. 194)

Introduction

Samuel Rutherford wrote of himself, 'I am made of extremes', and few who are acquainted with his writings would deny it.[1] Author both of the spiritually intense *Letters* and of densely argued Latin works of Reformed scholasticism,[2] he was, in Taylor Innes's oft-cited phrase, 'St Thomas and St Francis under one hood'. He lived from 1600 to 1661, an incurable activist in ecclesiastical politics, an acute scholar in the higher reaches of Reformed theology, and an intense seeker of intimacy with his 'lovely Jesus, fair Jesus, King Jesus'.[3] Loved and hated with equal vehemence in his own day, he has been familiar to later generations chiefly through two of his 'extreme' works: the spiritually passionate *Letters*, which were not published until after he had died, and the politically radical *Lex, Rex*, which could easily have had him executed in 1661 if he had not died first.

One inescapable aspect of a consideration of *Saints and Society* is that of the role of the civil government, and although it might be argued that Rutherford was not an original thinker in this area, his status as a widely known and outspoken representative of one particular strand of Christian political thought suggests that he might make an interesting case study. What follows, therefore, is an attempt to summarize Rutherford's thinking about civil government as presented in his 1644 work *Lex, Rex*. With the exception of the relevant chapter in John Coffey's superb book *Politics, Religion and the British Revolutions: The Mind of Samuel Rutherford*,[4] such summaries as are available tend to concentrate

---

1. *Letters of Samuel Rutherford*, CLXVIII.
2. Such as *Exercitationes Apologeticae pro Divina Gratia*, 1636, which provoked his banishment to Aberdeen, and *Disputatio Scholastica de Divina Providentia*, 1649.
3. *Letters*, CLXVII.
4. Cambridge: CUP, 1997. Most relevant is chapter 6, 'The political theorist', although there is a wealth of helpful material throughout the book. Other books and articles of interest are listed in 'Further reading' at the close of this chapter.

upon the polemical purpose of the book: namely, the theological defence of armed resistance to the tyrant. What distinguishes what follows from Coffey's work (apart from vastly less knowledge of Rutherford!) is my endeavour to present Rutherford's thinking, so far as is possible, in his own words, as well as the deliberate organization of the summary around Aristotle's four causes, to which Rutherford refers in the opening sentence of the book.

There are several interesting and valuable things, then, that this chapter is not. It is not a study of Rutherford's political theory in relation either to the rest of his thought or to other Christian political theory. It is not an attempt to identify Rutherford's dependence upon others nor an explanation of the ways in which his thought is distinctive.[5] It is not, sadly, a piece of constructive Christian political theology[6] produced in conversation with Rutherford and others, nor even a critical

---

5. In *Politics*, p. 157, Coffey states that 'Rutherford said little that had not been said before by the conciliarists, the Spanish Thomists and earlier Calvinist writers. However, he integrated their arguments in a unique manner, providing an unusually comprehensive statement of Calvinistic political thought, and at times taking up more radical positions than were normal within the constitutionalist tradition.' A look at Aquinas, Althusius, Buchanan or Baxter confirms that Rutherford is dealing in a common currency of ideas. Parallels could be drawn at point after point and the perilous task of assigning intellectual causes and effects attempted, but it would add little to the fundamentally descriptive endeavour of this chapter.

6. In 'Further reading' at the close of this chapter I have listed some of the works which have most shaped my own political thought. There can be few better starting points, for the serious reader, than Oliver O'Donovan's magisterial *The Desire of the Nations*, along with *From Irenaeus to Grotius: A Sourcebook in Christian Political Thought*, which O'Donovan co-edited with his wife, Joan Lockwood O'Donovan. For those with less time to devote to these matters, Peter Leithart's *Against Christianity* is a most stimulating and highly readable introduction to some key themes in Christian political thought.

evaluation of *Lex, Rex*.[7] It is, quite simply, a layman's look at *Lex, Rex*, a book of which many have heard but which few have read and yet a book which richly repays close and multiple readings.[8]

Lex, Rex: *The Law and the Prince*

Rutherford's work first appeared in October 1644. At the time Rutherford was one of the Scottish Commissioners at the Westminster Assembly and much occupied with what he saw as the antinomian threat of the sectaries, the necessity of establishing divine right presbyterianism, and the ongoing priority of affectionate practical divinity.[9] The book's full title was:

> *Lex, rex:* The Law and the Prince. A Dispute for the just Prerogative of King and People. Containing the *Reasons* and *Causes* of the most necessary Defensive Wars of the Kingdom of Scotland, and of their Expedition for the ayd and help of their dear Brethren of England. In which their Innocency is asserted, and a full Answer is given to a Seditious Pamphlet, Intituled, *Sacro-sancta Regum Majestas*, The Sacred and Royall Prerogative of Christian Kings; Under the Name of J. A. But penned by *Jo: Maxwell* the Excommunicate P. Prelat. With a Scripturall Confutation of the ruinous Grounds of *W. Barclay, H. Grotius,*

---

7. In addition to Coffey's work, the pieces by Raath and de Freitas, by David Hall, and by J. D. Ford are useful in providing critical perspectives on Rutherford's work. Those by Burns and Goldie, by Skinner and by Tuck provide invaluable background.

8. At the beginning of 'Further reading' at the end of this chapter, I have listed the three main forms in which *Lex, Rex* is available. It is to be hoped that a critical modern edition may be produced before long.

9. Amongst Rutherford's publications in the five years or so after his arrival at Westminster were the following: *The Due Right of Presbyteries*, 1644; *The Tryal and Triumph of Faith*, 1645; *The Divine Right of Church Government and Excommunication*, 1646; *Christ Dying and Drawing Sinners to Himself*, 1647; *A Survey of Spiritual Antichrist*, 1648; *A Free Disputation against Pretended Liberty of Conscience*, 1649.

H. Arnisæus, Ant. de Domi. popish Bishop of *Spalato,* and of other
late *Anti-Magistratical Royalists*; as, The Author of *Ossorianum,* D. *Ferne,*
E. *Symmons,* the Doctors of *Aberdeen,* etc.[10]

This, then, was a defence of the Scots' military action against
Charles, both in the so-called Bishops' Wars of 1639–40 and from
1643 onwards in support of the Parliamentary side in the English
Civil War. John Maxwell, Bishop of Ross until the Glasgow assembly of December 1638 excommunicated him, and subsequently
chaplain to Charles I, had written a Royalist defence of the
king's actions, emphasizing 'The Sacred and Royal Prerogative of
Christian Kings'. Rutherford's reply was published with the
outcome of the war still very much in the balance: the Parliamentary
forces had scored a notable victory at Marston Moor in July, but
Montrose had won well for the king at Tippermuir and Aberdeen in
September, while later in October the second battle of Newbury
proved to be yet another indecisive engagement. Rutherford's title
also spoke of prerogative but, in deliberate contrast to Maxwell, this
was the '*just* prerogative of King *and* People'.

The argument of the book is laid out in answers to forty-four
questions. Coffey's summary of the main focus of the questions is
helpful:

> Questions I to XIV dealt with the origins of government, and Questions
> XV to XXI with the relation between king and people, especially the
> institutions of parliament and the judiciary. The heart of the book is
> found in the answers to Questions XXII to XXVII, where Rutherford
> discussed the relationship between the king and the law, placing *rex*
> firmly under *lex*. Then in Questions XXVIII to XXXVII he defended
> the defensive wars of the Scots, and in Questions XXXVIII to XLIV he
> concluded by discussing a miscellaneous range of issues such as how his
> theory related to that of the Jesuits and how it fitted with the history of
> Scotland.[11]

---

10. The title page also carried the citation: 'I Sam.12.25. *But if you shall still do
    wickedly, ye shall be consumed, both ye and your King.*'

11. Coffey, *Politics,* p. 152.

Lex, Rex is a curious book which approaches its subject from various angles. Close exegesis of particular biblical passages and phrases, with reference to numerous commentators, lies hard up against interaction with Jesuitical political thought, while constant appeal to natural law sits alongside detailed accounts of Scottish history and reference to a range of Reformed confessions. Rutherford applies rigorous logic to Maxwell's arguments, frequently taking him to task for his loose thinking, and then a few pages later engages in something between preaching and demagoguery, comparing the king with Nero and lamenting on behalf of the poor oppressed people of Scotland. The book is repetitious and at times it almost rambles through its 470 quarto pages.[12] Rutherford's contempt for Maxwell is stinging[13] and, for those not familiar with the range of Rutherford's work, it is hard to believe

---

12. The pagination of the original is slightly muddled, but there are 40 pages of title, preface and contents followed by 434 pages of text (numbered 1–467 but jumping from p. 280 to p. 313). Quotations and references in this chapter will be to the more readily available 1843 edition, which modernized spelling and renumbered some paragraphs but made virtually no other changes. This edition has been recently reprinted by Sprinkle Publications. The page number in the original follows in square brackets. Additionally, Bible references have been standardized.

13. Rutherford refers to Maxwell as, amongst other things, 'the excommunicated prelate' (p. 9 [16]), 'the unchurched Prelate' (p. 10 [16]), 'this Demas [who] forsook us and embraced the world' (p. 25 [43]), 'this pratler' (p. 27 [46]), 'this calumniator' (p. 205 [411]), 'the windy man' (p. 205 [411]), and a 'black-mouthed calumniator' (p. 205 [412]). He writes frequently of Maxwell's Arminianism, calls him a 'rotten papist' (p. 207 [415]), and accuses him of drunkenness (p. 181 [367]). Repeatedly he accuses Maxwell of plagiarism, calling him 'the plagiary Prelate' (p. 29 [50]), 'the poor Plagiarius' (p. 63 [114]), and declaring that 'in his book there is not one line which is his own, except his railings' (p. 65 [118]). On p. 30 [52] Rutherford writes: 'The P. Prelate might thank Spalato for this argument also, for it is stolen; but he never once named him, lest his theft should be apprehended. So are his other arguments stolen from Spalato; but the Prelate weakeneth them, and it is seen stolen goods are not blessed.'

that this could come from the same hand that penned the famous *Letters*.

What is clear, however, is that the book hit the mark. Coffey writes:

> According to the Scottish moderate, Henry Guthry, every member of the 1645 General Assembly 'had in his hand that Book lately published by Mr Samuel Rutherford . . . [which was] so idolised that whereas Buchanan's treatise *De Jure Regni apud Scotos*, was looked upon as an oracle, this coming forth, it was slighted (as not anti-monarchical enough) and Rutherford's *Lex, rex* only thought authentic'.[14]

And, as is well known, in September 1660, not long after the restoration of Charles II, copies of *Lex, Rex* were burned in Edinburgh and outside New College in St Andrews. Rutherford himself was due to face charges of treason, but died in March 1661 before he could do so, reputedly saying: 'I have a summons already from a superior Judge and adjudicator, and I behove to answer my first summons, and ere your day arrives, I shall be where few kings and great folk come'.

Lex, rex and Aristotle's 'four causes'

The first sentence of *Lex, Rex* outlines the subject matter of the book and sets our agenda. Rutherford simply states:

> I reduce all that I am to speak of the power of kings, to the author or efficient, — the matter or subject, — the form or power, — the end and fruit of their government, — and to some cases of resistance.[15]

Rutherford is working with the four *aitias* of Aristotle, often referred to as the four causes: the efficient cause; the material cause; the formal cause; and the final cause. In his 'cases of

---

14. Coffey, *Politics*, p. 151.
15. p. 1 [1].

resistance' he discusses the grounds, occasions, and manner of restraining, restricting or withdrawing the king's power, and this discussion flows from what he has said about the four causes.

If we reorder the causes (to final, efficient, formal and material), rephrase them as questions, and take 'cases of resistance' to be 'forms of limitation', then we approach Rutherford's 1644 work with these questions: What is the purpose or goal of government? Who or what brings government into being? What is it that makes government government, or what is the essence of government? What is government made out of? Each carries with it the implied further question, what are the due limitations of civil government?

What is the purpose or goal of civil government? (The final cause)

God, as a good creator, intends the well-being of his creatures and so programmes human beings with a natural inclination to their own good and a natural instinct for their own self-preservation. Further, he grants them both the power of self-preservation and the duty of self-defence. Rutherford writes, 'all living creatures have radically in them a power of self-preservation, to defend themselves from violence'.[16]

This duty of self-preservation, which, from a good Creator's hand, amounts to a duty to seek the good and to be happy, is binding, and thus the right of self-defence is inalienable. Human beings do not have the power to destroy themselves and they 'can no more resign power of self-defence, which nature hath given them, than they can be guilty of self-murder'.[17] Just as no-one has power to murder another or let another be murdered but rather has the duty to prevent murder, so no-one has the power to murder himself or let himself be murdered but rather has the duty to prevent harm to himself.[18]

---

16. p. 6 [10].

17. p. 178 [361].

18. p. 34 [59–60]. See also pp. 46 [81–83], 159 [325–326], 162 [330–332], 185 [373–375].

Government is about self-preservation

Government, at its most basic, may be considered as the exercise of power for a person's self-preservation and well-being and, therefore, is natural. Self-government is the first form of government – one's own exercise of power to defend against evil and to secure the good. Equally naturally, the second form of government is domestic government, in which the father, by virtue of being a father, has the power and the duty of defending his family members and seeking their well-being.

Beyond self-government and domestic government, however, a third form emerges. Although the duty of self-preservation is inescapable and although the right of self-defence is inalienable, a person or group of people may delegate their power in order better to secure their well-being. This delegation of the power of self-preservation is the basis of civil government. God intends for men to live peaceably and so, 'supposing that men be combined in societies . . . it is natural that they join in a civil society'.[19] In fact, a community's failure to 'set . . . rulers over themselves' would be 'a breach of the fifth commandment'.[20] In particular, the entrance of sin makes civil government a necessity and without 'kings and other judges . . . all human societies should be dissolved'.[21]

Rutherford believes that without humanity's fall into sin there would have been no civil government.[22] Under sin, however, human beings are marked by irrational and lawless selfishness and, for this reason, there is a need for an effective agency able to prevent one person from harming others, an agency which is stronger than any single person alone.[23] And this agency, civil government, formed with the purpose of preventing evil and with the community's delegated power of self-preservation, is a blessing from God. Rutherford reminds us that 'not to be under governors

19. p. 2 [2].
20. p. 5 [8].
21. p. 25 [44].
22. p. 79 [142].
23. pp. 111 [201–203], 227–228 [453–456].

and magistrates is a judgment of God, (Isa. 3:6–7; 3:1; Hos. 3:4; Judg. 19:1–2)'[24] stating that:

> A community of itself, because of sin, is a naked society that can but destroy itself, and every one eat the flesh of his brother; therefore God hath appointed a king or governor, who shall take care of that community, rule them in peace, and save all from reciprocation of mutual acts of violence.[25]

The supreme law

Repeatedly and emphatically, Rutherford asserts that the health or safety of the people is the supreme law for civil government: '*salus populi, suprema lex*. The safety of the people is the supreme and cardinal law to which all laws are to stoop.'[26] And this is worked out and illustrated in several ways. Good rulers, such as Moses and David were, are those who are willing to suffer themselves in order to secure the safety of the people.[27] The power and use of royal prerogative is measured by its potential for furthering the welfare of the people.[28] All laws are to be understood and evaluated in the light of the supreme law: 'The law hath one fundamental rule, *salus populi*, like the king of planets, the sun, which lendeth star-light to all laws, and by which they are exponed.'[29]

And if laws, then certainly rulers are to be judged by the same criterion:

> The genuine and intrinsical end of a king is the good, (Rom. 13:4) and the good of a quiet and peaceable life in all godliness and honesty (1 Tim. 2:2) . . . [his] genuine end is to preserve the law from violence, and to defend the subject; — he is the people's debtor for all happiness

---

24. p. 65 [116].
25. p. 69 [124].
26. p. 119 [218]. See also pp. 142 [262–263], 210 [421], 228 [455–457].
27. p. 119 [218].
28. p. 124 [228].
29. p. 137 [252].

possible to be procured by God's sword, either in peace or war, at home or abroad.[30]

Civil rulers as servants

The logic of this may have sounded somewhat demeaning to Royalist ears, but Rutherford did not shy away from it. Put simply, the civil government, and more specifically the king, is a means to an end. Far from possessing any sort of absolute power, the monarch is – in just these terms – relativized:

> The king, as king, hath all his official and relative goodness in the world, as relative to the end. All that you can imagine to be in a king, as a king, is all relative to the safety and good of the people, (Rom. 13:4) 'He is a minister for thy good'. He should not, as king, make himself, or his own gain and honour, his end.[31]

> The king, as a king, is formally and essentially the 'minister of God for our good,' (Rom. 13:4; 1 Tim. 2:2) and cannot come under any notion as a king, but as a mean, not as an end, nor as that which he is, to seek himself . . . And God's end in giving a king is the good and safety of his people.[32]

Phrased differently, the personal means is a servant and Rutherford uses this language too: 'He is the commonwealth's servant objectively, because all the king's service, as he is king, is for the good, safety, peace and salvation of the people, and in this he is a servant.'[33]

Freedom and the 'health of the people'

This, of course, invites the question as to what constitutes the 'good, safety, peace and salvation of the people' and Rutherford answers in several ways. First, he asserts the natural dignity, freedom and equality of all human beings in striking tones.

---

30. p. 103 [187–188].
31. p. 83 [150].
32. p. 120 [219].
33. p. 70 [126].

Human equality and liberty consists in the fact that, considered simply as humans, no-one is born under civil subjection to another: 'subjection politic is merely accidental'.[34] There is a natural subjection but it is domestic, within the family.[35] There are not separate natural classes of humans, rulers and ruled. Rather, 'liberty is a condition of nature that all men are born with'.[36]

> A man being created according to God's image, he is *res sacra*, a sacred thing, and can no more, by nature's law, be sold and bought, than a religious and sacred thing dedicated to God . . . Every man by nature is a freeman born, that is, by nature no man cometh out of the womb under any civil subjection to king, prince, or judge, to master, captain, conqueror, teacher, &c.[37]

In fact, civil or political subjection is characteristic only of a fallen world and is 'a penal fruit of sin, and against nature . . . because all men are born by nature of equal condition'.[38] One aspect of the good and safety of the people is the maintenance of these freedoms, and when the actions of the civil government either allow or themselves bring about unnatural and unjust subjection then those actions are contrary to the God-given end of government.

A second aspect of the good and safety of the people relates to this. A person's freedom and well-being are defined by the law of God and are violated when another human being breaks that law as it bears upon the relationship between them. God's law prohibits theft and thus not-to-be-stolen-from is part of human freedom and well-being. The restraint and punishment of thieves is the promotion of human good and safety and is therefore a key component of the community's delegated power of self-preservation which is the basis of civil government.[39]

---

34. p. 51 [91].
35. p. 51 [91–92].
36. p. 66 [119].
37. p. 51 [91].
38. p. 64 [116].
39. pp. 59 [105–107], 64–65 [115–118].

A pure and protected church and the health of the people

Clearly, then, the *salus populi* will include freedom from theft, rape, murder and the like. But the first commandment is to worship the true God and the next three commandments require that he be worshipped truly. In this, supremely, the people's good and safety consists. And since the church is the promoter and guardian of the true worship of the true God, the civil government's relationship with the church will be an important aspect of its faithfulness or unfaithfulness in discharging its God-given responsibility of seeking the health and peace of the people.

The boundaries of responsibility between church and civil government are not given much attention in *Lex, Rex*, although this was a question to which Rutherford devoted a great deal of thought. Minimally, however, Rutherford believes that the civil government should, in some ways, protect and nurture the church. It should recognize the limits of its jurisdiction and not compromise the 'crown rights of King Jesus' in the government and ordering of the life of the church. And it should not interfere with the church; and should never allow, far less encourage, far less require the church to depart from the true worship of the true God:

> A king is a special gift from God, given to feed and defend the people of
> God, that they may lead a godly and peaceable life under him,
> (Ps. 78:71–72; 1 Tim. 2:2).[40]

Since the health of the people is most bound up with pure worship, then the most intense, indeed, the archetypal failure of civil government would be to require the church to institute false worship. Only one thing worse could be imagined: the attempt to impose false worship by force:

> He is made by God and the people king, for the church and people of
> God's sake, that he may defend true religion for the behalf and salvation
> of all. If therefore he defend not religion for the salvation of the
> souls of all in his public and royal way, it is presumed as undeniable that

---

40. p. 48 [85].

the people of God, who by the law of nature are to care for their own souls, are to defend in their way true religion, which so nearly concerneth them and their eternal happiness.[41]

This, of course, is exactly what Rutherford and others understood Charles to have been doing from 1633 onwards. Their interpretation of the heinousness of surplice-wearing or of the imposed Prayer Book may be disputed but the line of argument from there is irresistible. Civil government is the community's delegated power of self-preservation and thus has the good and safety of the people as its supreme law. The good and safety of the people was to be secured by preserving their liberty and natural equality and by restraining and punishing the evildoer; but, above all, it was secured by protecting and supporting the church in her calling to promote the true worship of the true God. If a civil government – against the liberty and natural equality of the people – imposed what was diametrically opposite to that people's good and safety, peace and salvation, then that civil government had altogether missed the end of government.

The health of the people a touchstone for questions of government

Rutherford's views upon the three main forms of government will be described later, but here it should be noted that the end of government, securing the good and safety of the people, also forms a criterion in selecting one rather than another form of government at any particular time:

> If a nation seeth that aristocratical government is better than monarchy, *hic et nunc*, that the sequels of such a monarchy is bloody, destructive, tyrannous; that the monarchy compelleth the free subjects to Mahomedanism, to gross idolatry, they cannot, by the divine bond of any oath, captive their natural freedom, which is to choose a government and governors for their safety, and for a peaceable and godly life.[42]

---

41. p. 56 [100].
42. p. 44 [78].

Again, in considering the role of the lesser magistrates, the key consideration will be the degree to which their presence or absence, effectiveness or ineffectiveness secures the end of government:

> These judges cannot but be univocally and essentially judges no less than the king, without which in a kingdom justice is physically impossible; and anarchy, and violence, and confusion, must follow, if they be wanting in the kingdom. But without inferior judges, though there be a king, justice is physically impossible; and anarchy and confusion, &c. must follow.[43]

It is no surprise, in view of the importance which Rutherford places upon the reasons for which government exists, that when he comes to define tyranny he does so less by reference to the way in which power is attained or maintained or to the demeanour of the ruler but by reference to the end of government. A tyrant is one who uses power for purposes other than those which God has assigned; a tyrant is defined not by how much power he has or uses but by the purposes to which he puts his power:

> Tyranny being a work of Satan, is not from God, because sin, either habitual or actual, is not from God: the power that is, must be from God; the magistrate, as magistrate, is good in nature of office, and the intrinsic end of his office, (Rom. 13:4) for he is the minister of God for thy good; and, therefore, a power ethical, politic, or moral, to oppress, is not from God, and is not a power, but a licentious deviation of a power; and is no more from God, but from sinful nature and the old serpent, than a license to sin.[44]

Simply, there is 'power to be a father' and 'power to be a tyrant'. The one is 'power to fight for the people' and the other 'power to waste and destroy them'.[45] At every turn Rutherford applies the test of the end of government, the good and safety of the people.

---

43. p. 94 [171].
44. p. 34 [59].
45. p. 38 [67].

And, as suggested above, he has no doubt that Charles has badly failed the test. The charges are repeatedly brought that the king has tried to 'press . . . upon the people a false and idolatrous religion'.[46] The 'idolatry of bread-worship and popery' which was being imposed was 'as hateful to God as dagon-worship'[47] and 'the Service Book commanded, in the king's absolute authority, all Scotland to commit grosser idolatry, in the intention of the work, if not in the intention of the commander, than was in Babylon'.[48] But what was 'hateful to God' and 'grosser idolatry than was in Babylon' must necessarily be dangerous to the people and entirely opposite to their peace and salvation. Thus, for the civil government to impose and command these things was to act contrary to the end of government. And this, as much as arbitrary or absolute powers, was what rendered that government a tyranny.

In response to the objection that these were merely matters of interpretation, Rutherford denies that 'tyranny can be obscure long' but, deliberately choosing the number thought to comprise the king's army against Scotland in 1639–40, makes the point that, 'if a king bring in upon his native subjects twenty thousand Turks armed, and the king lead them, it is evident they come not to make a friendly visit to salute the kingdom, and depart in peace'.[49]

The health of the people as warrant for removing a government
One step remains. The end of government is the good and safety of the people. The form of government, the assessment of rulers, the civil government's relationship with the church and the definition of tyranny are all to be judged in relation to this. The final step is the recognition that if the community's delegation of the exercise of power for self-preservation is defined by and limited to the safeguarding of the community's health and peace, then it is understood to be a conditional grant and one which may be withdrawn if the civil government does not meet the conditions of the grant.

---

46. p. 55 [99].
47. p. 166 [339].
48. p. 110 [200].
49. p. 117 [213–214].

This flows naturally from the inalienability of the duty and right of self-defence. If I transfer my power of self-defence to an agency and that agency then exercises power against me, then, since my transfer of power did not and could not involve the alienation of the (inalienable) duty of self-defence but merely the temporary and conditional delegation of executive power, I must resist that agency and, so far as I am able, reverse the grant of power. Rutherford is clear that 'they transfer their power to the father [i.e. the king], for their own safety and peace, (not if he use the power they give aim to their destruction)'.[50] The people are able to recognize when they are 'in an extraordinary exigent' such as 'when Ahab and Jezebel did undo the church of God, and tyrannise over both the bodies and consciences of priest, prophet and people', and in such a case they may, as Rutherford puts it, 'resume their power'.[51]

Again and again, Rutherford asserts that the grant of power is conditional and makes it clear that the condition is defined by the end of government, the good and safety, peace and salvation of the people:

> If the estates of a kingdom give the power to a king, it is their own power in the fountain; and if they give it for their own good, they have power to judge when it is used against themselves, and for their evil, and so power to limit and resist the power that they gave.[52]

> The community . . . may resume its power, which it gave conditionally to the ruler for its own safety and good; and in so far as this condition is violated, and power turned to the destruction of the commonwealth, it is to be esteemed as not given.[53]

In summary, then, government is the exercise of power for self-preservation. Civil government receives a conditional transfer of

---

50. p. 39 [68].
51. p. 36 [63].
52. p. 143 [264].
53. p. 69 [125]. See also p. 141 [261].

such power from the community, which does not thereby forfeit its right or escape its duty of self-defence. The end of government is the good of the people and is achieved by preserving their natural liberty and equality, by restraining and punishing the evildoer and by protecting and supporting the church. Since the people's highest good is found in the true worship of the true God, the civil government's most vicious and reprehensible abuse of power would be in hindering such worship or, worse still, imposing false worship. Nothing could be more contrary to the health and safety of the people. In such a case, the people's duty of self-defence would require – at this point – resistance to the civil government and renunciation of its power.

Who or what brings civil government into being? (The efficient cause)

God is the supreme and almighty sovereign and all power is his. Since government is the exercise of power, this means that all government, originally, is also God's. Every creature owes its existence and every other sort of power to God:

> Certain it is, God only, univocally and essentially as God, is the judge, (Psal. 75:7) and God only and essentially king, (Psal. 97:1; 99:1) and all men in relation to him are mere ministers, servants, legates, deputies; and in relation to him, equivocally and improperly, judges or kings, and mere created and breathing shadows of the power of the King of kings.[54]

God, then, ultimately, is the efficient cause of government, the one who brings it into being. However, further distinctions are possible. A distinction, first, may be drawn between the fact of government, the form of government, and the particular persons designated to serve in government. The fact of government is from God and, since God is the source of all power, then the

---

54. p. 107 [195].

civil ruler's power is from God. Quite simply, 'all civil power is immediately from God in the root'.[55]

Which form of government is it to be?

Civil government may, however, take various forms. Rutherford, following tradition, writes of monarchy, aristocracy and democracy. He declares that these are 'not governments different in nature' and all are, in themselves, legitimate.[56] All three forms are related ('there is no one government just that hath not some of all three'),[57] the attempt to 'warrant any one in its rigid purity without mixture'[58] is unreasonable and unscriptural and the boundaries between the forms are fuzzy. Each has its advantages and each its disadvantages.[59]

How is it, then, that one form rather than another will hold place in a given community? That, says Rutherford, depends upon the free will and choice of the people.[60] Just as 'single life and marriage are both the lawful ordinances of God'[61] so with the forms of government, and one is to be chosen rather than another 'according as the necessity and temper of the commonwealth do most require'.[62]

If, then, we were to ask of a particular society which had chosen one of the three forms of government over against the others who or what had brought the government into existence, we would have to answer in various ways. The fact of government

---

55. p. 1 [2].
56. p. 5 [7].
57. p. 116 [212].
58. p. 116 [212].
59. p. 192 [387].
60. pp. 30 [53], 52 [94].
61. p. 5 [8].
62. p. 25 [44]. Later, Rutherford states his preference: 'A limited and mixed monarchy, such as is in Scotland and England, seems to me the best government, when parliaments, with the king, have the good of all the three. This government hath glory, order, unity, from a monarch; from the government of the most and wisest, it hath safety of counsel, stability, strength; from the influence of the commons, it hath liberty, privileges, promptitude of obedience', p. 192 [387].

was immediately brought about by God. The range of lawful
options also came from God. The selection of one form rather
than another came from the people and yet, since the powers that
be are instituted by God, it was also from God, only in this dimension it came from him mediately.

Who should rule?

A similar distinction must be drawn with reference to the appointment of particular persons to positions of governmental
responsibility. Rutherford claims that 'we cannot but put difference
betwixt the institution of the office, viz. government, and the designation of person or persons to the office'.[63] He illustrates using
other roles in society:

> For the pastor's and the doctor's office is from Christ only; but that
> John rather than Thomas be the doctor or the pastor is from the will
> and choice of men — the presbyters and people [and so . . .] The
> office is immediately from God, but the question now is, What is that
> which formally applieth the office and royal power to this person rather
> than to the other five as meet? Nothing can here be dreamed of but
> God's inclining the hearts of the states to choose this man and not
> that man.[64]

So, when a particular person finds himself in office, then he may
say that as to the fact of government, it is immediately from God;
as to the form of government, it is in general from God but
through the choice of the people; and as to his being in office
rather than another, it, too, is from God but mediated through the
choice of the people.

Who grants power?

And the power which he wields, likewise, is ultimately and originally
power from God, but as to its nature and immediate grant, it is from
the people. The power which the civil ruler has, has been delegated

---

63. p. 1 [1].
64. pp. 6 [10], 9 [16].

to him by the members of the community. The power of the civil government is 'virtually' in the people[65] and, indeed, is theirs as those made in the image of God: 'as for the official authority itself, it is virtually in all in whom any of God's image is remaining since the fall'.[66] Rutherford states that 'we defend ourselves by devolving our power over in the hands of one or more rulers'[67] or again that people 'put this power of warding off violence in the hands of one or more rulers, to defend themselves by magistrates'.[68]

All power comes from God and he has given the power of self-preservation to all people. They then delegate that power to their rulers. Thus the ruler's power *is* the people's power, the people's law-making, war-declaring, self-preserving, health-promoting, evil-resisting power: 'the first, and ultimate, and native subject of all power is the community'.[69] But God is also the one who has instituted civil government as such and thus the ruler's power is from God that way too.

How do the people 'make kings'?

The people's bestowal of power and designation of particular persons to office take place at the same time and this means that the people really do 'make kings'.[70] Thus, 'by the authoritative choice of the states the man is made of a private man and no king, a public person and a crowned king: 2 Sam. 16:18; Judg. 8:22; Judg. 9:6; Judg. 11:8, 11; 2 Kgs 14:21; 1 Sam. 12:1; 2 Chr. 23:3'.[71]

> As the people's act of coronation is distinctive, so is it constitutive: it distinguished Saul from all Israel, and did constitute him in a new relation, that he was changed from no king to be a king.[72]

---

65. p. 11 [19].
66. p. 25 [43].
67. p. 2 [2].
68. p. 6 [10].
69. p. 34 [58].
70. pp. 12 [20–21], 203 [407–408].
71. p. 7 [11].
72. pp. 229 [457].

The key to this process, and essential to the selection and authorization of the civil government or the 'making of the king' is the 'free consent'[73] or 'free suffrages of a community',[74] the 'intervening consent of the people'[75] or 'the people's election'[76]. Along with the power of self-preservation which the people bestow, the people have the power of bestowing it. And this *is* the power of making kings which they 'put forth in act'[77] freely, voluntarily and actively:

> The people hath virtually all royal power in them, as in a sort of immortal and eternal fountain, and may create to themselves many kings.[78]

The demand that the people consent to the designation of a particular ruler and the notion that that consent formalized in a contract or covenant is what actually establishes the ruler in office and bestows power upon him is essential to Rutherford and it is expressed in other ways too. For example, if the people choose monarchy as their preferred form of government, then the appointment of the king by election is the method which most clearly expresses what is really going on in the formation of civil government:

> He who is made king by suffrages of the people, must be more principally king than he who hath no title but the womb of his mother.[79]

Birth alone is insufficient:

> And if he have not the consent of the people, he is an usurper, for we know no external lawful calling that kings have now, or their

---

73. pp. 52 [93], 8 [13–14].
74. pp. 45 [80], 63 [113].
75. pp. 27 [46], 38 [66].
76. pp. 39 [68–69], 45 [79–80], 47 [83].
77. p. 29 [50].
78. p. 69 [125]. See also pp. 6 [10], 11 [19].
79. p. 45 [80].

family, to the crown, but only the call of the people.[80]

Conquest alone is insufficient. It is the people's consent which renders even a just conqueror the duly appointed ruler of a community:

> If the people never give their consent, the conqueror, domineering over them by violence, hath no just title to the crown . . . Mere conquest by the sword, without the consent of the people, is no just title to the crown.[81]

Thus it is the people's consent which makes the king. Birth and conquest do not as such make a person a king – it is the people's 'suffrages' which do that.

This is at odds with the Royalist view, which Rutherford summarizes as 'he is not king because he is crowned, but he is crowned because he is king'.[82] Rutherford holds the opposite: the free consent of the people, expressed in the coronation, is what makes the man a king.[83]

The people's consent can come in various ways such as through the estates, by the original choice of a king and a conditional commitment to his bloodline, by acquiescence to certain laws; and by acquiescence to certain conquerors. But that consent is essential. Unless and until the people have consented the person is not a king. Quite simply, 'there is no title on earth now to the crowns to families, to persons, but only the suffrages of the people',[84] 'a king is made by the free consent of the people',[85] 'no man can be formally a lawful king without the suffrages of the people'[86] and so the people are the 'efficient and constituent cause' of the king.[87]

---

80. p. 33 [58]. See also p. 9 [15].
81. p. 47 [83].
82. p. 200 [402].
83. pp. 9 [14–15], 17 [30].
84. p. 8 [14].
85. p. 52 [93].
86. p. 9 [15].
87. p. 80 [144].

How can both God and the people bring government into being?
One possible objection to this, however, is that recognizing the
people's consent as that which brings government into existence
contradicts or compromises the claim that God is the one who
brings government into existence. Which is it to be? Does the
ruler's position and power come from God or from the people?

What might be termed a 'zero-sum' understanding of causation lies behind these questions and was expressed in the
Royalists' view that, since the king indisputably received his
appointment and power from God, his appointment and power
could not be attributed to the people. Rutherford sees that this
objection flows from his opponents' Arminianism and he has
little patience with it. Nevertheless, he sees it as pervasive in
Maxwell's argument:

> This is all one argument from the Prelate's beginning of his book to the
> end: In a most special and eminent act of God's providence kings are
> from God; but, therefore, they are not from men and men's consent. It
> followeth not.[88]

Rutherford's chief response is that of providing the vocabulary
to show that God acts but does so through secondary causes or
mediately through human agency. Of course, God is the 'first
agent in all acts of the creature',[89] the 'principal cause'[90] and the
'*causa causarum*, the Cause of causes'.[91] But the point for
Rutherford is that the acts of human agents may be at one and the
same time the acts of God and the acts of those human agents:

> Power of government is immediately from God, and this or that definite
> power is mediately from God, proceeding from God by the mediation of
> the consent of a community.[92]

---

88. p. 21 [36].
89. p. 7 [11].
90. p. 70 [127].
91. p. 23 [40].
92. p. 3 [5].

It is not in the people as in the principal cause; sure all royal power that way is only in God; but it is in the people as in the instrument, and when the people maketh David their king at Hebron, in that same very act, God, by the people using their free suffrages and consent, maketh David king at Hebron.[93]

Rutherford gets close to exasperation:

All power is from God only, as the first Author, and from no man. What then? Therefore men and people interpose no human act in making this man a king and not that man. It followeth not.[94]

And at these points, he argues from other instances of God's mediate action. God saved the world, God gave Canaan to Israel, God rescued Israel from Egypt and from Babylon, but he did each of these things 'by the ministry of men'.[95] He makes the point repeatedly:

The victory the Lord's [sic]; therefore Israel never fought a battle. So Deut. 32, The Lord alone led his people — the Lord led them in the wilderness — their bow and their sword gave them not the land. God wrought all their works for them, (Isa. 26:12) therefore Moses led them not . . . It followeth not. God did all these as the first, eminent, principal, and efficacious pre-determinator of the creature (though this Arminian and popish prelate mind not so to honour God). The assumption is also false.[96]

Not only does he insist that both God and the people can be the efficient cause of civil government (God as principal and people as instrument, God as first cause, people as secondary cause), he also draws out the implication for the tyrant. The fact that the ruler's power is from God does not mean that the people must

---

93. p. 70 [127]. See also pp. 7 [11], 12 [20].
94. p. 14 [24].
95. p. 21 [36].
96. p. 18 [31]. See also pp. 12 [20–21], 22–23 [38–40], 33 [57–58].

wait until God immediately removes the tyrant. The ruler's power was from God through the people's consent, and so the people may withdraw their consent, and that itself will be the way in which God removes the tyrant.[97]

In summary, properly understood, it can be said that both God and man make kings.[98] Once this is reckoned with, a key plank in the Royalist argument has broken: 'But the truth is, take this one argument from the Prelate, and all that is in his book falleth to the ground, — to wit, Sovereignty is from God only'.[99]

A failure to grasp the twofold but ordered efficient cause of civil government could be seen to mirror-image misconstructions of political authority. If God's causation and human causation are mutually exclusive (that is, to the degree that God is the cause of an event, humans are not and vice versa), then one of three things will result. If God's causation is determinative then divine right absolutism results. If human causation is determinative, then popular majoritarianism or the victory of the violent follows. If divine and human causation are both determinative then they are so in competition with each other. Tyranny of one sort or another is inevitable. Put otherwise, whereas in the Calvinist version of contractarianism, God is active in both contracting parties (which is why the contract is actually better understood to be a covenant), this is not the case in an Arminian version in which God must stay on his side of the fence. In fact, Arminianism plus contractarianism may well lead to secularism, just as Arminianism plus divine right monarchy leads to royal absolutism. Divine right royal absolutism is a consequence of severing the king's relationship with the people and locating everything in his relationship with God. Secular majoritarianism flows from severing the government's relationship with God and locating everything in its relationship with the people. The logic of Rutherford's position is that only a Reformed doctrine of providence and causation secures the public square from tyranny and for God (and therefore for true human welfare).

---

97. p. 26 [45].
98. p. 80 [144–145].
99. p. 14 [24].

Covenant and duality

As suggested in the previous paragraph, a further expression of the twofold but ordered efficiency of God and people is found in the notion of covenant. Several strands make up the notion. A covenant, even that between king and people, which Rutherford strongly asserts,[100] is made in the presence of God. It lays 'mutual civil obligation upon the king to the people and the people to the king' and is therefore, by definition, conditional.[101]

> The people maketh . . . a king covenantwise and conditionally, so he rule according to God's law, and the people resigning their power to him for their safety, and for a peaceable and godly life under him, and not to destroy them, and tyrannise over them.[102]

Made in the presence of God, by a people subject to God and a king who 'swear[s] by the most high God, that he should be a father and protector of the church of God',[103] the terms of the covenant between king and people are determined by the law of God. Even if this is not explicit, it is to be assumed:

> If there be no conditions betwixt a Christian king and his people, then those things which are just and right according to the law of God, and the rule of God in moulding the first king, are understood to rule both king and people, as if they had been written.[104]

And, of course, the criteria by which the king is selected are themselves those revealed by God; the people must act 'following the rule of God's word'.[105] In every way that he can, Rutherford shows that the appointment and empowering of the king is neither from

---

100. pp. 54 [96–97], 56 [99–101], 202 [405–407].
101. p. 54 [96]. See also p. 60 [107–108].
102. p. 57 [103].
103. p. 54 [97].
104. p. 59 [106].
105. p. 14 [23].

God acting immediately and apart from the people nor from the people acting principally or independently of God.[106]

People and parliament

A word of clarification may be due. Rutherford's insistence that the people make kings and that their consent is an essential element in the efficient causation of government is not to be mistaken for mass democracy or popular rule. While the 'sovereign power [is] eminently, *fontaliter*, originally and radically in the people',[107] it is as they are 'parliamentarily convened'[108] that they have the authority to make the king. Or, more precisely:

> The first, and ultimate, and native subject of all power, is the
> community . . . but the ethical and political subject, or the legal and
> positive receptacle of this power, is various, according to the various
> constitutions of the policy. In Scotland and England, it is the three
> estates of parliament.[109]

Similarly, the legislative power of the people does not mean rule by referendum, because it is invested in the parliament[110] and the people's silence in the face of duly promulgated laws is to be understood as approbation.[111]

Politics is inescapable, neutrality impossible: Some implications

If it is God and the people who bring the government into being, then several inferences may be drawn. The first inference is the familiar covenanter position that politics is inescapable, neutrality

---

106. Neither mass democracy nor popular rule have any place in
     Rutherford's thought, in spite of his insistence that the people 'make
     kings'. The people act as 'parliamentarily convened', p.25 [43]. The place
     of the 'people' is clarified on pp. 86 [156], 34 [58], 80 [144–145], 34 [60].
107. p. 86 [156].
108. p. 25 [43].
109. p. 34 [58].
110. p. 80 [144–145].
111. p. 34 [60].

is impossible, and some form of 'Christendom' is desirable. If God is the one who brings government into being, then that government will be accountable to God; must rule according to his purpose and his law; must relate to other institutions as he requires; may not exceed the boundaries of its God-given function; and, above all, may not act as though it were self-empowering and self-authorizing. The government is hedged in by the powers which God has given and the laws which God has laid down.

The power to do evil is no God-given power, for 'God can give no moral power to do wickedly: for that is licence, and a power to sin against a law of God, which is absolutely inconsistent with the holiness of God'.[112] But if God is the source of all the power which the government does have and he is not the source of power to do evil, then the government has no power to do evil. 'When the magistrate doth anything by violence, and without law, in so far doing against his office, he is not a magistrate. Then, say I, that power by which he doth, is not of God.'[113]

The same applies to judicial pronouncements and to the government in its legislative function:

> The king hath no power from God to pronounce what sentence he pleaseth, because the judgment is not his own but God's.[114]

But just as the fact that God brings government into being limits government, so the fact that the people bring government into being also limits government. This is because the *way* that the people bring government into being is by the transfer of powers to it. The only powers, however, which the people have to give, are those of self-preservation and the advancement of their own wellbeing. Since the people do not have the power of self-harm, they are not able to transfer or sign away the power of self-harm. And this in turn means that the government cannot have the power of harming the people. It cannot have that power from God because

---

112. pp. 72–73 [131].
113. p. 103 [186].
114. p. 88 [160].

it would be against God's purpose and laws. It cannot have that power from the people because it is not theirs to give: 'they cannot give what they never had, and power to destroy themselves they never had'.[115]

Once again, this makes kingship conditional and reversible:

> He who is made a minister of God, not simply, but for the good of the subject, and so he take heed to God's law as a king, and govern according to God's will, he is in so far only made king by God as he fulfilleth the condition; and in so far as he is a minister for evil to the subject, and ruleth not according to that which the book of the law commandeth him as king, in so far he is not by God appointed king and ruler . . .
> Rom. 13:4; 2 Chr. 6:16; Ps. 89:30–31; 2 Sam. 7:12; 1 Chr. 28:7, 9.[116]

It also makes the relationship between the civil government and the church a matter of interest. Institutional pluralism there may be, but this is emphatically alongside ethical monism. The same God who instituted civil government for the health of the people established the church too, and this means that the civil government is not absolute in relation to the church and also that the limitation of the king's powers or the removal of the tyrant is something which intimately concerns the church. As Rutherford puts it in his preface, 'I hope this war shall be Christ's triumph, Babylon's ruin.'[117]

Further, since God is the efficient cause of government, he will not have given to government powers which conflict with the powers he has given to other human agencies and institutions. In particular, the conscience of the individual is inviolable.[118] The exclusive responsibilities and sanctions of the church must not be trespassed upon by the king.[119] And lesser magistrates or inferior judges are directly empowered by and accountable to God and in

---

115. pp. 102 [184–185], 210 [420–421].

116. p. 57 [102].

117. p. xxi [A3 +1].

118. p. xxiii [a2+3 and a2+4].

119. p. xxiii [a2+3].

no way to be regarded merely as instruments or agencies of the supreme magistrate.[120]

That the people are the efficient cause of government means that they have the power to 'resume their power'. 'Those who have power to make have power to unmake kings.'[121] God may act immediately in removing a tyrannical king by a special providence, but unless he does so then the tyrant remains king 'in titulo, so long as the people and estates who made him king have not recalled their grant'.[122] Since it was their consent which made the king, it must be their voluntary and duly expressed common dissent which must unmake him.

All this amounts to a prescription for Christendom so long as Rutherford's doctrine of providence is admitted. God's action and human action refer to the same space – the public square – but not in such a way that the one dislodges the other. It is therefore the case that God can make absolute and universal demands upon a community without that community either becoming mono-institutional or losing its mutual and interlocking responsibilities. The one purpose of God, which has no no-go areas in human life, is utterly integrated. God addresses the multiple institutional and social audiences of a community with one voice, and each individual, stratum and organization is to hear God's voice to others as well as to itself in order the better to occupy its own space and sustain its own relationships as it ought.

What *is* government? What is the essence of government? (The formal cause)

The third of Aristotle's *aitias* which Rutherford discusses in relation to civil government is the 'formal cause' or 'power'; which

---

120. The key features of Rutherford's thought on the immediacy and
     independency of the lesser magistrate may be found on pp. xxiii [a2+3],
     5 [8], 94 [169], 89–92 [160–167], 137 [253].
121. p. 126 [232].
122. p. 58–59 [105].

is to say, he asks what is it that makes government government? What is the essence of government? All created things have powers, and defining the nature of those powers correctly is the way of identifying the essence of a thing. In summary, Rutherford's position is that civil government is the embodiment and the instrument of the rule of law.

The distribution and limitation of the three powers of government

The traditional three powers of government are recognizably present and distinguished in *Lex, Rex*. The enactment and promulgation of law is the legislative power, which Rutherford normally calls the 'nomothetic' power. The application of law to restrain the evildoer and praise the good in individual cases is the judicial power. And the administrative and penal enforcement of law is the executive power. What makes government government is its role of enacting, applying and administering the law.

These powers, as will be seen, are radically in the people and devolved by them to the civil government. And although all government is defined by the exercise of these powers, various arms of government have particular responsibility for one element or another of them. Specifically, parliament has greater legislative power and the king greater executive power. These propositions are best expressed in Rutherford's own words.

The people (under God) are the source of the powers of government to and through the parliament ('the states') and to the king:

> The people being the fountain of the king must rather be the fountain of laws. . . . The king is the only supreme in the power ministerial of executing laws; but this is a derived power, so as no one man is above him; but in the fountain-power of royalty the states are above him.[123]

The various powers are distributed variously:

> They make laws who make kings: therefore, this nomothetic power

---

123. p. 114 [208]. See also p. 35 [61].

recurreth into the states, as to the first subject.[124]

The power for actual execution of laws be more in the king, yet a legislative power is more in the estates.[125]

And this means that the king is independent neither of the people nor of the parliaments which represent them:

The royal power to make laws with the king, and so a power eminent in their states representative to govern themselves, is in the people; for if the most high acts of royalty be in them, why not the power also?[126]

The parliaments of both kingdoms standing in possession of a nomothetic power to make Laws, proveth clearly that the king is in no possession of any royal dignity conferred absolutely, and without any condition, upon him.[127]

This conferment of powers, however, is for the people's own sake and not for the sake of the rulers. Rulers are selected and are granted powers for the good of the people. It is true that real power is delegated, but the people 'put this power of warding off violence in the hands of one or more rulers, to defend themselves by magistrates'.[128] Rutherford denies 'dominion' to rulers precisely because he defines it as being for the good of the ruler, whereas true rule is 'to take care of the good of those over whom the ruler is set'.[129] And he draws a picture of the people deciding together that it would be most to their advantage to select one of their number and give him particular powers and responsibilities as a

---

124. p. 114 [208].
125. p. 99 [179].
126. p. 80 [145].
127. p. 59 [106].
128. p. 6 [10].
129. p. 65 [116].

watchman for all.[130] At bottom, the 'people give themselves to the king to be looked after'.[131]

The civil rulers' possession and exercise of the powers of government is therefore qualified. Above all, it must be understood that:

> The law is not the king's own, but given to him in trust. He who receiveth a kingdom conditionally, and may be dethroned if he sell it or put it away to any other, is a fiduciary patron, and hath it only in trust.[132]

The people remain the source of power: 'the most eminent and fountain-power of royalty remaineth in the people as in an immortal spring'.[133] Moreover, the powers of government are never held solely by one individual. If the form of government is monarchy then the king must rule with parliament and with inferior judges, recognizing that the power which both parliaments and the inferior judges possess is theirs from God and through the people no less than his own. Parliament does not receive its power from the king; the king is obliged to convene parliament; and parliament's grant of power to the king is to execute the law which parliament itself enacts.[134]

Beyond this, 'the king is not the sole and final interpreter of the law'[135] because the lesser magistrate is directly accountable to God for his interpretation and application of the law. Similarly, the power of the sword is given by God to the inferior judges as well as to the king,[136] and the parliament has power to declare war even though it may give that power to the king.[137]

In addition to this distribution and limitation of powers, there

---

130. p. 26 [45].
131. p. 69 [124–125].
132. p. 72 [129–130].
133. p. 82 [148]. See also p. 85 [153–154].
134. p. 98 [178].
135. p. 137 [252].
136. p. 184 [372–373].
137. p. 185 [373–375].

are the limitations, described in the previous sections, associated with the requirement that the civil ruler exercise power according to God's purpose for government and do so with an accountability to the twofold and ordered authors of government: namely, God and the people.

The civil ruler as servant and 'means'

Following naturally from this understanding is Rutherford's repeated descriptions of the civil ruler as 'servant' and 'means', already referred to above. The power that he has has been entrusted to him and is power to serve the people who have entrusted it:

> The king hath no proper, masterly, or lordly dominion over his subjects; his dominion is rather fiduciary and ministerial, than masterly.[138]

The 'king is for his kingdom as a mean for the end, as the watchman for the city, the living law for peace and safety to God's people'.[139] He is 'an adopted father, tutor, a politic servant and royal watchman of the state'.[140] In various respects Rutherford compares the king to pastors and doctors, whose power, it is plain, is the power to serve.[141] Everything the civil ruler does is to be related to the health of the people and measured by its effectiveness in securing that end. So in some respects the king is 'nothing but an eminent servant of the state'[142] and, quite simply, 'what the king doth as king, he doeth it for the happiness of his people'.[143]

Because the civil ruler is a servant of the people, a means to the end of their well-being and measured always against their interests, it can be said that the people are 'greater' or 'more precious' than the king.[144] It is true that he 'hath an authoritative

---

138. p. 64 [116].
139. p. 43 [75]. See also pp. 72 [129], 120 [219–220].
140. p. 59 [105].
141. p. 62 [112].
142. p. 127 [233].
143. p. 123 [226].
144. See especially pp. 77–79 [139–144].

power above the people, because royalty is formally in him, and
originally and virtually only in the people', but still the people
'create the man king, they are so above the king, and have a virtual
power to compel him to do his duty'.[145] Even as the king is
'really a sovereign above the people' it is 'in the executive power
of laws'.[146] Just as the owner and managing director of a
multi-billion-pound company may be told to stop talking and
leave the room by a lowly safety officer in the event of a fire, in
spite of having appointed that safety officer and given him such
authority as he has, so the people may be told what to do by their
servant the king by virtue of the executive power which has been
vested in him. Neither the safety officer nor the civil ruler are
thereby understood to be greater than the ones who appointed
them and gave them their authority. As Rutherford put it:

> The king is above the people, by eminence of derived authority as a
> watchman, and in actual supremacy; and he is inferior to them in
> fountain-power, as the effect to the cause.[147]

It must always be remembered that 'a kingdom is not the prince's
own'.[148]

The rule of law – which law?

However, of all the limitations placed upon the civil ruler's power
arising out of a consideration of the formal cause of government,
the most stringent is the requirement that in the understanding and
exercise of its power the civil government is to do everything
according to and in subjection and conformity to the law of God.
Government is defined in relation to law. The essence of government is the embodiment of the demands and functions of the
law. Government is the instrument of the rule of law. And each of
these statements raises the question of which law it is that the

---

145. p. 56 [101].
146. p. 208 [417].
147. p. 115 [209–210].
148. p. 42 [74].

civil government identifies, promulgates, applies, administers and enforces.

The answer, of course, is 'God's law'. Rutherford was not unaware of the further questions raised by this answer, but seemed relatively untroubled by the use of natural law and more than ready to apply principles and practices from the Old Testament to seventeenth-century Britain. This was not, however, because he placed undue confidence in unaided human reason, for, to him, natural law was not an independent source of truth but a reading of the way the world was put together, and so functioned in the light of Scripture. In this way the law of nature was God's law and the court of nature was God's court.[149] Nor was Rutherford under any illusion that there was no difference between government in pre-exilic Israel and government in seventeenth-century Britain. With regard to the divine identification of kings he explains that 'the Jews had this privilege that no nation had'.[150]

He concedes that:

> God indeed, in the time of the Jews, was the king of Israel in another
> manner than he was the king of all the nations, and is the king of
> Christian realms now.[151]

He asserts that aspects of government had 'vanished with the commonwealth of the Jews'[152] and that the application of various laws had changed with the change of redemptive-historical moment.[153]

The difficulty of these further questions about where that law was to be found and how it was to be interpreted was not to obscure this basic point: civil government was the embodiment and instrument of the rule of law, the law in question was the law of God, and this amounted to the single most important limitation on the civil government which could be made. As might be

---

149. p. 5 [8].
150. p. 13 [22].
151. p. 24 [41].
152. p. 43 [76].
153. p. 232 [462–463].

expected, this theme is expressed repeatedly and variously throughout *Lex, Rex.*

Legislatively, a human law is only really a law if it conforms to and expresses the law of God and therefore, 'what civil laws parliaments make against God's word, [the church] may authoritatively declare them to be unlawful'.[154] Judicially, the interpretation and application of human law must be subject to the law of God, for 'the king hath no power from God to pronounce what sentence he pleaseth, because the judgment is not his own but God's'.[155] The king was to have 'the law of God as his rule'.[156] Executively and administratively, as the king 'may not command what he will, but what the King of kings warranteth him to command, so may he not punish as he will, but by warrant also of the Supreme Judge of all the earth'.[157]

The people's grant of power was on the condition that the king rule according to the law of God.[158] The civil ruler is 'obliged to command and rule justly and religiously for the good of the subjects, and is only set over the people on these conditions'.[159]

The only power which God granted was the power to act lawfully: God never could or does give moral power to sin and therefore, as seen above, the only power which the king has from God is power under the law of God.[160]

Similarly, any prerogatory powers the king possessed could not be defined as 'beyond the law', because in all events, 'the king, as king, can do no more than that which upon right and law he may do'.[161]

The king as the embodiment of law

One of Rutherford's preferred ways of describing the relationship

---

154. p. xxiii [a2+3]. See also p. 138 [254–256].
155. p. 88 [160]. See also p. 137 [252–254].
156. p. 35 [62]. See also p. 109 [198–199].
157. p. 232 [463].
158. p. 57 [101–103].
159. p. 141 [261].
160. p. 73 [131]. See also p. 191 [385].
161. p. 106 [193].

between the law of God under which the king operated and the king, or civil ruler, himself was in asserting that the king was to be the embodiment of the law:

> If the king as the king, be *lex animata*, a breathing and living law, the king, as king, must do by obligation of law what he doth as king, and not from spontaneous and arbitrary grace.[162]

> *Rex est lex viva, animata, et loquens lex*, the king as king, is a living, breathing, and speaking law . . . so is the king the law reduced in practice.[163]

> A royal power is the good gift of God, a lawful and just power. A king acting and speaking as a king, speaketh and acteth law and justice.[164]

All this not only answers the question as to the formal cause, the essence of government; it also means that in some respects, it is the law that is the real ruler. This is merely another way of stating that the civil ruler is the deputy of God; that a deputy has no power other than that given to him by the one whose deputy he is; that obedience to the deputy is actually obedience to the sovereign; and that subjection to the sovereign does not entail obedience to the deputy as and when the deputy is acting against or beyond the will of the sovereign.

Tyranny and absolutism

With this in place, it is not hard to guess how Rutherford will define tyranny and on what grounds he will oppose the absolutist rule of the civil government. A king is only a king in so far as he 'fulfilleth the condition', which is to 'take heed to God's law as a king, and govern according to God's will'.[165] The exercise of power beyond God's law is illegitimate, because 'God hath given no absolute and

---

162. p. 98 [178].
163. p. 101 [184].
164. p. 177 [358]. See also pp. 111 [201], 125 [230], 146 [269].
165. p. 57 [102].

unlimited power to a king above the law'[166] and to this degree 'when the magistrate doth anything by violence, and without law, in so far doing against his office, he is not a magistrate'.[167]

The measure of a tyrant is solely and simply departure from the law which the king is to embody:

> A tyrant is he who habitually sinneth against the catholic good of the subjects and state, and subverteth law . . . and so much as he hath of law, so much of a king; and in his remotest distance from law and reason he is a tyrant.[168]

This limitation is not merely theoretical, however. If the king acts beyond or against the law of God, then the people are 'in these acts . . . not to acknowledge him as king'.[169] Moreover, tyrannical power – that is, power exercised beyond or against the law of God, of which the civil ruler is meant to be the embodiment – is 'evil . . . and can tie none to subjection . . . and if it tie not to subjection, it may be lawfully resisted'.[170]

Summary

What makes government government is that it embodies the rule of God's law for the good of the people. Definitions of government necessarily involve reference to power, but in Rutherford's view it is always power at the service and under the direction of God's law and it is always power exercised for the good of the people. 'The law, rather than the king, hath power of life and death',[171] and since the law is for the good of the people then, as we have seen above:

> The king, as king, hath all his official and relative goodness in the world, as relative to the end. All that you can imagine to be in a king, as a king,

166. p. 101 [183].
167. p. 103 [186].
168. pp. 119 [217], 101 [184].
169. p. 58 [103–104].
170. p. 141 [261]. See also p. 220 [441].
171. p. 102 [184].

is all relative to the safety and good of the people, (Rom. 13:4) 'He is a minister for thy good'. He should not, as king, make himself, or his own gain and honour, his end.[172]

Rutherford's understanding of the formal cause of civil government thus, quite literally, relativizes it. There is no place for autonomous, arbitrary or absolute rule by a special class. Rather, 'the kingdom . . . is superior to the king';[173] the king is a 'life-renter, not a lord, or proprietor of his kingdom';[174] and in his every activity and intention the government is bounded by the law of God, who grants power through the consent and for the well-being of the people.

What is the civil government made out of? (The material cause)

The fourth and last of the 'What makes government?' questions is that of the material cause: 'Out of what stuff is government made?' In brief, Rutherford's answer is that the civil government is made out of ordinary human beings, equal with all others by nature, and themselves sinful. The limitations on the civil ruler which flow from this answer revolve around his relationship with other agencies in society and the distinction between the civil ruler as civil ruler and the civil ruler as a man: between his office and his person.

All human beings are naturally equal: Civil rulers are not a class apart

As was seen above, Rutherford strongly asserts the natural equality of all human beings: 'all are born alike and equal . . . for king and beggar spring of one clay'.[175] Every human being is born free and his only *natural* subjection is domestic, within the family.[176] This

---

172. p. 83 [150].
173. p. 69 [125].
174. p. 86 [155].
175. pp. 25 [43], 2 [3].
176. p. 51 [90–92].

means that the civil ruler is not another species or a special class of human being. No-one is ruler by nature and, in that sense, there is no reason in nature why one man should be king and lord over another.[177] As Rutherford graphically puts it, 'no man cometh out of the womb with a diadem on his head or a sceptre in his hand'.[178] Rulers are made, not born.[179]

Not a class apart in relation to the church

This means that the civil government is not made out of qualitatively different stuff from other God-given agencies in society, such as the church and the family, and nor does one stratum of civil government have unqualified authority over another.

If the church were the institution for ordinary humans and the civil government were composed of those who by nature were more than human, then the civil rulers might be exempt from the nurture and discipline of the church. However, since by nature the ruler is merely a human being, equal with all other human beings, then he can expect no special favours in the life of the church:

> Kings are under the co-active power of Christ's keys of discipline,
> and . . . prophets and pastors, as ambassadors of Christ, have the keys
> of the kingdom of God, to open and let in believing princes, and also to
> shut them out, if they rebel against Christ; the law of Christ excepteth
> none, (Mat. 16:19; 18:15, 16; 2 Cor. 10:6; Jer. 1:9).[180]

Of course, it is not the task or calling of the church to 'repeal civil laws',[181] but it is emphatically the church's job to 'preach against unjust and grievous laws'[182] and, as she does so, the civil ruler is reminded of his accountability to the Lord who rules all

---

177. p. 31 [53–54].
178. p. 6 [10].
179. pp. 11 [18–19], 38 [67], 40–43 [70–77], 45 [79–80].
180. p. xxi [A3+2].
181. p. xxii [a2+3].
182. p. xxii [a2].

human institutions. As he sits listening to the word of God in church, the king's office is honoured but his behaviour, if unlawful, is rebuked: that is, in a distinction to which we must shortly give more attention, he is rebuked 'as a man'.

> The king's sceptre is his royal office, which is not subject to any judicature . . . but if the king, as a man, blaspheme God, murder the innocent, advance belly-gods . . . above the Lord's inheritance, the ministers of Christ are to say, 'The king troubleth Israel, and they have the keys to open and shut heaven to, and upon the king, if he can offend'.[183]

Not a class apart in relation to lesser magistrates

In the same way, the fact that the king is made of the same stuff as the lesser magistrate rules out any thought that the higher the stratum of government, the greater the intrinsic authority. The highest and the lowest level of civil government alike have authority given by God over people specified by God for tasks described by God according to rules revealed by God. Certainly, as mere man, the highest civil ruler will work with other rulers:

> Wherever God appointed a king he never appointed him absolute, and a sole independent angel, but joined always with him judges.[184]

And Rutherford insists that these inferior judges or lower levels of civil government, including 'parliaments, mayors, sheriffs, provosts and constables',[185] received their power from God and not from the king. It was not that God gave power to the king which he then shared out with lower levels of government:

> The judges of England rule not by the king of Britain, as their author, efficient, constituent, but by Jesus Christ immediately . . . All these, and their power, and persons, rule independently, and immediately by Jesus

183. p. xxii [a+1].
184. p. 5 [7].
185. p. 13 [22].

Christ. . . . All inferior judges are . . . the ordinances of God not
revocable.[186]

The king could not impose laws upon lesser magistrates; they
were to judge according to the law of God. The king could not
rule over the consciences of the lower levels of government; they
were subject directly to God. And the king could not appoint or
remove inferior judges by some absolutist will, but rather only
according to criteria which God had laid down:

> And in a moral obligation of judging righteously, the conscience of
> the monarch and the conscience of the inferior judges are equally
> under immediate subjection to the King of kings; for there is here a
> co-ordination of consciences, and no subordination.[187]

Quite simply, Rutherford's insistence on the natural equality of
all human beings and on recognizing that the stuff out of which
the ruler was made was the same stuff out of which the ruled
were made amounts to a refusal of some 'great chain of being'.
Rather:

> Inferior judges are no less immediate deputies of God . . . than the
> king . . . inferior judges are no less essentially judges, and the immediate
> vicars of God, than the king . . . [they have] immediate subjection of
> their conscience to the King of kings. And their judgment which they
> execute is the Lord's immediately, and not the king's.[188]

When the king dies, the judges are still judges because their
authority and appointment is from God.[189] If the king fails in
his duty, this does not excuse the inferior judges because
they are directly accountable to God.[190] If the king threatens its

---

186. p. 13 [22–23].
187. p. 5 [8]. See also p. 13 [23].
188. p. 18 [30–31], 88 [159], 92 [166–167], 94 [169].
189. p. 94 [170].
190. p. 97 [175–176].

well-being, then parliament is 'to take course for the safety of the kingdom'.[191] Parliament's power is not granted to it by the king, and 'his convening of them is an act of royal duty, which he oweth to the parliament by virtue of his office, and is not an act of grace'.[192]

Thus, over and over, Rutherford insists that the fact that the raw material of the highest civil ruler is the same as the raw material of all other civil rulers limits his power over them.[193]

Civil rulers are sinners

Rutherford goes further. Not only is the civil government composed of mere human beings who are naturally equal to those over whom they rule; it is composed of sinful human beings who are not, by virtue of office-holding, any more morally upright than those they rule. Of course, if rulers are chosen by the people according to the criteria which God lays down, then the rulers will be more morally upright than those they rule, but this is something that brings them to office rather than something which comes to them by virtue of holding office. Rutherford is plain-speaking and forceful on these points:

> All the good kings that have been may be written in a gold ring . . .
> There be more foolish kings in the world than wise . . . Histories teach
> us there have been more tyrants than kings . . . Because all kings, since
> the fall of the father, king Adam, are inclined to sin and injustice, and so
> had need to be guided by a law, even because they are kings, so they
> remain men.[194]

This itself provides a reason for the limitation of the civil government's power. The more power, the greater the likelihood of really harmful abuse of power by those sinners who hold it.[195]

---

191. p. 97 [176].
192. p. 98 [178].
193. See also pp. 99 [179–180], 113 [206–207], 173–174 [352–353].
194. p. 121 [221], 122 [223], 132 [243], 191 [385].
195. p. 194–197 [390–398].

Or, as Rutherford puts it, 'omnipotency in one that can sin is a cursed power'.[196] Again:

> It is the manner of inferior judges, as we see in the sons of Eli and
> Samuel, to pervert judgment, as well as king Saul did; but the king may
> more oppress, and his tyranny hath more colour, and is more catholic
> than the oppression of inferior judges.[197]

Distinguishing between the office of the king and the king who holds office

At this point Rutherford makes a move which is by no means original to him but which is integral to the argument of the whole of *Lex, rex*. If the formal cause of civil government is its embodiment of the rule of God's law, and if the material cause of civil government is the stuff of sinful human beings, then the probability of there being a discrepancy between how God intends the ruler to behave and how the ruler actually does behave is very high indeed. If, further, the power of office which God has granted is the power to serve as an instrument of the rule of his law, then when the ruler uses power beyond or against God's law it should be understood that he does so beyond or against his office. The distinction which Rutherford draws here is between the ruler acting according to his office and the ruler acting beyond or against his office. Rutherford uses two ways of describing this discrepancy. First, he speaks of the king *in abstracto* (the office as God intends and authorizes it: that is, the king considered as exercising power precisely under and according to God's law) and the king *in concreto* (the person who holds the office in his historical reality, which may include the exercise of power against or beyond God's law). Second, he speaks simply of the king, as a king, over against the king, as a man. Some examples may clarify his usage.

He describes the position which he opposes like this: 'the power lawful and the sinful person cannot be separated'.[198]

---

196. p. 191 [385].
197. p. 195 [392].
198. p. 141 [259–260].

And he summarizes his own argument in this way:

> This distinction, rejected by royalists, must be cleared. This is an evident and sensible distinction: — The king *in concreto*, the man who is king, and the king *in abstracto*, the royal office of the king.[199]

For this reason, resisting the tyrant is not resisting the ordinance of God: subjection to the powers is subjection to God as he authorizes the powers. But God does not give the powers authority to impose false religion, for example, and thus the subject who obeys for conscience's sake will obey according to the law of God. The ruler is to be obeyed as the embodiment of the law of God, but when he acts beyond or against the law of God he does not embody the law of God and so at those points he is not to be obeyed:

> It is evident from Rom. 13 that all subjection and obedience to higher powers commanded there, is subjection to the power and office of the magistrate *in abstracto*, or, which is all one, to the person using the power lawfully.[200]

> We must needs be subject to the royal office for conscience, by reason of the fifth commandment; but we must not needs be subject to the man who is king, if he command things unlawful.[201]

Another way of stating this is to say that judges are only 'formally judges, in so far as they . . . act conform to the will of the King of kings'.[202] Rutherford illustrates the way in which the rulers' failure to 'act conform to the will of the King of kings' changes the way in which the ruled should relate to them. If a pastor turned robber,[203] if a king turned parricide,[204] or if a

---

199. p. 143 [265].
200. p. 144 [265–266].
201. p. 145 [268].
202. p. 221 [443].
203. p. 10 [17].
204. p. 127 [234].

'father in a distemper would set his own house on fire, and burn himself and his ten sons',[205] then resisting and restraining such rulers in their madness and wickedness would not be resisting the ordinance of God, simply because God's ordinance consisted in the power to act according to his law and for the good of the ruled. Similarly, if the actions of the ruler tend to anarchy, then they are actions beyond or against God's law and therefore beyond or against his office. Resistance to the ruler in such a case would be resistance to the man and not to the ruler as such.

In response to the charge that the distinction is ultimately unsustainable, Rutherford presses the logic. If, for example, the king required conversion to pagan religion, then, according to those who deny the distinction, refusal to convert to paganism would be resistance to God. But this in turn would mean that God had contradicted himself. Rutherford shows that such distinctions are commonplace in Scripture.[206]

The civil ruler has been given a 'sword' – the power by which he upholds the rule of law. The distinction between the 'king as king' and the 'king as man' is simply that between legitimate and illegitimate uses of the sword. Even though the sword has truly been given over to the ruler, it is necessary to identify and resist its wrongful use:

> But when he abuseth his power to the destruction of his subjects, it is lawful to throw a sword out of a madman's hand, though it be his own proper sword, and though he have a due right to it, and a just power to use it for good; for all fiduciary power abused may be repealed.[207]

Responding to the unlawful discrepancy between the conduct of the man and the demands of the office

How then are the subjects – who are, after all, naturally equal with their rulers and directly accountable in their conscience to

205. p. 115 [209].
206. pp. 147–148 [272–273].
207. p. 84 [152].

God – to deal with the discrepancy between the civil government as it should be and the civil government as it actually is? The first thing is to regard the unlawful use of power as a form of madness.[208] Second, the subjects must not allow that the tyrannous acts (those beyond or against the law of God) are lawful or that the king is acting as king when he performs them:

> Tyranny being a work of Satan, is not from God, because sin, either habitual or actual, is not from God: . . . and, therefore, a power ethical, politic, or moral, to oppress, is not from God, and is not a power, but a licentious deviation of a power; and is no more from God, but from sinful nature and the old serpent, than a license to sin.[209]

'Not a power, but a licentious deviation of a power': this is the civil ruler when not acting under and according to the law of God. More simply still, 'when the magistrate doth anything by violence, and without law, in so far doing against his office, he is not a magistrate'.[210] And if at that point he is not a magistrate, then he is to be given neither the recognition nor the obedience due to him as magistrate:

> He that commandeth not what God commandeth, and punisheth and killeth where God, if personally and immediately present, would neither command nor punish, is not in these acts to be subjected unto, and obeyed as a superior power.[211]

Indeed, to be subject to the ruler in the ruler's rebellion against God would be to share in his rebellion against God. The king can

---

208. p. xxi [A₃]. This claim, along with the claim that the king has been misled by evil counsellors, represents a commonly used way of critics of the monarch asserting their loyalty. See also p. 104 [188] and Rutherford's protestations of loyalty on p. 190 [383]. Further instances may be found on p. 140 [259] and p. 146 [269–270].

209. p. 34 [59].

210. p. 103 [186].

211. p. 144 [266].

have no legitimate claim upon the subjection of the ruled at those points where he departs from the law of God:

> Every act of a king . . . in so far as it is lawless, the person in that act repugnant to law loseth all due claim of actual subjection in that act, and in that act power actual is lost, as is clear, Acts 4:19; 5:29.[212]

What comes next is unsurprising. Refusal to recognize the ruler in his acts of tyranny leads to refusal to be subject to him in those acts, and this in turn leads to the right and duty of resisting rulers 'when they command things unlawful, and kill the innocent'.[213] With the all-important distinction in place this means, of course, resisting not the king in his office but the king as a man acting outside of his office. The office and the power may not be resisted, but by going beyond or against his office the ruler has put himself outside of it, and the ground upon which resistance takes place is precisely the ground 'outside the office'.[214] Resisting the king when the king commands 'that which is against God' is actually resisting Satan: 'a man commanding unjustly, and ruling tyrannically, hath, in that, no power from God'.[215]

In a passage which Coffey describes as taking us to the 'emotional heart' of *Lex, Rex*,[216] Rutherford reiterates the principles, underlines the distinctions and draws the conclusions by a description of the late 1630s and early 1640s as he and his fellow radicals saw them:

> The lawful ruler, as a ruler, and in respect of his office, is not to be resisted, because he is not a terror to good works, but to evil; and no man who doth good is to be afraid of the office or the power, but to expect praise and a reward of the same. But the man who is a king may command an idolatrous and superstitious worship — send an army of

---

212. pp. 149–150 [276].
213. p. 144 [266–267].
214. p. 145 [268–269].
215. p. 144 [267].
216. Coffey, *Rutherford*, p. 182.

cut-throats against them, because they refuse that worship, and may reward papists, prelates, and other corrupt men, and may advance them to places of state and honour because they kneel to a tree altar, — pray to the east, — adore the letters and sound of the word *Jesus* — teach and write Arminianism, and may imprison, deprive, confine, cut the ears, and slit[217] the noses, and burn the faces of those who speak and preach and write the truth of God; and may send armies of cut-throats, Irish rebels, and other papists and malignant atheists, to destroy and murder the judges of the land, and innocent defenders of the reformed religion, &c., — the man, I say, in these acts is a terror to good works, — an encouragement to evil; and those that do good are to be afraid of the king, and to expect no praise, but punishment and vexation from him; therefore, this reason in the text will prove that the man who is the king, in so far as he doth those things that are against his office, may be resisted; and that in these we are not to be subject, but only we are to be subject to his power and royal authority, *in abstracto*, in so far as, according to his office, he is not a terror to good works, but to evil.[218]

What, then, was civil government made of? It was made of sinful human beings, not belonging to a special class but rather equal by nature with those whom they ruled. Since they formed no special class, their power must sit alongside and work with other God-given powers such as the church and the various levels of governmental hierarchy. These sinful human beings would, in their sin, act against and beyond the office which God had given them, which was the embodiment and implementation of his law, and at those points a distinction must be drawn between the rulers as rulers and the rulers as men, sinners and tyrants. The rulers as rulers, acting according to their office, must be honoured and obeyed. The rulers as men acting against their office must not, in those acts, be recognized or obeyed but rather resisted.[219]

---

217. In the original 'slit' is 'rip'.

218. p. 145 [267–268].

219. A summary of Rutherford's explanation of the conditions under which
     armed resistance is permissible and of his response to Christian

Summary and transition

The civil government, then, according to Rutherford, is brought into being by God and the people. It exists for the well-being, and especially the protection of the people, whose highest good is found in the practice of true religion. It is made of the stuff of ordinary, sinful human beings, neither separate from nor superior to those they rule. And the essence of civil government is its embodiment of the law of God, which it is to declare legislatively, apply judicially, and enforce executively. The answers to these four questions generate reasons to limit civil government, to keep it under jealous observation and to pray for those given responsibility in it. Moreover, the answers themselves, as well as Rutherford's route to them, produce further questions for our consideration: questions for Rutherford from us and for us from Rutherford. It is to a description of those questions that we now turn.

Some questions for Rutherford

There are many practical questions we would like to ask Rutherford about the relationship between institutions in society; about how precisely the distinctions which he lays down are to be applied; about whether organizing the material in relation to Aristotle's four causes did not lead inevitably to a certain set of answers; about particular phrases and concepts within *Lex, Rex*; about what we are to do for and in response to persecuting authorities and persecuted brothers and sisters; and about what he, Rutherford, would do if he were with us under judgment, where the marginalized church experiences – and even embraces – cultural impotence and irrelevance. However, the key questions which twenty-first century Christian readers wish to bring to the work cluster around issues of salvation history. Modern readers would wish to question Rutherford along the lines outlined in the following paragraphs.

'pacifist' arguments from the life of Jesus, the early church and key New Testament texts have had to be omitted. A copy may be had from the author at davidf@oakhill.ac.uk.

Apart from the necessary geographical spread of true religion, in what ways have the cross and resurrection of Jesus and the outpouring of the Holy Spirit shaped – or made a difference to – your political theory? *Lex, Rex* gives the impression that the principles of civil government are timeless laws rather than historical reflections of and upon God's saving work in Christ.

Similarly, what eschatological perspectives do you bring to bear upon the nature and function of civil government? Does *Lex, Rex* reflect the realities of which Joel Garver writes:

> Ecclesial order and civil order . . . do not occupy two different spaces, but two different *times*: the church having an eternal end, rooted in God's past saving acts in Christ, made present now in word and sacrament; the civil order having a temporal function within the present *saeculum*, ordained to continually pass away, though its treasures are carried in the bosom of the church into the eternal kingdom (Rev. 21:24).[220]

Another way of asking the same question would be to reflect upon O'Donovan's determination to 'place political history within the history of God's reign'.[221] Does *Lex, Rex* do this?

There is an ecclesiological angle on this, too. How does your view of the church shape your view of the state, and how does your view of the state shape your view of the church? To what extent is *Lex, Rex* simply presbyterianism in civil affairs? What difference does the fact that the church is a nation, a political entity and the only eschatological social unit make to our understanding of the nation-state; to the possibility that a nation may, as such, be in covenant with God; and to the relationship between the civil authority in a nation and the church in that nation? Do you follow through the political implications of your declaration that the church is 'a free kingdom that oweth spiritual tribute to none on earth, as being the freeborn princess and daughter to the King of kings'?[222]

---

220. *There is another King*, 'Conclusions'.

221. O'Donovan, *The Desire of the Nations*, p. 19.

222. Rutherford, *Letters*, CCLXXXI.

Aspects of biblical interpretation also arise. Surely, no Christian would disagree with your view, as summarized by John Coffey, that the Old Testament is 'the magistrate's most important textbook'.[223] However, it would be reassuring to have an explanation of the methods by which you draw relevant distinctions about the applicability and conceptual transfer of passages located in one cultural and redemptive-historical moment to situations in a very different cultural and redemptive-historical moment.

Still on the question of authority, some more definite biblical warrant would be welcome for the natural law axiom upon which you lay so very much stress: namely, the duty of the individual human person to seek his own well-being. The way that you combine it with emphatic theocentricity reminds us of Baxter in your day and those who call themselves 'Christian hedonists' in ours. Both work as though there were an unqualified command lawfully to defend ourselves and pursue our own good.

Putting these concerns together, we recognize that the political theory of *Lex, Rex* is Christian, in so far as it is built upon the propositions of Christian dogmatics. What is less clear is how far it is evangelical in the sense that it expresses and is shaped by the gospel story which is the shape of history itself. Admittedly, the whole approach makes sense only if orthodox Christian teaching about 'God' and 'humankind', and 'sin' and suchlike are true, but does this political theory reflect the newness and the strangeness of the kingdom of God embodied in Jesus the servant and established by his death and resurrection?

It is not hard to imagine that Rutherford would have answers to these questions – and probably very long and detailed answers. In brief, however, a defence of *Lex, Rex* against the charges which these questions imply may proceed by responding positively to Peter Leithart's questions:

> The issue is whether the hope of forming Christian culture in the wider society is inherent to the Church's mission, or a deviation from the

223. Coffey, *Politics*, p. 157.

Church's mission. Should the Christian *ekklesia* want to remake the earthly city in her image?[224]

The centrality of the church; the universal Lordship of Christ as the beloved of the Father; the civil authority's accountability not to the church but to Christ himself; and the subordination of all human institutions to God's redemptive purposes are all assumed by Rutherford. It is not that he is behind us in these matters, but rather that he is so far ahead that, unless we hurry up, he is about to lap us. He knows full well that:

> The church's one project is to witness to the Kingdom of God. Christendom is *response* to mission, and as such a sign that God has blessed it. It is constituted not by the church's seizing alien power, but by alien power's becoming attentive to the church.[225]

What we are relearning, he assumes. Lessons of Christian politics are lessons of redeemed society; stern words to the powers that be are part of fulfilling the Great Commission, to disciple the nations and teach them to observe all that Christ has commanded.

Some questions from Rutherford

In his turn, Rutherford presents us with a number of questions, some of which may prove a little embarrassing. He may even enlist Oliver O'Donovan to express some of his interests and concerns! His first question is, of course, about the five questions which *Lex, Rex* itself sets out to answer:

- What is the purpose of civil government?
- What brings it into being?
- What is the essence of civil government?

---

224. Leithart, *Against Christianity*, p. 125.
225. O'Donovan, *Desire*, p. 195.

- What is the stuff of which it is made?
- Under what conditions, if any, may the civil government be resisted?

Rutherford's meta-question is simply whether it is possible to have a coherent political theory without an answer to these questions. But he asks with a purpose because if, as seems likely, we acknowledge the coherence and relevance of these questions for a consideration of civil government, then he will want to know our answers to them.

This leads to his second major question to us: how can we pretend that those who differ on these foundational questions of government may still act together as though there is something deeper still which unites them? This, of course, is the question by which he exposes the myths of neutrality and pluralism alike. The purpose of civil government is to secure the well-being of the people by protecting them and the church so that they may attain their highest good in the knowledge of God in Christ. True or false? The God who rules all things through his exalted Son brings government into being using the consent of the people as a means. True or false? What makes government government is its submission to and embodiment of the law of God discovered through study and application of his infallible and sufficient word, the Bible. True or false? Government is made of sinful human beings, each one of whom is directly accountable in conscience and on judgment day to the one true living God. True or false? Rutherford's answers to the 'questions of government' do not appeal to some 'shared values or objectives' which try to get behind the supremacy of Jesus Christ. Boldly and explicitly they thus eliminate possibility of neutrality. As O'Donovan puts it:

> In the Christian era there is no neutral performance on the part of rulers; either they accommodate to the energy of the divine mission, or they hurl themselves into defiance.[226]

---

226. O'Donovan, *Desire*, p. 217.

Every actual society reaches answers to these questions which it treats as normative, and so makes definite religious judgments about the proper content of religious belief and practice. The false consciousness of the would-be secular society lies in its determination to conceal the religious judgments that it has made.[227]

What follows is obvious: a question for those who seek to affirm the possibility or legitimacy of neutrality or pluralism in civil government. If, Rutherford might ask, one set of answers to the questions above is correct and other sets incorrect, then how, for right-minded people, could the recognition and implementation of the correct answers not be the goal for the future and the critical measure of the present? In a few short steps Rutherford takes us to the Christendom question. Coffey calls Rutherford a 'full-blooded defender of Reformed theocratic ambition'.[228] Rutherford would wish to ask what else he could be while remaining consistent with his answers to the original questions.

Pressing his point, Rutherford might then ask whether, far from there being a tension in his thought between the 'Whig constitutionalist' and the 'Presbyterian theocrat', it is not rather the case – in a politically presuppositionalist sort of way – that all that is good and proper in his political theory hangs or falls together. Coffey describes how *Lex, Rex* is experienced as an 'ambiguous book' by modern readers:

On the one hand, Rutherford's arguments for popular sovereignty, the rule of law, and the right of resistance to tyranny, remind us of Locke, and can lead to the impression that the author of *Lex, Rex* was something of a modern liberal. On the other hand, his desire for a covenanted nation purged of heresy, idolatry and unbelief, makes him appear thoroughly reactionary, utterly committed to the ideals of Christendom.[229]

---

227. O'Donovan, *Desire*, p. 247.
228. Coffey, *Politics*, p. 29.
229. Coffey, *Politics*, p. 187.

Rutherford might reply that those features of his thought which are attractive to moderns (the 'modern liberal' Rutherford) – its contractarianism, division of powers, checks and balances, emphasis on the rule of law, person–office distinction – cannot be separated from the Reformed systematics and covenantal reading of Scripture (the 'thoroughly reactionary' Rutherford) with which they are associated in *Lex, Rex*. This is because they are not merely 'associated'. Rather, Rutherford's affirmation of modern aspects of political thought and practice wholly depends upon its theological underpinning. Unless there is a sovereign, righteous God, unless the Calvinist doctrine of providence is true; unless the church is the bearer of salvation news and Christ is Lord over all human institutions; unless the law of God clearly and authoritatively describes human maturity and social well-being; then what the successors of the 'Whig constitutionalist' so appreciate in *Lex, Rex* is lost to them and to the rest of us. This is presuppositionalist by affirming politically what is also true epistemologically and ethically and personally: the only sure foundation for ordered and good thinking and living is the rule and rules of the triune God; where those who deny that rule and those rules nonetheless prosper (think straight, live well, or do politics properly), it is because they are being inconsistent with their denial; and sanity and well-being are found and human flourishing experienced best by submissive and dependent acknowledgment of God and by living, thinking and politicking consistently with that.

Taking this further: if, for a few moments, Rutherford could set aside his own refusal of toleration, he might even ask modern Christians who are so keen on toleration for an explanation of how they think that pluralism can provide a basis for it. Imagine that the constitution sets out the principles by which a society determines what is to be tolerated and what to be criminalized: that is, what should be placed on the statute book. A full pluralist constitution will say something like 'Everyone is right and no-one is right and none of us can ever know for sure.' This makes any toleration which is offered 'out there' in the public square or on the statute book either arbitrary or unfounded. In contrast – and somewhat ironically – a commitment at the level of the constitution to the recognition of the authority of Christ provides solid grounds for extending toleration exactly as far as he commands. The constitution will read, 'Jesus Christ is King of Kings and we are to do what he says.' The statute book can then say with a proper basis in the constitution, 'The King says that behaviours X and Y are to be tolerated (with respect to sanctions from the magistrate) and that behaviours A and B are to be punished.' And, depending on answers to a multitude of exegetical questions, it is a distinct possibility that X and Y will include 'belief in a false god'. Toleration has a foundation in a 'Christendomite' constitution which it does not have in a pluralist constitution. This, too, demonstrates that those wishing for 'Whig constitutionalist' benefits such as toleration need the 'Reformed theocrat' Christendom ideal (the 'professedly Christian civil order') to underpin such benefits.

This means, of course, that Rutherford is not a modern political theorist if Skinner's two tests of individualism and secularism are applied. Quite the opposite: being a Presbyterian, he has a covenantal understanding of social structures not an individualistic one, and being a theocrat, he has an inescapably and pervasively religious view of what constitutes a well-ordered society. His question to us, then, is: how do you propose to establish the good things of 'Whig constitutionalism' without their necessary underpinnings in 'Reformed theocracy'?

Rutherford's remaining questions to us flow from this. If you acknowledge that the good news of which the church is the bearer and the right worship of God for which the church is the proper setting are themselves essential to the well-being of a people, and also recognize that the civil government has been established by God in order to further (some aspects of) the well-being of a people, then is it not inevitable that the civil government's attitude to the church will be different from the civil government's attitude to groups and institutions which bear a message or promote practices which are highly destructive of human welfare? On some – but by no means all – issues, Rutherford would be quoting Oliver O'Donovan at us. And certainly here:

> If the mission of the church needs a certain social space, for men and
> women of every nation to be drawn into the governed community of

God's Kingdom, then secular authority is authorised to provide and
ensure that space . . . the goals and conduct of secular government are
to be reconceived to serve the needs of international mobility and
contact which the advancement of the Gospel requires.[230]

Again, since the instruments and powers of the highest well-
being of a community rest with the church rather than with the
civil government, how have you allowed political discourse to
proceed on the assumption that the civil government itself is
the provider, promoter and protector of the highest goods?
O'Donovan again:

When believers find themselves confronted with an order that, implicitly
or explicitly, offers itself as the sufficient and necessary condition of
human welfare, they will recognise the beast. When a political structure
makes this claim, we call it 'totalitarian'.[231]

Rutherford's repeated use of Nero as an example of absolutism and tyranny is abundant testimony to his agreement with
this perspective. Further questions he might ask us relate to this:
how is it that a servant who was employed in order to provide
social space for real good to be done by others has been allowed
to become the master of the house, making none too subtle
claims to be the Lord and Saviour of all on the estate and requiring that the goods of the estate be put to his service? How did
you get to the position where other institutions are understood as
subordinate to and at the service of the civil government? Why
are all other strata in the hierarchy of civil government understood to come under the jurisdiction of the executive? How did
you get to the position where – to use the words of one of your
politicians – there is no such thing as society, only the state and
the agencies of the state?
Rutherford's questions to conservative evangelicals are easily
guessed. At what point and for what reason did you abandon the

---

230. O'Donovan, *Desire*, pp. 146–147.
231. O'Donovan, *Desire*, p. 274.

theological sub-discipline of Reformed political thought? If the 'Christendom project' could be distilled, illustratively, to writing 'Jesus Christ is ruler of the kings of the earth' as the first line of the constitution and over the doors of parliament, then at what point in the argument do you depart from such a project? Is Jesus Christ the ruler of the kings of the earth? Is it desirable that the kings of the earth should acknowledge this? Is it desirable that the kings of the earth *qua* kings should publicly confess this? Since you wish for Christ to have first place in all things, why do you exclude national constitutions from these 'all things'?

He might continue: when and why did you start acting as though Christ was king only of the church? When and why did you stop instilling a distrust of princes as a fundamental rule of healthy social life? Or reminding believers and civil rulers alike that the authorities do not have personal power but are rather the embodiment of the law and legitimate only to the degree that they discharge that responsibility faithfully? And addressing the ruling power with the word of Christ? After all, 'the church has to instruct it [the ruling power] in the ways of the humble state'.[232]

More anxiously, he might experience a brief crisis of confidence as he notices two things to which O'Donovan refers: that the great tradition of Christian political theology was in flow from 1100 to 1650,[233] and also that:

> In the seventeenth century philosophy came to lose confidence in the objectivity of final causes . . . now there arose a tradition of explaining societies entirely by reference to efficient causes . . . Individual agents had their ends; but objective structures only had their origins. Moral purposes and goals, questions of human virtue and fulfilment, seemed intrusive, another form of theocratic temptation.[234]

Rutherford might ask, 'Was it something I did or said?' What

---

232. O'Donovan, *Desire*, p. 219.
233. O'Donovan, *Desire*, p. 4.
234. O'Donovan, *Desire*, p. 8.

went wrong with the Puritan revolution? Was it that the political endeavours of the puritans and covenanters were based on the right principles and aiming at the right objectives but prematurely and too forcibly realized? How far were the philosophical turn from final causes and the theological turn from political thought reactions to the mid-century turmoil? How could it have been otherwise? Surprised at the self-loathing and fear of some modern Christians (as if the admittedly awful mistakes of previous 'Christendom' attempts bore any comparison whatever to the tyrannies and mass murders of 'secular' states), he might ask what is so very terrible about 'official' acknowledgment of the lordship of Jesus in the public square. Does the failure and harm of one attempt in the 1650s mean that for ever after it is better to deny or ignore the lordship of Jesus in constitutional matters? Is a nation a safer or healthier place under a denial of Christ's lordship than under an acknowledgment of it?

His questions continue: Why are you so docile before the civil government, as though it was spiritually dangerous to be politically critical or as though the civil ruler was not a servant of the same Christ who is bridegroom to the church? What is the legitimacy of the civil government? Do you agree with me that it is only legitimate so far as it is lawful, and that as and when and where it contradicts the law of God, it is not legitimate authority but only a beast? What do you make of O'Donovan's claim that:

> The state exists in order to give judgment; but under the authority of Christ's rule it gives judgment *under law*, never as its own law. One might say that the only sense of political authority acknowledged within Christendom was the law of the ascended Christ, and that all political authority was the authority of that law.[235]

When did you last declare that an action of the civil government was against the law of God, therefore tyrannical, and to be denounced, ignored or resisted by the people of God? Are you not – perhaps through not having thought through issues of

---

235. O'Donovan, *Desire*, p. 233.

legitimacy and of the person–office distinction – so biddable that you are in danger of performing unrighteous actions and then claiming that you were 'only following orders' as if God's requirement that you submit to the authorities were unqualified?

Rutherford might, therefore, challenge us to think of contemporary examples of the civil government acting tyrannically and – more specifically – of what would provoke us to supplication, to flight, to non-violent resistance, and to armed resistance. He might ask us to complete the sentence 'We are to submit to the authorities so far as . . .'

He would ask us to explain why we act as though democracies cannot be tyrannical. Since the opposite of tyranny is 'obedience to God's law' rather than 'majority support', why do we act as though majority support legitimates the actions of a civil ruler? If all those under sixty years of age voted to expropriate the goods of all those over sixty years of age, would that not be an act of tyranny? He might raise the question of how far and why we place establishing democratic institutions and habits of public life above or before the building of the church as the key to a stable and prosperous society. Challenging us with what we could not deny – that democracy is not the hope for the world – he might ask in what ways the church declares the danger of idolizing democracy. If health and wholeness and true humanness are secured for individuals by the gospel rather than by the establishment of democracy, then would not the same be true for societies? What leads us to put our hope for world peace (to the extent that we have such a hope) in the spread of democracy rather than in the Isaiah 2 spread of the kingdom?

It would be surprising if Rutherford, visiting Britain early in the twenty-first century, did not have more immediate questions for us. Why is the civil government involved in almost every area of life, banning activities such as smoking in public places, fox-hunting, and advertisements for high-fat foods? What is this about compulsory identity cards, and the disqualification of people from public office on the basis that they regard homosexual behaviour as sinful and the protection of his wife as one of a husband's primary duties? How can civil government which is the servant of God declare that the Bible, which is the word of God, contains hate-speech; or permit the slaughter of 170,000 babies each year while getting ever closer to forbidding parental chastisement of children? How does armed resistance, which is the use of minimal defensive force in the absolute last resort and in the face of a direct and actual assault on one's life, sit with the idea of regime change under the doctrine of 'overwhelming force' and nation-building? How much attention has been paid in Iraq to the principle that the legitimacy of a conqueror depends both upon the justice of the conquest and upon the consent of the conquered? Three hundred and sixty years after its first publication, a reading of Rutherford's *Lex, Rex* is uncomfortable, provocative, instructive and inspiring.

Conclusion

For all the words which we might put into Rutherford's mouth, it is better that the last words should really be his. With the various twists and turns of the arguments, what drove Rutherford's political theory was love for his King Jesus and jealousy for his glory, secured properly not only as sinners received forgiveness from him but also as rulers rendered homage and due submission to him. 'The golden reign and dominion of the Gospel, and the high glory of the never-enough-praised Prince of the kings of the earth' was Rutherford's great ambition.[236]

This was what he suffered for: 'I suffer for my royal and princely King Jesus, and for his kingly crown, and the freedom of his kingdom that his Father hath given him'.[237]

This is what he prayed for:

> The kings of Tarshish and of the isles must bring presents to our Lord Jesus (Ps. 72). And Britain is one of the chiefest isles; why then but we may believe that our kings of this island shall come in and bring their

---

236. *Letters,* CCLXXXVIII.
237. *Letters,* LXI.

glory into the new Jerusalem, wherein Christ shall dwell in the latter days? It is our part to pray, 'That the kingdoms of the earth may become Christ's'.[238]

This is what he longed for: 'Let never dew lie upon my branches and let my poor flower wither at the root, so that Christ were enthroned and His glory advanced in all the world and especially in these kingdoms.'[239]

And this is what he urged others to stand firm for: 'Be courageous for Him . . . The worms shall eat kings'.[240] 'It is our part to back our royal King, howbeit there was not six in all the land to follow Him.'[241]

We may agree with little or with much of the political theory of *Lex, Rex*, but it would be a blessing to us, to our church and to our nation if we could have just a fraction of the spirit of Samuel Rutherford, its author, who, more than anything else, lived with the desire that as 'the beginning, the firstborn from among the dead' Jesus Christ should have the first place in all things.

Further reading

Editions of Lex, Rex

Samuel Rutherford, *Lex, Rex, or The Law and the Prince*, London, 1644 (467pp. qto).

Samuel Rutherford, *Lex, Rex, or The Law and the Prince*, Edinburgh, 1843 (234pp.). Reprinted by Sprinkle Publications. (PO Box 1094, Harrisonburg, VA 22801) in 1980 and 1982.

Samuel Rutherford, *Lex, Rex, or The Law and the Prince*, online at http://www.constitution.org/sr/lexrex.htm (accessed 24 November 2004).

---

238. *Letters*, CCLXXXVIII.
239. *Letters*, CCLXXXIV.
240. *Letters*, CCLXVIII.
241. *Letters*, CLXXI.

Other publications

Althusius, Johannes, *Politica*, an abridged translation of *Politics Methodically Set Forth and Illustrated with Sacred and Profane Examples*, ed. and trans. Frederick S. Carney, Indianapolis: Liberty Fund, 1995.

Aquinas, Thomas, *Summa Theologica* Ia.XC–CVIII, 'Treatise on Law'.

Atkinson, James (1982), *Church and State under God*, Latimer Studies 15, Oxford: Latimer House.

Bahnsen, G. L. (1984), *Theonomy in Christian Ethics*, 2nd ed., Phillipsburg, NJ: Presbyterian and Reformed.

Barker, W. S. and Godfrey, W. R. (eds.) (1990), *Theonomy: A Reformed Critique*, Grand Rapids: Zondervan Academic.

Barry, N. P. (2000), *An Introduction to Modern Political Theory*, 4th edn, Basingstoke: Macmillan.

Bartholomew, Craig, Chaplin, Jonathan, Song, Robert and Walters, Al (eds.) (2002), *A Royal Priesthood? The Use of the Bible Ethically and Politically – A Dialogue with Oliver O'Donovan*, Carlisle: Paternoster Press.

Bastiat, Frédéric (1850), *The Law*, available online at http://bastiat.org/en/the_law.html (accessed 24 November 2004).

Baxter, Richard (1994), *A Holy Commonwealth*, ed. William Lamont, Cambridge: CUP.

Burns, J. H. and Goldie, M. (eds.) (1991), *The Cambridge History of Political Thought 1450–1700*, Cambridge: CUP.

Calvin, John, *Institutes of the Christian Religion* (ed. John T. McNeill, 1960) Philadelphia: The Westminster Press, 4.20.

Campbell, W. M. (1941), 'Lex rex and its author', *Records of the Scottish Church History Society* 7: 204–228.

Clarke, J., 'Rutherford and Resistance' in *The Standard Bearer*, April 1989 online article at http://www.hopeprc.org/reformedwitness/1993/RW199307.htm (accessed 24 November 2004).

Coffey, John (1997), *Politics, Religion and the British Revolutions: The Mind of Samuel Rutherford*, Cambridge: CUP.

—(2004), 'Samuel Rutherford' in *Oxford Dictionary of National Biography*, Oxford: OUP.

Collins, G. N. M. (1975), 'The Scottish Covenanters', in *The Christian and the State in Revolutionary Times*, papers from the 1975 Westminster Conference, pp. 45–59.

Conway, David (1995), *Classical Liberalism*, Basingstoke: Macmillan Press.

Culver, R. D. (1974), *Towards a Biblical View of Civil Government*, Chicago: Moody Press.

de Jasay, Anthony (1991), *Choice, Contract, Consent: A Restatement of Liberalism*, London: IEA.

DeMar, Gary (1982–1986), *God and Government*, 3 vols., Atlanta, GA: American Vision Press.

Engelsma, D. J. (1993), 'Conditional Submission?' in *Reformed Witness*, 1.7, (July), two online articles at http://www.hopeprc.org/reformedwitness/ 1993/RW199307.htm#part2 (accessed 24 November 2004).

Estrada, David, 'Samuel Rutherford as a Presbyterian Theologian and Political Thinker', *Christianity and Society* 13.4.

Fagothey, Austin (1959), *Right and Reason*, Rockford, IL: Tan Books.

Flinn, Richard (1978–1979), 'Samuel Rutherford and Puritan Political Theory', *Journal of Christian Reconstruction* 5, pp. 49–74.

Ford, J. D. (1994), 'Samuel Rutherford on the Origins of Government', in Roger Mason (ed.) *Scots and Britons: Scottish Political Thought and the Union of 1603*, Cambridge: CUP.

Foulner, M. A., 'Samuel Rutherford and Theonomy', online articles at http://www.kuyper.org/news/page_wc2.html, http://www.kuyper. org/ news/page_wc3.html and http://www.kuyper.org/news/page_wc4.html (accessed 24 November 2004).

Frame, John (1989), 'Towards a Theology of the State', *Westminster Theological Journal* 51.2, pp. 199–226.

Garver, S. Joel, *There is Another King: Gospel as Politics*, online article at http://www.lasalle.edu/~garver/gospel.htm (accessed 24 November 2004).

Hall, David, *Savior or Servant? Putting Government in its Place*, ch. 10, 'From Reformation to Revolution: 1500–1650', online article at http://www. capo.org/premise/96/mar/p.960304.html (accessed 21 July 2004).

Hengel, Martin (1977), *Christ and Power*, Belfast: Christian Journals.

Heywood, Andrew (1999), *Political Theory, An Introduction*, 2nd edn, Basingstoke: Palgrave.

Hoppe, Hans-Hermann (2001), *Democracy, The God that Failed: The Economics and Politics of Monarchy, Democracy, and Natural Order*, London: Transaction.

Jenson, R. W. (1999), *Systematic Theology*, 2 vols., Oxford: OUP.

Johnson, Paul (1983), *Modern Times: The World from the Twenties to the Eighties*, New York: Harper & Row.

Jordan, J. B. (1988), *Through New Eyes*, Brentwood, TN: Wolgemuth & Hyatt.

Kishlansky, Mark (1996), *A Monarchy Transformed: Britain 1603–1714*, Harmondsworth: Penguin.

Koestler, Arthur (1940), *Darkness at Noon*.

Leithart, P. J. (2003), *Against Christianity*, Moscow, ID: Canon Press.

Lewis, C. S. (1945), *That Hideous Strength*.

Maclear, J. F. (1965), 'Samuel Rutherford and *Lex, rex*', in G. L. Hunt and J. T. McNeill (eds.), *Calvinism and the Political Order*, Philadelphia: Westminster Press.

McConville, J. G. (2002), *Deuteronomy*, Leicester: Apollos.

McDermott, G. R. (1992), *One Holy and Happy Society: The Public Theology of Jonathan Edwards*, University Park, PN: The Pennsylvania State University Press.

North, Gary (1989), *Political Polytheism: The Myth of Pluralism*, Tyler, TX: Institute for Christian Economics.

O'Donovan, Oliver (1996), *The Desire of the Nations*, Cambridge: CUP.

O'Donovan, Oliver and O'Donovan, Joan Lockwood (eds.), (1999), *From Irenaeus to Grotius: A Sourcebook in Christian Political Thought 100–1625*, Grand Rapids: Eerdmans.

Orwell, George (1945), *Animal Farm*.

— (1949), *1984*.

Ovey, Michael (2004), *Beyond Scrutiny? Minorities, Majorities and Post-modern Tyranny*, Cambridge Papers 13.2, June 2004.

Owen, John, 'Sermons to the Nation', *Works*, ed. W. H. Goold, Edinburgh, 1967, vol. 8.

Pearce, A. S. Wayne (2004), 'John Maxwell', in *Oxford Dictionary of National Biography*, Oxford: OUP.

Perks, S. C. (1998), *A Defence of the Christian State*, Taunton: The Kuyper Foundation.

Raath, Andries and de Freitas, Shaun (2001), 'Theologico-political Federalism: The Office of Magistracy and the Legacy of Heinrich Bullinger', *Westminster Theological Journal*, 63, pp. 285–304.

Rothbard, M. N. 2000 [1974], 'Anatomy of the State', in *Egalitarianism as a Revolt Against Nature and Other Essays*, Auburn: Mises Institute, pp. 55–88. Available online at http://www.mises.org/easaran/chap3.asp (accessed 24 November 2004).

Rutherford, Samuel, *Letters of Samuel Rutherford*, ed. Andrew A. Bonar, Edinburgh: Banner of Truth Trust, 1984.

Ruwart, M. J. (2003), *Healing our World in an Age of Aggression*, 3rd edn, Kalamazoo, MI: SunStar Press.

Schlossberg, Herbert (1983), *Idols for Destruction*, Wheaton, IL: Crossway Books.

Skinner, Quentin (1978), *The Foundations of Modern Political Thought*, 2 vols., Cambridge: CUP.

Smart, I. M. (1980), 'The political ideas of the Scottish covenanters, 1638–88', *History of Political Thought*, 1:167–193.

Stevenson, W. R. (2004), 'Calvin and Political Issues', in D. K. McKim (ed.) *The Cambridge Companion to John Calvin*, Cambridge: CUP, pp. 173–187.

Tuck, Richard et al. (eds.) (1993), *Philosophy and Government 1572–1651*, Cambridge: CUP.

Whyte, Alexander (1894), *Samuel Rutherford and Some of His Correspondents*, Edinburgh: Oliphant Anderson and Ferrier.

Wright, C. J. H. (2004), *Old Testament Ethics for the People of God*, Leicester: Inter-Varsity Press.

Wright, N. T. (1996), *Jesus and the Victory of God*, London: SPCK.

—(1999), 'Paul's Gospel and Caesar's Empire', *Center of Theological Inquiry Reflections* (Princeton) 2 (Spring), 42–65, and online article at http://www.ctinquiry.org/publications/wright.htm   (accessed 24 November 2004).

—(2004), 'God and Caesar, Then and Now', in Martyn Percy and Stephen Lowe (eds.) *The Character of Wisdom: Essays in Honour of Wesley Carr*, London: Ashgate, 2004, pp. 157–171.

4. A VICTORIAN PROPHET WITHOUT HONOUR
Edward Miall and the critique of nineteenth-century British Christianity

David W. Smith[1]

Born in 1809 in Portsmouth and departing this world seventy-two years later at Sevenoaks in Kent, Edward Miall's life spanned most of the century that has been identified as both the 'Evangelical century' and the 'great century' of Christian missions.[2] These

---

1. I would like to acknowledge the help of the staff at the National Library of Scotland, Edinburgh, and International Christian College, Glasgow in the research for this study. I am particularly grateful to Gwenda Bond for her help in tracking down relevant materials.

2. The historian David Bebbington has suggested that the 'hundred years or so before the First World War deserve to be called the Evangelical century'. See his *Evangelicalism in Modern Britain: A History from the 1730s to the 1980s* (London: Unwin Hyman, 1989), p. 149. In relation to missions, Kenneth Scott Latourette observed that at the close of the nineteenth century 'Christianity was now taken to more peoples than ever before and entered as a transforming agency into more cultures than in all the preceding centuries.' Thus he gave the fourth volume in his magisterial

phrases reflect the growth in fervent religious belief and allegiance in the Victorian era, an expansion of Christianity made visible on the skylines of British cities and towns through massive church-building programmes of which at least physical evidence remains even today.

However, while Edward Miall's ministry was itself, at one level, evidence of the numerical growth and spiritual and intellectual confidence of British Nonconformist religion, it also reveals a man unusually aware of the ambiguities of church growth and sensitive to other currents running within the wider culture which, he believed, posed serious questions concerning the depth and quality of the expanding Evangelical movement. The same century which witnessed spiritual revivals, a steady increase in church attendance, and significant Christian social action, *also* saw the rise of revolutionary political movements and the beginnings of a major recession from the Christian faith as growing numbers of people, educated in what came to be known as 'modern thought', found themselves struggling with religious doubts.[3] Miall, as we shall see, was aware of these currents, which at first ran below the surface of the culture, but eventually spread to become a veritable tidal wave threatening British Christianity as a whole.

I have used the term 'prophet' in relation to Edward Miall for reasons that will, I hope, become clear. People possessing genuinely prophetic insight are rarely easy to live with and frequently find themselves sidelined by the guardians of the traditions subjected to their searching critical analysis. Miall, who was not unhappy to be described as a 'strolling agitator', was a controversialist whose words and actions inevitably made him enemies and led to his being viewed with more than a little suspicion within Anglicanism and by some Evangelical groups. Marginalized during his life, he has been largely forgotten after his death, his name omitted from prestigious dictionaries and found only occasionally in the indexes of specialist

---

History of the Expansion of Christianity the title *The Great Century in Europe and the United States of America* (Grand Rapids: Zondervan, 1970).

3. See Elizabeth Jay, *Faith and Doubt in Victorian Britain* (London: MacMillan, 1986).

studies of nineteenth-century church history. I wish to argue not only that Miall spoke in his time with unusual insight and clarity, but that his work is relevant to British Christianity a century and a half later, when the trends he so clearly identified have resulted in the emergence of a new culture in which believers find themselves playing a diminished and seemingly marginal role.

Life and times

Edward Miall's childhood was marked by both the experience of real poverty and the pervading ethos of the devout Evangelical faith of his parents. His father, Moses, was a merchant who moved to London as a schoolteacher in search of an income that might sustain his large family. The effort proved unsuccessful, and when Edward was in his eighteenth year the family home was broken up and the young man sent to work as a school usher, first in Braintree in Essex, and later at Nayland in Suffolk. In that same year Miall experienced personal religious conversion in a manner that clearly reflects the fact that he lived in the afterglow of the Great Awakening. On his eighteenth birthday he recorded the event in the form of a signed covenant between himself and God: 'By the blessing of God and under His Divine assistance, I, Edward Miall, solemnly dedicate myself, body and soul, unto the Lord.' He later recalled the deep spiritual struggle that had preceded this solemn act of consecration: 'I entreated in agony of soul that this emotion might not prove transitory. I devoted every leisure moment to the hearty pursuit of God. My impressions were deepened, my desires increased . . . A glow of love to the Redeemer pervaded my heart.'[4] The language bears the classic marks of an *experiential* faith; Christ known within the heart and then followed and obeyed as an expression of the love and gratitude which are the wellsprings of genuine discipleship.

---

4. Quoted in Clyde Binfield, *So Down to Prayers* (London: J. M. Dent, 1977), p. 108.

Both of these features of Miall's early life were to shape his future ministry and service: the early encounter with poverty and the painful experience of his father's insolvency gave him a deep sympathy with the British working classes and clearly inspired his radical social and political thought and action, while the evangelical experience of what has been called a 'felt Christ' never left him, with the result that his Christianity took a mystical form and made him suspicious of mere doctrinal formulas. Preaching at a memorial service in honour of Miall in 1881, R. W. Dale commented that he had been a man whose political and social actions flowed from a relationship with God so close and intimate that he always gave the impression that 'he had authentic tidings from unseen worlds'.[5]

The utter dedication of the young Miall led him to undertake theological education at Wymondley, where he is known to have read the works of Gibbon, Locke, Adam Smith, Bishop Butler and Jonathan Edwards. He considered going to Africa as a missionary, but a growing awareness of social injustices within Britain during brief ministries in Ware and Leicester convinced him that his calling was to a different kind of mission *within Christendom*. When William Baines and twenty-six members of Miall's Leicester congregation were sent to prison for refusing to pay church rates, he was outraged and determined to devote the rest of his life to the cause of liberating the gospel from its identification with the class structures of a hierarchical society. Within months he resigned his pastorate and founded a newspaper, the *Nonconformist*, which was 'uncompromisingly radical'.[6] In 1844 Miall founded the 'Anti State Church Association', which became popularly known as the Liberation Society and was the vehicle for his lifelong campaign for an end to the formal establishment of religion.

It is important to note at this stage that Miall's antipathy toward established religion was not based simply on a desire to advance

---

5. A. W. W. Dale, *The Life of R. W. Dale of Birmingham* (London: Hodder & Stoughton, 1899), p. 369.

6. See J. S. Newton, 'The Political Career of Edward Miall, Editor of the *Nonconformist* and Founder of the Liberation Society', unpublished PhD thesis, University of Durham, 1975.

the self-interests of the rising middle classes associated with his own Nonconformist constituency. As we shall see, he was severely critical of Nonconformist churches, which he judged to be guilty of an unbiblical syncretism involving the attempt to worship both God and Mammon. Miall's concern was much broader and more principled, in that he wished to liberate what he called 'the religion of Christ secularized' from state patronage and control. He believed that such an arrangement was disastrous for Christianity in general, *including even those ecclesiastical bodies which, outwardly at least, seemed to benefit from it.* Miall twice entered Parliament, first as the member for Rochdale in 1852 and then for Bradford in 1869, and his speeches on the subject of disestablishment constantly stressed that the severing of the connection between State and Church would be in the interests of the Church of England. His hostility was not directed toward Anglicanism as such, but to what he viewed as the 'fatal incubus of state patronage'.[7] It was the country as a whole, Miall argued, that is the loser as the result of the division of the British people into two great sections: the one privileged, the other tolerated.[8] Moreover, not only did Dissenters suffer injustices as the result of the state patronage of particular religious institutions, but so too did that still larger class of people aptly designated by Miall as the *Absenters*: the masses of people who had no share whatever in 'the proceeds of that large estate which has been appropriated to the religious teaching they decline'.[9]

In the years immediately before the appearance of Miall's *Nonconformist*, the struggles of the British working classes had reached something of a climax in a series of Chartist demonstrations between 1838 and 1842. Eileen Yeo has shown that these struggles should not be understood as involving a secular radicalism pitched against a religious conservatism, since Christianity was

---

7. *Dictionary of National Biography*, XIII, p. 325.

8. See an excerpt from an important speech in the House of Commons on 9 May 1871, in David M.Thompson (ed.), *Nonconformity in the Nineteenth Century* (London: Routledge & Kegan Paul, 1972), pp. 187–192.

9. Ibid, p. 132.

not understood to be the possession of one particular social group, but rather was 'contested territory'. This was evident in the Sunday demonstrations of 1839, when working men marched on parish churches in thirty-one towns across England and Wales with the declared intention of challenging what they perceived to be the perversion of Christianity by the ruling and rising classes. Their decision to attend worship in working clothes and to occupy pews set aside for the rich and powerful involved the assertion of the value of labour in the sight of God and the absurdity of their exclusion on the basis of dress or poverty. Seen from the other side, working aprons and clogs were an affront to the respectability which was becoming equated with godliness, while the occupation of rented pews was 'a gesture of menace to private property and the disruption of a carefully contrived display of social hierarchy'.[10] Commenting on the reaction of the clergy, Yeo observes that by 'heaping fulsome praise on the existing social order' and denying the demonstrators 'a shred of dignity or a vestige of a case' they merely confirmed Chartist suspicions that they were wolves in sheep's clothing 'who legitimized oppression while pretending to speak the word of God'.[11]

This was the social context of Edward Miall's career. He recognized the justice of the Chartist cause and understood the damage being done to Christianity among working people by the reactionary behaviour of many conservative churchmen. His resignation from the pastorate in the year following the Chartist demonstrations was prompted not only by the desire to

---

10. See Eileen Yeo, 'Christianity in Chartist Struggle 1838–1842', *Past and Present* 91 (1981), p. 109. William Dale Morris observed that working-class movements between 1830 and 1842 clearly drew their inspiration from their faith; he quotes Mark Hovell, who writes: 'The leaders of the movement drew their inspiration from the Bible . . . This tendency to hark back to the Bible and to Christianity as a basis for political and social practice is the most interesting phase of the whole Chartist movement.' William Dale Morris, *The Christian Origins of Social Revolt* (London: George Allen & Unwin, 1949), p. 168.

11. Ibid, p. 134.

right the wrongs done to Dissenters, but by a growing concern about the alienation from all the churches, Nonconformist as well as Anglican, of the *Absenters*. Miall knew perfectly well that, had the Chartists chosen to enter many of the chapels in his own denomination, their reception would have been very little different. Congregationalism's chronic identification with the middle class is well documented; by the late 1840s the denomination's *Yearbook* can be found urging the repudiation of the plain meeting houses of the past and the building of churches with 'taste and judgement' so as 'to attract rather than repel persons of intelligence and respectability'.[12] Against this background Miall attempted to enter into dialogue with the Chartist leaders in 1842 and began to reflect on the condition of British Christianity, an investigation which, as we shall see, resulted in an analysis which was an even-handed and deeply perceptive critique of all Evangelical religion, not least within his own denomination.[13]

Christianity and politics

Edward Miall's lifelong commitment to the cause of disestablishment inevitably led him into the political arena. He both

12. *The Congregational Yearbook* for 1847, cited by Binfield, *So Down to Prayers*, p. 165. Calum Brown has studied the growth of evangelicalism in the city of Glasgow in the nineteenth century and comments: 'The adequate supply of church accommodation suitably isolated from the industrial working classes was vital in the context of a rapidly expanding city.' Glasgow's growing middle class moved to the new West End, where splendid church buildings 'permitted social segregation and the self-elevation of the middle-class groups'. 'Religion and the Development of an Urban Society: Glasgow 1780–1914', unpublished PhD thesis, University of Glasgow, 1981, p. 336.

13. The material in the previous few paragraphs is based on my earlier article, 'Church and Society in Britain: A Mid-Nineteenth Century Analysis', in *Evangelical Quarterly* 41. 2 (April 1989), pp. 141–158.

defended such a move and provided a detailed statement of his political philosophy in a series of articles which appeared in the *Nonconformist* in the late 1840s and were published under the title *The Politics of Christianity* in 1863. Aware that some Christians regarded politics as off limits to believers and wished to maintain a rigid separation between faith and social action, Miall dismisses such a view as a 'mischievous absurdity'. Once again, it is clear that his motivation in political life was closely linked to his awareness of the great damage being done to the cause of Christ among Britain's working people by churches that appeared to offer a halo of sanctity to a socio-political system that he regarded as being manifestly unjust. Evangelicals, he suggests, 'have never been earnest in their advocacy of social justice', with the result that working people increasingly view Christianity 'as a deceiver'. The separation of politics from faith 'has induced the rejection of religion by the myriads whose interests political exclusiveness has betrayed and well nigh ruined'.[14]

Christianity does not, in Miall's view, provide a detailed blue-print for social and political action. Rather, the revelation given to the world in Christ, displaying divine love and holiness in a perfect human life, works like leaven, gradually and mysteriously trans-forming peoples and cultures. Politics done consistently with the confession that 'Jesus is Lord' will therefore be shaped and driven by gospel imperatives, and this must result in the rejection of a narrow partisanship serving sectional interests, while inspiring an absolute determination to 'do good unto all men'.

Miall thus makes no attempt to discover a specific political programme within the pages of the Bible. He notes that the New Testament affirms that political power is granted to those who are called to positions of authority in order that they may be 'ministers of God to thee for good'. Thus, stamped upon the brow of polit-icians by God himself are the words '*for good*', which implies that politics is to serve the good of the entire human race. Clearly the opposite is often the case, because such power corrupts many who

---

14. Edward Miall, *The Politics of Christianity* (London: Arthur Miall, 1863), pp. 5–6 (hereafter '*Politics*').

attain to it, and yet 'human perversity has not been able wholly to make void the divine intent'.[15]

Interestingly, Miall does not argue that Christianity sanctifies or requires one particular form of government; he can even say that 'absolutism, constitutional monarchy, government by representation, aristocracy, chartism or republicanism' are all 'mere forms of civil rule', none of which can be said to be 'more scriptural' than the others. What Christianity does offer, however, are the 'great principles of equity, justice and benevolence', by means of which it is possible in any particular context to determine 'whether the machinery of civil government as constructed in our own times, is in unison with the object and spirit of divine revelation'.[16] Judged against these fundamental criteria, Miall has no doubt that the existing system in Britain is both corrupt and unjust. It is worth quoting at some length his description of the British political system at the mid-point of the nineteenth century:

> A machinery deliberately put together with a view to the political ascendancy of only one order, an external form that is meant to give expression to the will of one class as paramount to that of all others, a structure that practically excludes the influence of the poor, and which, consequently, leaves them unprotected from the oppressive habits and exactions of the rich, – legislation which is sure of siding with property

---

15. *Politics*, p. 16.

16. *Politics*, p. 55. It needs to be remembered that Miall is writing in a context in which many Christians showered praise upon the British constitution as though it were divinely sanctioned and beyond any possible change or improvement. There are many instances of churchmen praising the class system in enthusiastic language and urging the poor to recognize that their place in society has been determined for them by the will of God. The redoubtable Francis Close, Vicar of Cheltenham, for example, responded to the Chartist demonstrations with a sermon that thundered against socialism as 'rebellion against God' and Chartism as 'rebellion against man'. See Nigel Scotland, 'Francis Close: Cheltenham's Protestant Patriarch', in James Thrower (ed.), *Essays in Religious Studies for Andrew Walls* (Aberdeen: Department of Religious Studies, Aberdeen University, 1986), p. 129.

against labour, – magistracy which must needs be partial to the
wealthy, – institutions and forms of rule which help the powerful to
crush the weak, instead of shielding the weak from the aggressions of
the powerful . . .[17]

One chapter in *The Politics of Christianity* bears the title 'Man
Above Property' and reveals the crucial importance of biblical
anthropology within Miall's politics. He describes Christianity as
'unflinching' in its teaching concerning the wretchedness of the
human condition, but then insists that the Bible constantly affirms
'the original dignity of our *nature*'. The doctrine of the *imago Dei*
thus means that human nature cannot be despised with impunity,
nor can value be set upon people in relation to their material
wealth or external dignity. While British society appears to admire
the 'splendid habitation, the ample patrimony, the blazing livery of
wealth', Christianity teaches an entirely different standard of judgment, seeing beneath such outward displays the existence of pride
and greed, while 'underneath the ruggedest and most loathesome
exterior, she welcomes humanity wherever she meets with it'.[18]
Such insights had radical political implications for a society which
conferred dignity and privileges on the owners of property, and
Miall is not slow to draw the appropriate conclusions: the 'national
exaltation of pounds sterling' will result in a stagnant political
system from which escape is possible only as we accept the truth
'prominent everywhere in the Gospel', that 'human nature is to be
honoured rather than wealth – *that man comes before property*'.[19]

I would like to notice two particular examples of Edward Miall's
political thought, which illustrate both his realism concerning
the dilemmas and tensions likely to face Christians who seek to
exercise political power and his integrity in endeavouring to allow
the gospel to shape policy decisions. Miall is acutely aware of the
tension between his calling as a Christian man to follow the
example of the suffering Saviour and the fact that political power

---

17. *Politics*, p. 63.
18. *Politics*, p. 69.
19. *Politics*, p. 71.

may involve the exercise of force in restraining wickedness, including the possibility of the waging of war.

In the last chapter of *The Politics of Christianity* Miall deals directly with the subject of war, adding two supplementary notes to respond to critics of the position he has taken. On the one hand, he has a horror of the violence of war, describing in a long, almost poetic passage the ghastly nature of conflicts between nations: 'WAR! Who that has witnessed it in its loathsome and revolting details would not, if a single spark of humanity has survived the ordeal, deprecate all that may, by possibility, lead to it?'[20] This being so, a Christian politician is bound to be committed to 'the unceasing and resolute cultivation of a pacific policy'. Later in the century, when he found himself in public life, Edward Miall consistently acted on the basis of such principles, opposing the Crimean War and supporting the Peace Society, a largely Quaker group which advocated arbitration rather than warfare.[21]

At the same time, Miall's awareness of the reality of human depravity and the necessity of defending the weak and vulnerable

---

20. *Politics*, p. 155.

21. J. S. Newton, 'Political Career of Edward Miall' (note 5 above). It is worth recalling here the strength of anti-war feeling expressed by another representative figure in nineteenth-century Nonconformity, Charles H. Spurgeon. Preaching to over 20,000 people at the Crystal Palace in 1857, he questioned Britain's role in India and, in the same year, attacked militarism in quite extraordinary language. The gospel, Spurgeon said, is a message of *peace* and when it achieves the success promised in Scripture, then 'wars must cease to the ends of the earth'. The recent appearance of the statues of military men in London is the result of 'the trickery of an ignorant age, the gewgaws of a people who loved bloodshed despite their profession of religion'. Later in the century, in 1870, Spurgeon's criticism of imperialism and his anti-war feeling are undiminished: we are eager, he says, 'to test our ability to kill our fellow men' and, while mythical British interests are set up as the excuse for foreign adventures, the truth is that 'the national bulldog wants to fix his teeth into somebody's leg'. See Albert Meredith, 'The Social and Political Views of Charles Haddon Spurgeon, 1834–1892', unpublished PhD thesis, Michigan State University, 1973, p. 96.

from the violence of evil people made it impossible for him to advocate a pacifist position. Civil government is established precisely for the purpose of restraining evil in a world in which selfishness often seems to be prevalent and the strong seek 'gratification regardless of the rights of others'. In such situations it is the task of politicians to 'organize and apply the physical force of the many for the protection of all', restraining the violence of people in a fallen world 'until the gentler appliances of Christianity shall have healed [humankind's] moral disease'.[22]

It seems clear that Miall is uncomfortable at this point; the use of physical violence against people made in the image of God is, he admits, difficult to square with the gospel, and yet such a policy cannot always be condemned as being evil. In attempting to resolve the dilemma, Miall comes close to a Lutheran two-kingdoms theology when he concludes that the institution of civil government carries with it 'Providential and Scriptural authority for shielding right from the lawless aggressions of might' and that the use of legitimate physical force will be necessary 'to the accomplishment of this purpose'.[23]

The second example of the manner in which Miall endeavoured to ensure that his politics were shaped by gospel imperatives brings us to what is perhaps the most remarkable aspect of a rather remarkable book: namely, his treatment of the subject of *colonization*. Miall's articles on politics appeared in the pages of the *Nonconformist* just as the build-up commenced toward the great Crystal Palace exhibition in 1851. Prince Albert, speaking at a banquet in the Mansion House, anticipated that this extravagant display would illustrate the global reach of British influence and would confirm 'that we are living at a period of most wonderful transition, which tends rapidly to accomplish that great end, to which indeed, all history points – the realization of the unity of mankind'.[24] In such a fevered atmosphere Miall's reminder of

---

22. *Politics*, pp. 150–151.
23. *Politics*, p. 153.
24. Prince Albert's speech is contained in J. M. Golby (ed.), *Culture and Society in Britain, 1850–1890* (Oxford: Oxford University Press, 1986), pp. 1–2.

'the crimes' that gave the British effective control over a large part of the globe must have seemed to many to strike a jarring note! He insists that if the history of the acquisition of the colonies is traced back to its original source, in almost every case it will be found to reveal a story of 'fraud, injustice, cruelty, and fiend-like atrocity such as few could read without mingled indignation and shame'.[25]

Once again, Miall's views are influenced by his anthropology, in that the compassion and respect he so evidently felt for the British working classes is now extended toward aboriginal peoples on the other side of the world. They too are human beings, made in the divine image and requiring protection 'from oppression by the colonists'. The manifest failure of the British government to defend such peoples and to uphold their human rights in the face of colonial depredation is a scandal which brings disgrace upon the name of Great Britain. In a memorable sentence Miall insists that Christianity 'nowhere gives countenance to the modern pretence that civilization may trample on barbarism, strength prey on weakness, or white-complexioned humanity play havoc with black'. The fundamental biblical assertion that 'God has made of one blood all the nations to dwell on the face of the earth' compels Miall to defend the interests of the colonized peoples, while also warning his fellow countrymen that the neglect of that truth in the making of foreign policy can only result in judgment and loss.

However, Miall's argument then takes a very surprising and remarkable turn as he muses on the future that might unfold in the colonies. Could it be possible, he wonders, that the coming centuries will witness developments in those distant lands that will provide 'a fresh start' for humanity? In new and remote regions of the world, untouched by the negative aspects of modern civilization, can we anticipate the emergence of forms of society that might offer a new model of social life and so prepare the way for 'those glorious triumphs of the moral over the material which we are taught to expect will signalize the

25. *Politics*, p. 147.

maturer age of this our world'.[26] In the background here, surely, is the postmillenial eschatology of Jonathan Edwards, which had inspired an earlier generation of Evangelicals with confidence that the whole earth would be transformed through the global spread of the message of Christ.

Sadly, Miall realizes that in his times what is actually being exported to the colonies is not the liberating and life-giving message of the grace of God, but a culture-bound version of Christianity that carries with it the seeds of a highly destructive modernity. If the hope for the future is to become reality, then politicians will need 'vigilant care' to ensure that 'the seeds of institutional vices which time has ripened in maturity at home' are not transplanted into foreign soils. Yet the existing colonial experience offers little ground for optimism: 'The same habits of extravagance, the same swarms of pensioned idlers, the same concentration of political power in a few hands, the same tricks of taxation . . . are transported by government agency to the colonies.' The result is that British colonial administrators and educators are simply 'training young nations into a studious imitation of our every fault'.[27]

Finally, Miall asks one more question concerning the colonies: should not the British government have one overriding aim in view in relation to colonized peoples, namely, their preparation for self-government? All the arguments that might be marshalled against such a view amount to the sacrifice of 'the most valuable rights of humanity' on the 'altar of a beggarly vanity'. The condescension and arrogance with which native peoples are treated represses their 'budding energies' in order to minister to British national pride. Miall's insight and language on this question may well take us by surprise when we recall that this voice reaches us from the late 1840s:

> We purchase a mean gratification of our selfishness at the cost of
> stunting the national development of our own flesh and blood. We keep

---

26. *Politics*, p. 143.
27. *Politics*, p. 145.

young nations swathed in our own old world institutions, and prevent their growth, merely that we may continue to call them our own.[28]

It is already clear, I hope, why the ministry of the forgotten man who is the subject of this study deserves the designation 'prophetic'.

The analysis of British Christianity

Alongside the explicitly political writing from the 1840s which we have examined above, Miall was also working on a series of studies in which he developed an acute critical analysis of the condition of the churches in Britain. Originally he had intended to deliver this material as a series of public lectures at the Exeter Hall in London, but when members of the committee there caught sight of an outline proposal of the contents they took fright and withdrew permission for the premises to be used for this purpose. The manuscript was published in 1849 with the title *The British Churches in Relation to the British People*. At one level, Miall's volume takes its place among a series of significant nineteenth-century theological works wrestling with the immense challenges thrown up by industrialization and urbanization. But, as the title suggests, this book went further, in that it analysed the condition of the churches *within the specific social and cultural context of mid-nineteenth-century Britain*. In this sense it broke fresh ground and might be regarded as a kind of precursor of a specifically social theology, or even of the sociological study of religion. In any event, it is an extraordinary work, full of unusual insights and offering a constructive critique of Evangelical Christianity which has lost little of its potency and relevance more than a century and a half later.

Miall's basic thesis is that Christianity in Britain, despite all its external earnestness and activism, was suffering from a pervasive and dangerous malaise. The fundamental cause of the problem was that contemporary religion was thoroughly anthropocentric;

---

28. *Politics*, p. 147.

it was driven by pragmatic and utilitarian concerns rather than by truly religious impulses. 'I apprehend', he writes, 'that in our reading of God's message, *man* occupies the first place in our attention, *God* a subordinate one'.[29] Those who crowd the churches seem less concerned with God than with the social and practical benefits that flow from their regular appearance in his house, their concept of salvation summed up in the characteristic Enlightenment phrase 'the greatest possible happiness'. Such man-centred religion was deficient both in its lack of spiritual depth and in the absence of moral earnestness. It failed to connect worship to the whole of life, isolating and marginalizing religion so that it had become 'a sort of enclosure railed off from the entire surface of existence'.[30] In modern sociological terminology, religion was becoming *privatized* as the result of its exclusion from the concerns of daily life.

Moreover, two years before the results of the 1851 religious census shocked the nation with the news that working people were largely outside the churches, Miall was already warning that Christianity was beginning to lose ground:

> Man's relation to the substantial verities of divine revelation is not changed . . . but . . . in this country at least, his susceptibility of impression by that aspect of the gospel that is presented to him from the pulpit and the press is slowly but steadily lessening.[31]

That is to say, the churches were failing to communicate the gospel faithfully or effectively; their truncated gospel appealed to human self-interest rather than to the moral sympathies of men and was perceived to be irrelevant to the lives of the masses, with the result that conversions from the world were very few. Miall

---

29. Edward Miall, *The British Churches in Relation to the British People* (London: Arthur Hall, Virtue, 1849), p. 132. This book will be cited as '*BCBP*'. In what follows I am again drawing on part of my *Evangelical Quarterly* article (see note 13 above).

30. *BCBP*, p. 141.

31. *BCBP*, p. 152.

suggests that if the central theme in preaching had been 'the transcendently glorious character of God, as imaged in Jesus Christ, instead of the benefit accruing to man from the Mediatorial work', the impact on the general population would have been considerable and the present situation, in which there seemed to be growing indifference to Evangelical religion, would have been avoided. In addition, the churches had substituted law for love as the spirit of Christianity; the Christian life had become a matter of adherence to a code of regulations and the churches were terrified of the freedom of the gospel. In this atmosphere zeal was a rare commodity; there was no 'exuberance of life' and prudence was 'elevated to the throne of the virtues'.[32]

Perhaps Miall's most significant (and controversial) theological critique relates to his concern that religion was being reduced to a matter of intellectual assent to a series of logical propositions. He does not deny that sound theological views are important to those who find 'delight in the manifested God' but, he says, 'an eye for the divine is of greater value than an accurate perception of form or letter'. Miall's own deeply mystical experience comes into play here and leads him to suggest that the *objective* aspect of Christianity had been greatly over-stressed, while its *subjective* element was disregarded. Just before the arrival of an era marked by growing religious doubts Miall was already sounding a warning and offering an alternative approach: 'overweening concern for what men shall believe has produced a carelessness as to the cause and character of their faith'.[33]

The final chapter of *The British Churches in Relation to the British People* is concerned with 'remedial suggestions'. He notes that church buildings, which as we have seen were assuming such importance in the thinking and planning of Miall's contemporaries at this time, were irrelevant to the advance of primitive Christianity. We never find the founders of the church 'at a standstill for want of a chapel building'. Indeed, Miall goes further and suggests that church buildings as conceived and used

---

32. *BCBP*, pp. 163–164.
33. *BCBP*, p. 172.

in Victorian Britain were an *obstacle* to the Christian mission: 'We might get rid of pews – we might get rid of pulpits . . . and we might turn to useful account during the week, the edifice in which we assemble for devotion and instruction on the Lord's Day.' The suggestion that the pulpit could be dispensed with was consistent with Miall's belief that effective communication with people who were hostile to the faith demanded 'a much freer character than a set of religious services implies'. He advocated open discussions with unbelievers in which all present would 'have full liberty to ask questions, to start objections, or to speak in opposition'. This dialogical approach to evangelism would form a bridge across the gulf dividing religious people from the *Absenters*, and it would benefit both sides by bringing Christ's disciples into closer contact with his foes.[34] It is surprising to discover proposals as radical as these in the middle of the nineteenth century, and we might ask whether British Christians have even yet learned the importance of the issues Miall raised in the context of Victorian society.

The issue of culture

We turn now from the general discussion of the malaise affecting Christianity in the mid-nineteenth century to notice two major themes in Miall's analysis of the British churches. The term 'culture' is, of course, a modern one, but it describes very well what he means when he says that contemporary Christianity in the Victorian era was being shaped by 'characteristics of local or national origin'. In one sense this is natural and normal; Christianity is a translatable faith and the church is a place to 'feel at home'. Problems arise, however, when the relationship to culture develops without critical reflection, so that culture becomes the normative source of values and practice. What we then have is a culture-*bound* church. And when, as Miall believed to be the case in his day, the cultural forces shaping Christianity are

---

34. *BCBP*, pp. 422–430.

unrepresentative of the nation as a whole and are shared only by a powerful minority of people, then the problems are considerable.

Miall uses a number of phrases to describe what was effectively the sub-culture to which the gospel was being accommodated; the first of these is *the aristocratic sentiment*. This he defines as 'value attached to man according to the circumstances of his worldly lot'.[35] People who possess noble titles seem to have been given a kind of concave mirror which magnifies 'the most diminutive forms of wisdom, virtue or piety'. On the other hand, those who lack all such external signifiers of dignity are ignored and despised, especially if they are poor, so that all actual human qualities, whether intellectual, moral or spiritual, 'are thrown into a balance, weighted on one side by the accidents of a man's lot'.

Of course, Miall recognizes that the Good News is to be preached to all classes of people, rich as well as poor, but what deserves the 'severest censure' is the widespread tendency in the churches 'to treat as unbecoming, and even as a desecration of revealed truth, all methods . . . not approved by those who call themselves the respectable section of society'.[36] In an important passage he contrasts the practice of the apostolic churches with those of his own day:

> Religion as embodied in the written word of God, and in that more emphatic living Word which 'was made flesh and dwelt among us', uniformly champions the cause of the weak, the friendless, the oppressed – religion, embodied in modern organizations, preaches up the rights of the powerful and dwells mainly upon the obligations of the powerless . . . Once her favourite occupation was to move as an angel of love among outcasts, to breathe hope into the spirits of the desponding, to wipe away tears as they rolled down the cheeks of the neglected – and when among the great, her theme of discourse was the vanity of perishable honours and possessions . . . In our day, she is more at home with the comfortable than with the wretched.[37]

---

35. *BCBP*, p. 185.
36. *BCBP*, p. 199.
37. *BCBP*, pp. 203–204.

What is under scrutiny here, of course, is the *class system*, or rather the fact that the churches have capitulated to that system, allowing it to determine conditions of membership, styles of worship and the content of preaching. Class distinctions of the most rigid kind have been carried 'into the house of God', so that in churches across Britain the 'poor man is made to feel that he is a poor man, while the rich are reminded that they are rich'.

Closely linked to the evils of the class structure is what Miall describes as the *trade spirit*. This he defines as 'the disposition to pursue trade with an exclusive, or even predominant view to the worldly advantage to be got by it – making it its own end'. Miall makes clear that in his view this is in fact *'the greatest and most pernicious practical error of the present day'*.[38] In the realms of business Christians act as though it is entirely legitimate to 'serve themselves', relegating Christ to a place at the margins of daily life. 'They go to the house of God' to seek him, but when entering 'their factories, counting-houses and shops' there is no desire or expectation to find him there. The result is that there is no difference between Christians and non-Christians in the practice of economic and commercial life; 'the lust of speculation is as rife in

---

38. *BCBP*, p. 299. The italics are mine. Recently the kind of culture Miall was describing has been called a *culture of economism*: that is to say, one in which economic causes or factors become 'the main source of cultural meanings and values'. As Jane Collier and Rafael Esteban have said, 'In Western culture it is to a large extent the economic that provides the ordinary-language terms and expressions that we use to give meaning to our world of daily life as we confront it, act in it, and live through it.' Elsewhere they observe: 'The minority in the West who are still practicing Christians experience the fact that their daily life is fundamentally shaped not by Christianity but by the cultural influence of economism, and that for only one hour a week do they remember that they are something more than consumers driven by self-interest.' Jane Collier and Rafael Esteban, *From Complicity to Encounter: The Church and the Culture of Economism* (Harrisburg: Trinity Press International, 1998), pp. 16–17; 45–46. Although Miall's language is different, these were precisely his concerns in 1849!

the one as in the other', because most religious people 'lay aside Christ's code of morals in their trade transactions'.

What is being described here is characteristic of an industrial, modernizing society operating a 'free market' on a capitalist basis and closing off economic activity from the norms and restraints of ethics derived from religious sources. Earlier in the nineteenth century it had been possible for an Evangelical theologian to justify this system with the astonishing claim that God himself intended human selfishness to be 'the grand principle on which the brotherhood of the human race is made to hang together'. Thomas Chalmers seems to have had no qualms about either the 'trade spirit' or the 'aristocratic sentiment', praising a social system which had 'a king upon the throne . . . borne up by a splendid aristocracy, and a gradation of ranks shelving down to the basement of society'.[39]

---

39. Quoted in N. Masterman (ed.), *Chalmers on Charity* (Westminster: Archibald, Constable, 1900), p. 167. Thomas Chalmers wrestled with the challenge of urbanization in *The Christian and Civic Economy of Large Towns* (3 vols., Glasgow: William Collins, 1826). Just how different his perspective is from that of Miall two decades later is evident in his heartless comments on the labouring poor: 'Had there just been a lesser population of these outcasts, their object would have been carried without any assertion on their part, and simply by the operation of the demand of capitalists upon a smaller supply. It is the redundancy of their own numbers, and nothing else, which is the cause of their degredation.' Chalmers, perhaps fortunately, does not suggest how this problem might be overcome! By contrast, Thomas Guthrie, an almost exact contemporary of Miall, recognized that Scotland's urban poor were 'doubly deprived' of justice, since the conditions in which they lived drove them to desperate measures for survival, and then respectable society exacted punishment on them for crimes traceable to its own heartlessness and indifference. 'We first condemn them to crime and then condemn them to punishment. And where is the justice of that?': Thomas Guthrie, *The City – Its Sins and Its Sorrows* (Edinburgh: Adam & Charles Black, 1851), p. 98. Guthrie's statue, depicting him shielding a poor child in his cloak, stands on Princes Street in Edinburgh and bears the description: 'The friend of the poor and oppressed'.

More than twenty years later, when the consequences of unbridled capitalism were becoming painfully evident in the exploding cities of industrial Britain, Edward Miall speaks an altogether different language and in a long and deeply moving passage offers a searching critique of the ideology of the market:

> [There are] individuals who figure perhaps, in the world's eye as men of active benevolence, but who, in the more private walks of commercial enterprise, push their products of money-making into any available corner, never stopping to reflect that they are snatching hard-earned bread out of other people's mouths and, perhaps, draining into their own well-filled reservoir, little streams which have been the only ones within reach of brethren who toil as hard, and deserve as well, as they do themselves . . . Many a bleeding, pining, broken heart – many a shattered family circle has borne witness before the merciful Ruler of all, against the desolation that has swept their hopes and prospects in consequence of the inconsiderate cupidity of the disciples of Jesus, and their exclusion of his gentleness of spirit, and kindness of disposition, from all their transactions in secular business.[40]

I mentioned earlier that Miall's original intention had been to deliver his material in a series of public lectures at the Exeter Hall in London. This was, of course, the great meeting place for Evangelicals, especially at the annual 'May Meetings', at which thousands of Christians came together from across Britain to be informed of the work of voluntary societies, including those spreading the gospel to the ends of the earth. When the committee refused Miall permission to use the hall they were probably worried by the general tenor of his critique of British Christianity, and even more alarmed by the fact that he intended to subject the missionary movement to critical examination. The May Meetings had already been attacked by magazines like *Punch*, which published articles suggesting that the Christians who flocked to London appeared to show love toward people in remote parts of the earth while neglecting the needs of the poor and destitute on

---

40. *BCBP*, pp. 322–324.

their own doorsteps![41] Miall, while clearly not opposed to foreign missions in principle, observed that the movement had ceased to arouse the suspicion it had earlier attracted and now benefited from 'fashionable patronage'. He criticized those who contributed funds to bring about 'the conversion of the heathen at the antipodes' while showing no compassion 'for the scarcely less degraded heathen at home'.[42] In other words, Miall believed that the missionary movement, like the British churches, was in danger of promoting a culture-bound version of the gospel which sanctified a socio-political system built on moral values at odds with the revelation of God given in Jesus Christ. Miall goes so far as to suggest that many of the people who lead Christian organizations and 'give princely sums to evangelical societies' are known to act in daily life 'almost exclusively upon the hard inflexible, inexorable maxims of commercial economy'.[43] The supporters of overseas missions, together with many preachers and Christian leaders, have

---

41. In 1844 an article appeared in *Punch* entitled 'Exeter Hall Pets'. It observed the way in which crowds of people would ascend 'the crystal steps' of Exeter Hall to testify their affection for 'the benighted sons and daughters of earth thousands and thousands of miles away'. For these folks, the writer claimed, sympathy is like Madeira in that it is 'all the better for a sea voyage': *Punch*, Vol. VI (1844), p. 210. A decade later *Punch* continued to critique the May Meetings, this time in the form of an ironic poem:

> Tis the sweet month of May love, the saints are all gay, love,
> Though they flee from the play love, the opera and ball;
> Then as this is our season, dost thou know any reason
> That should hinder our meeting at Exeter Hall?
> Be thou sure to be there love, and I will repair love,
> To the portals right early thy coming to bide,
> In order to find thee, and sit close behind thee,
> If I may not attain to a seat by thy side.
>   (*Punch*, Vol. XXX (May 1856), p. 209)

42. *BCBP*, p. 206.
43. *BCBP*, p. 329.

thus accepted uncritically both the 'aristocratic sentiment' and the 'trade spirit' of the age, so creating 'the impediments' to evangelism 'which they strive in vain to surmount'.[44]

Religion and politics

Having dealt with cultural barriers to the effectiveness of the Christian mission, Miall turns to examine the specifically *socio-political* hindrances to the success of the British churches. First, he describes in some detail the socio-economic conditions of the urban poor and argues that 'a thick sediment of physical destitution' acts as an impenetrable barrier to the message of Christianity. At the bottom level of society human beings exist in conditions in which they must survive on garbage, are preyed upon by vermin and are herded together for shelter in 'dark, damp cellars'. People who live in such a 'frightful abyss' are as much 'beyond the reach of the gospel, as the better tended cattle that are driven to the shambles'.[45]

---

44. *BCBP*, p. 341. Elsewhere Miall writes: 'It is hard to compute the extent to which a single mean and dirty transaction in trade, practised by a reputed disciple of Christ, operates to create increased hostility to the truths he is assumed to revere and receive'; *BCBP*, p. 339.

45. *BCBP*, p. 349. Miall was not alone in drawing attention to the extreme poverty of millions of urban dwellers in post-industrialized Britain and insisting on the urgent priority of political action to remedy this situation. Ian Shaw has shown the social dimensions of the ministries of high Calvinist preachers in this period, including William Gadsby of Manchester, who wrote: 'It is extreme distress which makes the poor people cry for redress of their grievances, and I believe that in time the Lord will hear their cries, whether anyone else will or not.' Shaw comments that when supporting the anti-Corn Law movement, Gadsby was 'prepared to sacrifice doctrinal preferences on what he saw as an issue of justice, morality and practical help, of benefit to "starving thousands" ': Ian Shaw, *High Calvinists in Action – 1810–1860* (Oxford: Oxford University Press, 2002), p. 135. In Edinburgh Thomas Guthrie argued passionately

Miall's point here is that preaching and evangelism that over-
looks both the causes and the results of such destitution on the
bodies, minds and emotions of the poor is doomed to failure. The
middle-class insistence on a strict observance of the Lord's Day as
a mark of genuine godliness, for example, revealed an ignorance
of the realities of life in the slums, where millions of people were
exhausted by relentless physical labour in the search for a 'bare
subsistence'. In such a situation the human body becomes
'exhausted of all nervous energy' and when 'the body is wronged
by overmuch employment during the week, depend upon it, it will
strive to right itself on Sunday'.[46]

Of course, Miall is aware of the good work being done in areas
of urban deprivation by the emerging city mission movement and

---

on behalf of the poor and oppressed: 'As a man, as well as a minister of
that blessed gospel which recognises no distinction between rich and
poor, I protest against the wrongs of a class that are to the full as
unfortunate as they are guilty. They deserve succour rather than censure.
They are to be pitied rather than punished': Thomas Guthrie, *The City – Its
Sins and Its Sorrows*, p. 80. Later in the nineteenth century, William Booth
could write in very similar vein: 'I leave to others the formulation of
ambitious programmes for the reconstruction of our entire social system;
not because I may not desire its reconstruction, but because the
elaboration of any plans that are more or less visionary and incapable of
realisation for many years would stand in the way of . . . dealing with the
most urgently pressing aspect of the question . . . There is nothing in my
scheme that will bring it into conflict with the Socialists . . . or any of the
various schools of thought in the great field of social economics –
excepting only those anti-Christian economists who hold that it is an
offence against the doctrine of the survival of the fittest to try to save the
weakest from going to the wall, and who believe that when a man is down
the supreme duty of a self-regarding society is to jump upon him':
William Booth, *In Darkest England and the Way Out* (London: Salvation
Army, 1890), p. 18. Booth confessed that when contemplating the depths
of the human tragedies in the cities it sometimes 'seemed as if God were
no longer in his world'.
46. *BCBP*, p. 356.

the establishment of such institutions as 'ragged schools'. Such efforts he describes as 'admirable', but he questions whether they can ever be successful in 'this region of the shadow of death' in the absence of *political* action to bring justice and dignity to the poor. What we have here is what would today be termed a *holistic* view of mission, one which affirms evangelism as being at the heart of Christian witness while also insisting on the necessity of political and social activity done in obedience to Christ the Lord, and providing credibility to the claim that the gospel is good news to the poor.

It is worth quoting Miall at length here, since the following passage brings us to the heart of his visionary and distinctive social theology:

[N]o multiplication of religious means will effectually meet the case. Scripture readings, chapel building, city missions . . . cheering as may be individual instances of success, do not fairly grapple with them and will never overcome or remove them . . . [P]eople huddled promiscuously together and crowded into filthy domiciles . . . *cannot* be made religious. It may be very well, and it seems very pious, to say, 'Preach the Gospel'. But . . . physical objects must be overcome by physical means – political obstacles by political means . . . The hindrances in the way are as irremovable by direct religious agency, as if they were geographical. We must therefore, set ourselves to attack . . . not depravity by a promulgation of the gospel, but crowded dwelling houses, filthy habits . . . we must carry our first warfare against all that unnecessarily augments the toil and penury of working men . . . and annihilate political religionism by getting rid of the state establishment of religion . . . They who are so perpetually urging the churches to confine all their attempts to the preaching of the gospel . . . [should] get clear of the childish error that religious acts are only performed by religious means . . . Any act, whether it be prayer to God, or street-cleansing for men . . . done from a religious motive . . . is as much an offering of affectionate and faithful homage to the Saviour, as if it had taken the most spiritual form.[47]

---

47. *BCBP*, pp. 396–399. The London City Mission had begun in 1835 and by the time Miall was preparing his lectures it was praised by people like Lord Kinnaird for pacifying the poor masses in the city and so delivering

The mention of *political religionism* in this passage leads us to the second specifically socio-political aspect of Miall's analysis and it also brings the argument full circle. It now becomes clear that Edward Miall's passionate opposition to the formal establishment of religion was driven not by a narrow sectarianism intended to increase the well-being of his own sector of society, but by the conviction that this arrangement sanctified an elitist and fundamentally unjust social structure. In the process, the message of Christ was horribly distorted because it was being used 'to mount guard over crowns, coronets, titles of distinction, exclusive privileges and sources of temporal wealth'. Political religionism is Christianity 'wielded by civil rulers for state purposes . . . the religion of love upheld by the sword, and the maintenance of its institutions enforced by a palpable violation of its mightiest precepts'. It is 'heavenly truth turned to earthly account'.[48]

Miall genuinely believed that the consequences of this arrangement were nothing short of catastrophic for the cause of biblical Christianity. We have already noticed his dialogue with the Chartist leaders, and there is no doubt that he had his ear constantly to the

---

London from the revolutionary movements that had swept Europe in 1848. The British establishment had good reason to be anxious when 10,000 demonstrators occupied Trafalgar Square for two days in March 1848 and the Chartists drew 100,000 to a demonstration in south London. It was widely believed that the work of the missionaries delivered London from revolutionary violence. However, one of the founders of the Mission, the Revd Baptist Noel, challenged the assumption that the society existed 'to be a sort of subsidiary moral police and to preserve the order of this community'. With insights not dissimilar to those of Miall, he insisted that if it was suspected within the slums that the workers of the London City Mission were inclined to 'teach the miserable to be content with misery and famine, while they themselves were supplied with all the comforts of life' then all credibility would be lost. Such was *not* the missionaries' object. Irene Howat and John Nicholls, *Streets Paved With Gold: The Story of the London City Mission* (Fearn, Rosshire/London: Christian Focus Publications/London City Mission, 2003), pp. 137–138.

48. *BCBP*, pp. 364–365.

ground in order to understand and assess the broad social and religious trends within the nation. Throughout his life Miall was continually on the move, preaching and lecturing in all parts of the British Isles, and so had opportunity to collect accurate information which enabled him to gauge the spirit of the times. What he learned in this process led him to challenge the fundamental and widely shared assumption that Britain was a Christian nation. On the contrary, Miall pointed out that a very large segment of British society, regarding established religion as complicit in the oppression 'which crushes them to the earth', were in the process of moving from a mere distaste for the outward forms of Christianity to a 'malignant hatred' of it. Once again, we are surprised to discover a warning concerning *secularization* as early as the 1840s but, although Miall obviously does not use this terminology, there can be no mistaking the fact that this is the reality of which he warns his contemporaries: 'We pass through life under the influence of a dream . . . We are a Christian people . . . And generation succeeds generation without the churches being thoroughly awake to the fact that very much of this is but a pleasant fiction – and that the spiritual life which really exists among us, is extremely small.' The great tragedy of Britain at the midpoint of the nineteenth century is that, notwithstanding the undoubted increase in church attendance, 'spiritual destitution' is 'concealed behind the screen of baptized nominalism' and the external show of religion hides and distorts 'the real state of the country Godward'.[49]

Perhaps it is not surprising that the fathers who controlled access to the Exeter Hall should have refused Miall the use of that building for the propagation of his views. He was, after all, a controversialist who did not mince his words: clerical titles and splendid vestments are dismissed as 'puerile trumpery'; Oxford and Cambridge universities are 'centres of abandoned profligacy' and 'schools of corruption' which send out an army of 'legally authorized expositors of Christianity' who are 'imbued to the core with worldliness'; and three-quarters of the clergy of the Church of England are 'ignorant of the great spiritual principles

---

49. *BCBP*, pp. 382–383.

of the Gospel'. Nonetheless, by closing its doors to Edward
Miall, Evangelicalism shut ears and minds to a prophetic voice
which, had it been listened to, might have made a considerable
difference to the subsequent history of religion in Britain.[50]

The relevance of Miall in the twenty-first century

Clearly the situation in Britain has changed beyond recognition in
the more than a century and a half since Edward Miall produced
his profound critical analysis of Victorian churches and culture.
Very few Christians in our deeply secular culture today imagine
that the context in which they confess their faith is one that is
basically friendly and hospitable to the gospel. However the
process of secularization is understood and explained, it seems
impossible to argue with the conclusion of the careful social historian Callum Brown that we have witnessed *the death of Christian
Britain*.[51] It is to Miall's great credit that, long before most other
people, he had, as we have seen, detected the early warning signals
of precisely this process and had pointed toward a theological
evaluation of its causes, which he found to lie in a truncated,
privatized and de-politicized gospel. Doubtless Miall would derive
great pleasure from the knowledge that, exactly 150 years after the
publication of *The British Churches in Relation to the British People*, a
speaker at a conference in an Anglican theological college could be
heard lamenting the manner in which the political content of the
Bible 'has been largely excised from Evangelical Bible study, theology and response'. In a manner that comes very close to Miall's
own analysis, Alan Storkey suggested that, from the time of Henry
VIII, the Church of England's relationship with the State had
been characterized by 'docility and servility'. Anglican theology is

---

50. See David W. Smith, *Transforming the World: The Social Impact of British
    Evangelicalism* (Carlisle: Paternoster Press, 1998), pp. 34–38.
51. This is the title of Brown's important book: *The Death of Christian Britain:
    Understanding Secularisation, 1800–2000* (London/New York: Routledge,
    2001).

said to have been 'lobotomized' as the church came under the control of the State and the landed gentry, while repeated attempts to suppress Dissent now require the Church of England to repent.[52]

I cite this not in any triumphalist, partisan spirit but simply to illustrate the fact that, as Christians confront the immense challenges of a secularized culture, there is likely to be growing convergence across many ecclesiastical traditions. This does not imply that all will be harmony and light; alas, a time like this is likely to witness increasing tensions, and the potential for disagreement and division is great. Nonetheless, as Christians come to terms with their new post-Christendom situation and strive to discover missiological responses in this context that are both faithful and relevant, they are likely to find themselves asking similar questions and moving in the same general directions. I strongly suspect that, could he address us today, Edward Miall would remind us that in our specific location in time and history we must seize the opportunity we have been gifted to rediscover what it means to be the People of God in a culture now totally dominated by the 'trade spirit' which he so brilliantly identified and exposed in Victorian England. Our present 'crisis' is in fact a door of opportunity, offering access to the real meaning of words like 'Christian', 'disciple' and 'mission'.

Moving from the British scene with which Miall dealt in nineteenth-century Britain, I want to ask whether his work might be of significance for *American* Christianity in the twenty-first century? In contrast to the situation in Europe, religion is strong in the United States and it is clearly politically powerful and active. North American Evangelical Christians are widely credited with playing a crucial role in the political process and seem confident that they are in a position to ensure that their moral values shape America's future and, through a foreign policy designed to bring 'democracy' to the world, influence the entire earth. In many

---

52. Alan Storkey, 'The Bible's Politics', in David Paterson (ed.), *Witness to the World: Papers from the Second Oakhill College Annual School of Theology* (Carlisle: Paternoster Press, 1999), pp. 63–92.

respects American Christians now find themselves at a point very similar to that experienced by the Victorian churches in nineteenth-century Britain. *And therein lies a warning!* Reading Miall one is struck again and again by the relevance of his critical and prophetic analysis to contemporary Christianity in the United States.

For example, Michael D. Evans, writing in a best-selling book which claims to read America's future destiny from the pages of the ancient Hebrew prophets, demonstrates his claim that America is 'the mightiest nation on earth and has long been a partaker of God's blessings' by the fact that, while his country claims only 7% of the world's population, it is in possession of more than half the world's wealth. America is blessed, according to Evans, because it produces 63% of the world's manufactured goods and 74% of the world's cars and 'consumes more than 35 percent of the world's energy'.[53] Here Miall's *trade spirit* is writ large and, given the global reach of American power, has an impact not merely on the poor in the cities of the USA, but on that even vaster ocean of derelict humanity to be found on the receiving end of economic globalization in the shanties and *favellas* of the southern hemisphere. If in a similar cultural context Edward Miall discerned the beginnings of a great collapse and a creeping secularization, then Christians in North America are in urgent need of the kind of analysis which his work offers.

Finally, I want to suggest that Miall has relevance to the emergent 'World Christianity', with its strength firmly located in the southern continents, which is such a distinctive and important feature of the world today. On the one hand, Miall can be read by these Christians as a salutary and necessary warning of the dangers that lurk for Christianity whenever it attains a critical mass within a society and so comes near to attaining political power. On the other hand, *is it possible that Edward Miall's dream that something genuinely new in the socio-political sphere might emerge from the distant regions of the world could be about to become reality?* Can believers who read the Bible without cultural lenses supplied by the Western

---

53. Michael D. Evans, *The American Prophecies: Ancient Scriptures Reveal Our Nation's Future* (New York: Warner Faith, 2004), p. 14.

Enlightenment and who place a sense of human belonging within community above the value of the isolated individual offer us a way out of the impasses of our desperate modernity? Or are Christians in the southern hemisphere, across the vast continent of Africa, amid the fervour of Pentecostalism in South America and within the growing church in China, in the end merely doomed to become *the next Christendom*?[54] These are critically important issues and the rising generation of non-Western leaders needs to give them urgent attention. In that process I suggest they might benefit from reading Miall's forgotten and neglected work.

I want to finish with a quotation from Richard Bauckham that captures exactly the spirit of Edward Miall's nineteenth-century work and warns us of the great dangers confronting the world church in the era of globalization, while also holding before us the wonderful prospect of a Christianity renewed in mission and holding before a suffering world an alternative and liberating model of what it might really mean to be a reconciled human family. In these words I suggest we discover how the critical analysis offered by a forgotten Victorian Christian has come to have a *global* relevance at the beginning of the twenty-first century:

> It may well be that, only if Christianity in the west becomes a movement of resistance to such evils as consumerism, excessive individualism and the exploitation of the global periphery, can Christianity be distinguished from the west's economic and cultural oppression of other cultures and peoples . . . Without international solidarity with the poorest of the world's poor the church's mission in any part of the globalized world is not only compromised but simply invalidated. It has departed from the biblical contours of God's way with the world.[55]

© David Smith, 2005

---

54. This is, of course, the title of Philip Jenkins's much-discussed book: *The Next Christendom: The Coming of Global Christianity* (Oxford/New York: Oxford University Press, 2002).

55. Richard Bauckham, *Bible and Mission: Christian Witness in a Postmodern World* (Carlisle: Paternoster Press, 2003), pp. 97–98.

5. CHRISTIANITY AND POLITICS IN A PLURALIST SOCIETY
An Augustinian approach

Paul Helm

The celestial society while it is here on earth, increases itself out of all languages, being unconcerned by the different temporal laws that are made; yet not breaking, but observing their diversity in divers nations, so long as they tend unto the preservation of earthly peace, and do not oppose the adoration of one God alone. And so you see, the heavenly city observes and respects this temporal peace here on earth, and the coherence of men's wills in honest morality, as far as it may with a safe conscience; yea, and so far desires it, making use of it for the attainment of the peace celestial.

(Augustine, *The City of God*, book 19, ch. 17)

In this chapter I shall attempt to look first at pluralism and then at Christian exclusivism, and then to argue that the two may be harmonious and even that, in the foreseeable political circumstances, the Christian exclusivist ought to be content with this arrangement. I shall finally discuss some of the issues raised by the idea of the 'privatization' of religion.

Pluralism

What is pluralism?

We live in a pluralist society, and so we need to spend a little time understanding the nature of pluralism and some of its implications. Let us distinguish between *descriptive* and *normative* pluralism. Pluralism in its descriptive sense recognizes that our society is socially and religiously permissive. In regard to many important areas of life it does not require conformity to some set of prescriptions backed by statute; it is not uniformitarian, and in particular it is not religiously uniformitarian. Rather, a person is free to come to a set of beliefs, even beliefs about the most important matters of life and death, and to express these individually or in a group. People in a pluralistic society are free to assemble, or not; to publish, or not; to proclaim publicly, or not. These freedoms are subject to certain conditions: there must not be incitements of various kinds, nor must the activities be reasonably construed as being incitements. Such freedoms extend to political and religious toleration, as well as to the freedom to enter or exit markets. Many of these freedoms (at least in England) are enjoyed by common law, others are granted by statute; pluralism in this sense goes with the rule of law. Pluralistic societies may or may not be democratic in the modern sense; such pluralism may flourish in a variety of political arrangements.

Pluralism, thus sketched, is a way in which certain societies exist, those usually contrasted with totalitarian societies. The gains from such pluralistic societies are notable: freedom from certain kinds of social oppression, and the provision of opportunities for self-expression. However, these freedoms carry with them responsibilities and so they exact a 'price': the responsibility to respect others' freedoms under law. We may debate the question of whether the scope of the freedoms we presently enjoy constitutes the freedoms we ought to have, but few dispute the benefits to be gained by such freedoms even if they dispute or are sceptical about some of the arguments they hear offered in defence of them.

This is the area of what may be called descriptive pluralism. It is to be clearly distinguished from normative pluralism. It does not follow that what a person believes and publicly expresses, or publicly advocates, must, in virtue of that fact, be agreed with or complied with by others. The plurality of views may be incompatible. Socially, various views are expressed side by side. But from this sociological fact it does not follow that all the views expressed are equally valid. To suppose otherwise would be to make pluralism inoperative; since all views are held to be equally valid, the point of pluralism would vanish. A necessary condition of pluralism flourishing in a society is that in that society there exist at least two competing or contrasting views about a matter which have advocates who want to give some form of public expression to those views, and that there is freedom of entry and exit. In practice, very many more views are given expression in modern pluralist societies. None of us are in practice uniformitarians.

Christians and pluralism

Christians are, by and large, exclusivists in their beliefs, and so they are normative pluralists. They are exclusivists in at least two senses. They believe that there is an objective truth of the matter, as far as their religious faith is concerned (and no doubt an objective truth of the matter in the case of many other issues as well). So they also stress the non-equivalence of the views legitimately expressed in a pluralistic society. It is important to recognize that these two positions are distinct. There are religious thinkers, such as John Hick, who hold that there is an objective truth of the matter in religion, and that there are several, or many – depending on how many 'great religions' there are – ways of referring to and coming into some kind of positive relationship with that objective truth. Just as it does not follow from pluralism that no one can know anything, so it does not follow that each view is as false or as true as the other.

We may see ourselves as members of a pluralist society and do so with different attitudes. One may be a welcoming or a grudging pluralist. If you are a welcoming pluralist then this is likely to be because you see in pluralism the necessary conditions for maintenance or perhaps the flourishing of certain virtues, or the provision of opportunities to which you attach great importance. If you are a grudging pluralist then this is likely to be so because you resent the idea of those who differ from you in matters which you regard as fundamental (but which they may not) being given the opportunity to express and propagate their views and rubbish or belittle or ignore yours. These different attitudes to pluralism will be of significance later on.

It is possible for the Christian to defend pluralism on a variety of grounds: for example, by appealing to the moral principles of Christianity, or to the instrumental value of pluralism, to historical precedent, or simply to the fact that live options to pluralism are less palatable than it is.

It might occur to me that if God is the basic source of value in the universe and has infallibly commanded a certain kind of life, the state should not only not undermine such a life, it should promote it. Little reflection is needed to see that this promotional stance cannot be achieved without restricting major offices – perhaps the highest ones – to religiously committed leaders. It may then occur to me that even in my own tradition there is disagreement about important elements in Scripture. I will also be aware of other Christian traditions. Would it not invite strife in my own tradition, and certainly between it and other religious traditions, to restrict political offices? And if I take to heart the injunction, 'Do unto others as you would have them do unto you,' I may be at least reluctant – from a sense of fairness as well as from prudence – to support a government that does not provide for representation from entirely different religious traditions with as deeply felt a devotion to their ideals as I feel to mine. If, in addition, I have thought about how power can corrupt and about how different are the missions of clergy and government officials, I may prefer a form of government in which all are free to pursue their religious ideals under the spiritual guidance of their choice and the clergy are not faced with secular concerns that may dilute their spiritual commitments or obscure their religious vision.[1]

But it would be mistaken, in my view, to beatify pluralism: to suppose that it is God-given above all other social and political forms. We must distinguish pluralism as one of many

1. Robert Audi, *Religious Commitment and Secular Reason*, p. 23.

forms – perhaps a particularly advantageous form – within which Christianity can exist and flourish, from pluralism as itself an expression of a form of religion: civil religion. Speaking generally, pluralism has this advantage: that in addition to the separation of powers between the judiciary, the legislature and the executive, and the freedom of the press, it helps to discourage the corrupting effects that the enjoyment of political power and of high office engenders, effects from which Christians are most certainly not exempt. It is one of the most depressing features of the history of the West that Christians have been willing to use the rack, the thumbscrew and the stake in order to secure a version of Christian uniformitarianism. There is no reason to think that should, say, the Christian moral majoritarians in the USA ever achieve power they would be free from these corrupting influences. The maintenance of a true pluralism does not guarantee that, say, particular people will not enjoy high office for long periods of time, and so be even more liable to succumb to persistent corruption, but it helps to prevent this.

If we as Christians look for a historical precedent for presently endorsing pluralism it is to be found, I believe, not in the Christian uniformitarianism of the past but in the behaviour of English Dissent for about 150 years following the Great Revolution of 1688–9. During that period Dissenters forfeited the opportunity of having discrimination against them lifted on the grounds that such an improvement in their lot would increase the chances of the Protestant Establishment being jeopardized. They valued the general advantages of such an arrangement more greatly than any particular advantages that they might gain for themselves. I argue that Christians in their turn should be prepared to tolerate the cost of secular pluralism – and it has a cost – lest a worse thing befall them.

Are there limits to the Christian's acceptance of pluralism? I think there are; or, more accurately, there is one limit. If in the pluralistic society legislation is passed that, were the Christian to comply with it, then he or she would sin, then it seems clear from the general thrust of the teaching of the New Testament that a Christian ought to refuse to comply. Here it is important to bear in mind the distinction between *enabling* and *requiring* legislation: between, say, legislation which permits abortion and legislation that requires it. A Christian may deplore the passing of enabling legislation and vote and campaign against it, but if such legislation is passed then we must acquiesce. But our reaction must clearly be different if a new law requires us to sin.

Of course, it is perfectly consistent with pluralism that within the welter of views that it is lawful to express is the advocacy of uniformitarianism. The uniformitarian thus has the political and social right to advocate the abandonment of pluralism. That is not the issue. Rather, what I am in the course of arguing is that Christians – even exclusivist Christians – ought, as citizens of the UK, to be in favour of pluralism. So the argument is not couched in terms of our present legal rights but in terms of Christian moral character. The moral character of Christian citizens should be such that they advocate or support pluralism; and that even in totalitarian or closed societies Christians should be on the side of the advocates of 'openness'. This is not so much because pluralism is defensible for its own sake, but because it ensures or makes more likely certain goods which would otherwise not be realized. They would not be realized because we are all imperfect; we are ignorant, prejudiced, and liable to be corrupted by power. More than this, for the Christian pluralism seems more congruent with how, according to the New Testament, men and women become Christians: not through the operation of the rack and the thumbscrew, but by the outward call of the gospel and the inward, efficacious call of the Holy Spirit. More daringly, perhaps, as Robert Audi claims, pluralism is one expression of the Golden Rule.

A speculative aside: we naturally think of pluralism in terms of the earthly city. Could there be pluralism in the New Jerusalem? After all, heaven is depicted a city. Nothing that we have in the portrayal of the heavenly state appears to rule out the occurrence of differences of opinion there. Heaven is also a world of love and an aspect of love is forbearance, as Paul teaches us (Eph. 4:2). So maybe our experience of pluralism here, with its attendant frustrations and messiness, is preparing us for the exercise of mutual forbearance in a refined and purified pluralism, the pluralism of heaven.

It is important also to see that the exclusivism that Christians profess, and that makes some Christians uneasy with the free-for-all of pluralism, is capable of being held with varying degrees of strength or intensity. Even modern conservative evangelical Christians give a tacit if not explicit recognition to the distinction between matters in their faith which are exclusively held – matters which, if you like, are non-negotiable – and other matters about which they hold there to be a truth of the matter which they by and large do not hold to dogmatically. Many such people think that there is a truth of the matter regarding ecclesiology, or the mode and subjects of baptism, or how to interpret the 'days' of creation, or how the Old Testament relates to the New Testament, but do not believe that they have such a firm grasp of these matters that they are entitled to exclude themselves from those who, though they otherwise hold similar views to them about the person of Christ and the way of salvation, differ from them on these other matters.

There are two further important features of the exclusivism which Christians typically hold, features they share with some others but not with everyone, which are relevant to our discussion. The first is the claim that the core of their exclusive faith is object-ively true. Christians have a stake in objective truth: first, in maintaining the idea of objective truth, and then in maintaining that their core beliefs are objectively true. So they have an interest in dissenting from other views which they regard as mistaken and dangerous. As we have seen, from a purely sociological point of view the Christian community or communities in the UK are 'faith communities' along with a whole host of other religious and charitable organizations. Each has a distinctive ideology and purpose, the Christians included. All are, or ought to be, treated equally before the law, with no discrimination. Here we need to distinguish between two among the many possible attitudes that the State may have to the church. The State may be *separate* from the church, neither intending to help nor helping to hinder any religion by its actions. This requires a strict separation between church and State. Or it may be *impartial* in regard to religion, treating all religions equally, not granting privileges (e.g. tax exemp-tions, or government grants) to one religion at the expense of others.[2] (Currently in England and Scotland, given the establishment by law of the Church of England and the Church of Scotland, the State is neither impartial nor neutral in religion, and so our pluralism as it affects religion is imperfect. But, echoing the attitude of early Dissent, one may argue for the continuation of such an imperfect arrangement on the grounds that its disturbance is likely to be less advantageous than the status quo; or one may not. One may combine the advocacy of pluralism with a Burkean caution about political disturbance because of its unforeseeable effects. So, from the point of view of sociology, or of the law, each religious community is not presently treated equivalently; each is not and does not see itself as equivalent with each of the others. Nonetheless, given this qualification, there is considerable religious pluralism at present in the UK.)

Similar points can be made about the values exhibited in pluralism, and the ideological tendencies of pluralism. We live in a society where various forms of lying are endemic in high places. In both politics and commerce there is deceit, usually going under the name of 'presentation'. And the current tendency is for the assertion of individual human rights to trump ancient common law rights of freedom of speech. If what I say offends you, that is increasingly regarded as an infringement of your right not to be insulted rather than exercise of my right to speak freely. These tendencies currently make it harder rather than easier for the Christian church – and for healthy debate in general – to flourish. But they do not make its existence and even its flourishing impossible. And he would be a rash person who claimed that such tendencies are a consequence of pluralism as such, or that their effects are to be found only in pluralist societies.

Christians, pluralism and relativism

However, it is one thing to advocate pluralism, to support pluralism on normative grounds; it is another thing to be seduced by it

2. For the distinction between separation and impartiality see Nicholas Wolterstorff, in Robert Audi and Nicholas Wolterstorff, *Religion in the Public Square: The Place of Religious Convictions in Political Debate*, pp. 76, 149.

into relativism or indifferentism or the advocacy of civic religion. The postmodern temper of our times strongly inclines us to see everything from this sociological point of view. Each ideology is equivalent, telling its own story, having its own narrative. The idea that one of these communities might make objective truth claims, and by its own lights have good reason to make them, claiming truth for its own confessional position and by implication denying the truth to other ideological positions, is strongly downplayed. This is either because of the scepticism that is inherent in much postmodernism – the denial that any of us can have knowledge of anything[3] – or because of a more fundamental objection to the very idea of knowledge claims: that they enshrine bids for power which are ideologically suspect. Knowledge is power, it is said, and so knowledge claims are bids for power, bids which should be resisted either on the grounds of the aforementioned scepticism or because of some version of the doctrine of individual human rights.

It is very important in this climate for Christians to maintain the objective truth claims of the faith, and that pluralism makes this difficult is one of its 'costs'. We may, initially, be attracted to the 'space' that postmodernism gives us, space in which to flourish and to tell our own story. But if the price of occupying that space and telling our own story is that we are denied the voice to claim that that story is true, to make the claim that we ourselves have reason to believe that it is true, then such space is not worth occupying, for it results in a gross distortion of the claims of the faith. To put the point provocatively, Christians may share with the postmodernists a negative estimate of the Enlightenment, but we need to remember that not everything that the Enlightenment stood for ought to be rejected. While we may be comfortable in rejecting the idea of autonomous human reason that lies at the heart of the 'Enlightenment project', we should not reject the Enlightenment's view of truth: of objective truth. This is not to claim, or to

---

3. There is nothing new here. In his *Outlines of Pyrrhonism* Sextus Empiricus (c. AD 200) defended scepticism by appealing to what he regarded as the mutually cancelling effects of cultural and religious diversity.

allow, that that concept was an invention of the Enlightenment, 'positivism' as it is sometimes labelled, but that the Enlightenment itself took over the idea of objective truth, or realism, from the Christian church and from aspects of ancient philosophy.

Christians as infallibilists?

The second feature of the exclusivism which is typical of Christians has to do with the sort of knowledge claims that they make. The basic thrust of the Enlightenment was infallibilistic. The rationalist and empiricist epistemologies devised by Descartes and Locke were reckoned by their practitioners to be infallible (or 'incorrigible') paths to knowledge, paths provided by the clear and distinct ideas of human reason or by sense experience. (The fact that these paths were different, and incompatible, and eventually led to the demise of the Enlightenment 'project' need not detain us here.) The Enlightenment, after all, offered itself as a rational alternative to the infallibilist claims of both Roman Catholics and Protestants.

As Christians, are we infallibilists? Here, I think, Christians walk something of a tightrope. On the one hand, we claim that God is himself infallible, and therefore that his word is infallible. But we go on to distinguish between the infallibility of the word of God and the fallibility of our own understanding of it. That councils have erred is part of the central epistemological thrust of the Reformation. Nothing, neither the Councils of the Church, nor the Pope, nor the Confessions of the Reformation period, supplants the infallible Scripture, the oracles of God. And so what of ourselves? Are we infallibilists about ourselves? Surely not; we reckon that our finitude, relative ignorance and defective cognitive apparatus make our own infallibility impossible. Councils have erred and so have we. Councils have erred and so have the 'Councils' which drew up the various Protestant Confessions of Faith, as they themselves confess.[4]

---

4. '[Councils] may erre, and sometyme haue erred, euen in thinges parteynyng unto God' (Thirty-nine Articles, Article 21, in John H. Leith, (ed.), *Creeds of the Churches*, p. 273). Compare the Westminster Confession of Faith, 31. 3.

Our present understanding of Scripture is fallible. To be fallible is not the same thing as to be completely in error. One can be fallible but have well-grounded certitude. So, having well-grounded certitude is not the same thing as being personally infallible.

Why is it necessary to reflect on this here, in a paper on Christianity and politics? Because recognizing our fallibility has social and therefore political consequences. Being fallible, and therefore possibly or likely in error on some matter, means that it may be wise to use human resources other than our own. The resources of the community are available for us to test our own ideas against and to learn from. Hence fallibilism should engender the toleration of opinions other than our own present opinions, however certain we may be of their truth. So it is appropriate that we spend a little time on toleration.

The defence of toleration

Toleration – and intolerance – may be considered and defended (and attacked) in at least three different ways. Most obvious nowadays is the *social good* defence: the idea that toleration is a good thing because of its effects on human well-being. That society is a better society in which human autonomy is respected and in which people do what they want to do and say and publish what they want to. Unlimited toleration is almost invariably proscribed, on the grounds that it will be harmful to children and to other vulnerable groups in society. The social good defence is often enforced by an appeal to human rights; people have the right to that degree of self-expression that is compatible with others exercising their right to self-expression.

Secondly, there is what might be called the *aretaic* defence: that toleration is a necessary condition of promoting certain virtues – a willingness to listen to others, to have one's position critically examined, to reconsider one's own point of view, to be prepared to be offended or hurt – the virtue of tolerance itself. We have recently been reminded by Lord Justice Sedley that free speech includes 'not only the inoffensive but the irritating, the contentious, the eccentric, the heretical, the unwelcome and the provocative provided it did not tend to provoke violence. Freedom only to speak inoffensively was not worth having.'[5]

Finally, there is what one might call the *epistemic* defence: that toleration is necessary for the better attaining of well-grounded beliefs, for the better pursuit of truth; for it provides a forum of debate against which we may test our own ideas and learn of other ideas which differ from our own.

Each of these approaches to toleration may be found in John Milton's *Areopagitica*, the classic defence of the freedom of the press. On social good:

> We should be wary therefore what persecution we raise against the living labours of public men, how we spill that seasoned life of man, preserved and stored up in books; since we see a kind of homicide may be thus committed, sometimes a martyrdom; and if it extend to the whole impression, a kind of massacre, whereof the execution ends not in the laying of an elemental life, but strikes at that ethereal and fifth essence, the breath of reason itself; slays an immortality rather than a life.[6]

Restricting the freedom of the press strikes at reason, a fundamental good.

On the virtue-producing effects of toleration:

> I cannot praise a fugitive and cloistered virtue unexercised, and unbreathed, that never sallies out and sees her adversary, but slinks out of the race, where that immortal garland is to be run for, not without dust and heat.[7]

Toleration demands the exercise of virtue against her adversaries, and so (presumably) publicizes and strengthens it.

And on the epistemic argument:

> There be who perpetually complain of schisms and sects, and make it

---

5. *The Times*, 28 July 1999, Law Reports, p. 25.

6. John Milton, *Areopagitica: A Speech for the Liberty of Unlicensed Printing, to the Parliament of England* (1644), in *Prose Works*, p. 104.

7. Milton, *Areopagitica*, p. 108.

such a calamity that any man dissents from their maxims. 'Tis their own pride and ignorance which causes the disturbing, who neither will hear with meekness, nor can convince, yet all must be suppressed which is not found in their Syntagma. They are the troublers, they are the dividers of unity, who neglect and permit not others to unite those dissevered pieces, which are yet wanting to the body of truth. To be still searching what we know not, by what we know, still closing up truth to truth as we find it . . . this is the golden rule in theology as well as in arithmetic, and makes up the best harmony in a church; not the forced and outward union, of cold, and neutral and inwardly divided minds.[8]

The practice of toleration aids us in the search for truth.

What we have in contention in our own cultural situation are two different conceptions of toleration and intolerance. There is, on the one hand, an intolerance of *judgment*, as when one judges that some claim is mistaken, and perhaps dangerous. If we think that we have the truth about some important matter we may also believe that it is irresponsible to tolerate dissent. While this is a mistaken belief, the assumptions underlying it – that issues to do with religion are issues of truth and falsity, and are capable of discussion by reason – are surely correct. While we may dissent from such intolerance of judgment, I hope that this is because we wish to advocate, and ourselves to exercise, a corresponding tolerance of judgment based upon the idea of objective truth and the prospect of gaining justified beliefs about it.

If the Christian religion and its relations with other religions and ideologies raises issues of truth and falsity, and can be reasoned about, and if religion is important, then the issue of toleration will arise because of a clash of judgments within a society about what is true and false, or about why certain actions ought to be forbidden and other actions ought to be permitted. This sort of toleration arises when there are differences over what people take to be true, and where these differences are not trivial but are over matters which may have important social consequences. In situations of wide differences of judgment over

---

8. Milton, *Areopagitica*, p. 115.

important matters there is a great temptation to fudge the issue of toleration and to err on the side of caution: on the side of unduly constricting its limits. The practice of toleration will be costly to the extent that one believes that one's judgments are correct, though only exorbitantly costly if one thinks that one's judgments, though correct, are incapable of reasonable defence or will not withstand renewed examination.

But there is another kind of toleration than the toleration that may arise when there is a difference of judgment. Suppose that there is a bluebottle buzzing loudly in the room where I am working. And suppose that I tolerate it, allowing the bluebottle the enjoyment of full freedom of expression during its short and unappealing life. This, I take it, is a genuine case of toleration, the toleration of noise. We might argue about the degree to which we ought to tolerate noise: bluebottles, lawnmowers, pop music. But however and wherever we draw the limits of such toleration, the toleration of noise is a different kind of toleration, because in deciding to tolerate the bluebottle I am not tolerating anyone else's cognitive judgment about what is true or false or reasonable or unreasonable. There is no cognitive content to the bluebottle's buzzing, or to the lawnmower, and little enough to the pop music. And when I tolerate the pop music I am not tolerating it because of its cognitive content. What is at issue here is the toleration of physical sensation rather than the toleration of belief and its expression. We do well to argue that religious toleration is the toleration of diverse beliefs, together with their associated practices and public expressions, not the toleration of manifold sensations. We shall return to this distinction later on.

The necessity of toleration

We have – as I claimed earlier – good but not infallible grounds for our views; and others think that they have good but not infallible grounds for their views. Even if some of us have infallible views, we cannot convince everyone else of the fact. And yet this fact, the fact of epistemological pluralism, does not (or ought not to) lead to us to think that scepticism is true or even that relativism, the first cousin of scepticism, is true either.

Toleration is necessary precisely because of our own epistemic fallibility. Because I may be mistaken in my beliefs, and you may be mistaken in yours, a framework within which our views can be disseminated and argued about is surely something that is of benefit to us both. As a result of such arguments each of us may be able to review his opinions and the reasons that he has for holding them, and the strength with which he holds them. It is such fallibilism which lies behind John Stuart Mill's well-known words:

> The peculiar evil of silencing the expression of an opinion is, that it is robbing the human race; posterity as well as the existing generation; those who dissent from the opinion, still more than those who hold it. If the opinion is right, they are deprived of the opportunity of exchanging error for truth: if wrong, they lose, what is almost as great a benefit, the clearer perception and livelier impression of truth, produced by its collision with error.[9]

Some have feared that if uniformity of worship and religious observance were not imposed there would be a collapse into scepticism and therefore wished to clamp down on all expressions of opinion but their own. But it might be argued that toleration is necessary precisely to avoid the collapse into scepticism. Worse, a belief which can only maintain itself by intolerance of its rivals is likely to be viewed sceptically by proponents and opponents alike. We need toleration of diverse opinions to make manifest that there is a spectrum of reasonableness and unreasonableness, and to afford us the time and space to make up our own minds.

Here I wish to return to the distinction made earlier between a toleration of sensation and a toleration of judgment. The reason for toleration is not that there is no prospect of approaching the truth because each opinion or 'perspective' is as valid as any other. The toleration of incommensurable perspectives is more like a

---

9. John Stuart Mill, *On Liberty*, p. 24. But it should be noted that one aspect
   of Mill's defence of toleration is that he believes that it is one means by
   which error will be progressively eliminated and a social consensus
   achieved. (See Rescher, *Pluralism*, p. 23.)

case of the toleration of sensation than it is the toleration of judgment. Rather, the reason for toleration is that the conditions of true toleration maximize the conditions under which fallible men and women and their fallible teachers can come to what they in turn regard as reasonable views.

Each of these points and the arguments offered in support are, it seems to me, especially important at present, when the recognition of fallibilism has a strong tendency to lead to insular forms of communitarianism and cultural relativism.

As we rejected the argument from scepticism so we need to reject the reverse argument: if tolerance, then scepticism; the argument that toleration is warranted because no one has any answers. The toleration that is desirable, that is worth having, is a toleration of judgment based on the idea of objective truth and the rejection of scepticism. Otherwise what we are left defending is a toleration of sensation, not a toleration of judgment.

Exclusivism and pluralism

Do exclusivism and pluralism go together? Well, they obviously do go together. There are exclusivists in pluralist societies (pluralist as defined above). So perhaps the question is: ought they to go together? Ought exclusivists grudgingly to tolerate toleration? Or ought they to welcome it, to be 'at home', comfortable with pluralism? Or perhaps, is there something about exclusivism that inevitably pulls in a uniformitarian direction? Can exclusivism flourish only in a uniformitarian society, one whose political ethos tolerates only the exclusivism of the Christian gospel?

Let us think a bit about such a uniformitarian society. What would it be like? We have had instances of this, when only one form of doctrine and worship was tolerated, and we know what happened. For example, for a time England became (in Jonathan Clark's words) 'a confessional State'[10] in which, even though there was a pluralism of worship, only varieties of Protestantism were

---

10. J. C. D. Clark, *English Society 1688–1832*, p. 411.

tolerated by an Anglican Establishment, and when Dissenters preferred to be disadvantaged in a Protestant England rather than be given privileges which might also be extended to Roman Catholics and so jeopardize the Protestant establishment. But in present circumstances such a confessionalism is irrecoverable, even were it desirable. The example shows us, however, that there are degrees of pluralism, of toleration. The limited pluralism of the English past, pluralism consistent with Protestant confessionalism, is irrecoverable not only because of the strength of secular pluralism in our society but also because of the strength of Christian pluralism.

So, since politics is the art of the possible, even if there were a consensus among Christians, a consensus even among exclusivist Christians that uniformitarianism was divinely mandated, there is the problem, or problems, of what form that Christian uniformitarianism ought to take, and what are the present political policies that are best calculated to achieve that. And – it is guaranteed – there would be different proposals about political means even when there was agreement on the exact shape of the political end. So the whole thing is crazy and I will not discuss it further here.

Pluralism and the Bible

However, Christian pluralists would be on stronger ground, it may be thought, if we could say that our pluralism is countenanced by the Bible. Is pluralism countenanced by the Bible? 'Countenanced' is a bit ambiguous. Is it easy to see that it is advocated by the Bible, or some part of it? Is it consistent with the Bible, or some part of it? I cannot see that pluralism is advocated by the Bible. But then I cannot see that uniformitarianism is, either; not at least by those parts of the Bible that we are likely to give priority to in such matters, namely the New Testament. Is there anything in Jesus' teaching that gives us a lead on the uniformitarianism–pluralism issue? Does he advocate one position or the other? If anything, his words seem to recognize pluralism, though if someone objects that I am pressing his words unnaturally then I might readily concede. His words about the kingdom – its natural, persistent, quiet, inevitable growth – seem to recognize that the kingdom grows in alien soil, and that wheat and tares go together, and that we must give to Caesar what is his as we give to God what is his. Christ's kingdom is not of this world, else would the servants of Christ fight. On top of that, Christ teaches that his followers must cultivate an ethic of service rather than of lordliness.

It follows that the Christian advocacy of pluralism requires a view of the kingdom of Christ which does not see it as having independent, visible expression until the return of the King. The covenanting assertion that the crown rights of the Redeemer ought here and now to have visible expression, and that the magistrate is as much a servant of Christ in the bringing about of his kingdom as is the minister of the gospel, seems to bring forward some of the features of the *eschaton* equally as much as do the Anabaptists. The Anabaptists see themselves as a visible expression of the kingdom of Christ, a righteous enclave in a sorry world, early realizations of the world to come. The Covenanters see society as the kingdom of Christ being overtly ruled by Christ, this rule made visible through the establishment of appropriate political structures; a development which may itself be regarded as an early stage of the consummation of all things. May not each extreme be making the same mistake: the mistake of not giving proper recognition to the fact that at present we are living 'in the interim'?

If someone objects that it is unwarranted to press such data from the Gospels in this direction, then I am willing to concede the point. But by the same token it looks implausible to press the teaching of Jesus in the opposite direction. If there are hermeneutical reasons for thinking that such teaching of Jesus does not warrant pluralism, then by the same token there are hermeneutical reasons for thinking that the teaching of Jesus does not warrant uniformitarianism in either its Anabaptistic or its Covenanting varieties, or in any other variety. And the same goes, I think, for the rest of the New Testament.

But some will say that we ought to extend our Bible study to the Old Testament, claiming that the patterns of Mosaic leadership or of Israelite kingship not only are descriptive of a uniformitarian society but are normative for us. They are certainly descriptive of a uniformitarian society, but are they in any way normative for us? Here exclusivists differ. So, before exclusivists can unite to pursue uniformitarian policies, they have to be of one mind on such a deep, meta-biblical question as the relation of the Old Testament to the New. So, no deliverance here. Or, at least, no immediate deliverance here.

Is pluralism countenanced by the Bible in our second sense: that if not taught by the Bible it is nevertheless (in some sense) consistent with it? Here I think we might hope to make more progress. I refer to two areas: to Paul's attitude to religious superstition and pagan philosophy at Athens, and to his teaching to the Corinthians. As regards his practice in Athens, it seems clear (to me) that he tolerated (and was tolerated by) the Stoics and Epicureans of the Areopagus. Neither he nor they sought the elimination of the views of the other by seeking to have the expression of their views outlawed or proscribed. And the same is true of the religious superstition of the Athenians. Paul's attitude to that superstition is clear, or fairly clear. He does not seek to ban it, or take even the first steps to having it banned.

In the case of the Corinthian correspondence there are a number of lines of evidence that converge to support this conclusion: the call for believers not to be yoked with unbelievers (a call to separation, whatever precisely this means) does not imply that the idol-worshippers ought to be put in prison, silenced or eliminated. Similarly with Christians going to law with Christians. There is no suggestion that Christians should not go to law with non-Christians, nor that they should not use any other rights that they may have as Roman citizens, and Paul for his part used his position as a Roman citizen to have his good name restored. (Acts 16:37–40). And in 1 Corinthians 5 Paul makes a distinction between associating with an immoral person who calls himself a Christian brother and associating with such a person who does not profess the faith. Shun the one, Paul says, but you may associate with the other. For if not, 'you would have to leave this world', plainly indicating that there are stable patterns of behaviour inconsistent with the Christian ethic which are likely to continue to exist; a recognition, if not an endorsement, of pluralism. Earlier I drew the distinction between welcoming and grudging acceptance of pluralism. There is not much evidence, if any, that Paul was a grudging pluralist.

The privatization of religion

The sort of position that I have been outlining and defending often leads to the charge that it results in the privatization of religion. This, as it stands, is a somewhat obscure claim. It clearly does not take religion out of the public realm; churches and other religious associations are public social organisms, and free, with some restrictions, to propagate their own views publicly. Religion is not relegated to private space like the family, much less to the realm of our private thoughts and desires. The privatization–nationalization contrast of political debate does not readily apply to the issue of Christianity and politics. Perhaps the point is this: that the view I have been defending implies that in endeavouring to contribute to political debate it becomes impossible to give reasons drawn from one's faith. I shall try to say something about this.

The other side of privatization is politicization. To the extent that our faith is not privatized will it be politicized? By 'politicization' I mean here the making of one or more political policies an essential part of the Christian message, or giving the impression of such a connection. There is grave danger that if Christian churches avow political policies then the liberty of Christians and the freeness of the gospel will be compromised. For I take it that though the gospel may commit us to certain social and political *ideals*, and even to certain social and political *ends*, it does not follow from this that the adoption of particular means to further these ideals or bring about these ends is part of the gospel. So if it is an implication of the gospel that Christians should be against injustice, it is not part of that gospel to prescribe means – at the level of political policy, and as an essential expression of allegiance to Christ – that Christians must take in order to further the cause of justice. The terms of the gospel do not include 'You must vote Tory' or 'You must vote Labour' or 'You must vote Liberal Democrat'. Even bearing in mind the secrecy of the ballot, voting for one of these parties, or being willing to do so, is not a condition of being a Christian in good standing, and an attempt to make it so ought to draw forth the same arguments as Paul used in his letter to the Galatians against making circumcision a condition for acceptance as a Christian.

So we must make a distinction between the visible church and organizations of politically like-minded Christians. Groups of Christians outside the life of the organized church must be free to lobby against what they regard as a social evil, even what the New Testament identifies as a social evil, and to advocate what they regard as appropriate policies to lessen or eradicate that injustice. But it would be an infringement of the liberty of other Christians to require them to adopt those policies as a part of their good standing as Christians. Here pluralism and the Christian faith strongly concur. For, properly understood, each finds a central place for people to think and act differently across a wide spectrum of political philosophy and policy. Not to give support to both the right and the necessity of Christians forming such para-church centres of policy formation both violates the pluralistic outlook of our times and – more seriously – misunderstands the nature of Christian freedom. It is part of the genius of Christianity that it can occur and flourish in a wide variety of circumstances.

Nicholas Wolterstorff illuminatingly distinguishes between two sorts of societal decision-making procedure, each of which is or may be 'democratic'. He calls them the *parliamentary session* and the *Quaker meeting*.[11] In the parliamentary session decision-making is by majority vote, and this may be variously understood. There are rules for debate and for the making of proposals. The vote is taken. The will of the majority of those voting is taken to be the decision of the entire body. The minority acquiesces in the verdict of the majority, even though it is entitled to protest the decision, and may do so. There is, as Nicholas Rescher puts it, acquiescence in disagreement. Such acquiescence is to be distinguished from consensus, which is a meeting of minds, 'a condition of intellectual uniformity'.[12] We acquiesce by 'going along' with another view while not agreeing with it, and we thus achieve that degree of peace and quiet in order that we may

11. See the discussion of this distinction in Nicholas Rescher, *Pluralism*,
    p. 159, a work to which Wolterstorff refers.
12. Rescher, *Pluralism*, p. 163.

pursue our own projects and fulfil our own callings, doing our best to live peaceably with everyone. By contrast, the Quaker meeting operates by consensus, by agreement, if there is no dissent from a proposal. So long as there is dissent no decision may be reached. Parliamentary sessions are thus messier than Quaker meetings; there is likely to be visible and active dissent, a majority and a minority. In order to be politically effective, arguments do not have to appeal to everyone but to a majority, however this is precisely understood. Some, such as Robert Audi, seem to define liberal democracy in Quakerish terms. Insofar as it is not Quakerish it is less than a fully liberal democracy. The majority cannot coerce the minority – typically, by passing legislation – except in the instance of preserving civic order.[13]

But, as Wolterstorff argues, Audi's position is surely unrealistically ideal. Every extant modern liberal democracy is parliamentarian, not Quakerish, even about matters which involve the coercion of some. On a whole range of matters there is pervasive disagreement, and deadlock or stalemate can be broken only by majority voting. If one holds to a parliamentary-session view of liberal democracy then at least one has the advantage of realism rather than unworkable idealism. In order to be a faithful citizen in a Quakerish society I could support only those policies which enjoy the secular Quaker-type consensus of all other citizens, assuming that they are fully informed and fully rational. For if such a person is coerced by a policy or law that he has not given agreement to then his autonomy is infringed. Liberal democracy as more traditionally understood certainly has an important place for autonomy, but it is a more chastened view of autonomy than the secular Quaker-meeting view delivers; it is the freedom of all citizens under law, equal protection afforded by the law, and an equal voice and vote.

What does all this mean, practically? It means the following: that I best respect my fellow citizen when I hear him (or at least allow him to speak) and when he hears me (or at least allows me to speak). When each of us hears the other, being informed by what

13. On this, see Audi, *Religious Commitment and Secular Reason*, p. 153.

each says about the matter in hand, then there is the opportunity of persuasion of the other's point of view and – putting this in parliamentary terms – of so framing the motion that I gain your agreement with it. So there is no a priori restraint on what kind of argument I might use in seeking to persuade you. The prime test of whether you may be listened to, and whether I may be listened to, is not that I am in some sense fully rational, whatever this may mean in this particular context, but that I have the right to express my view as well as the right to vote. In no extant liberal democracy do I qualify for the vote only by passing a rationality test. Given the parliamentary character of liberal democracy, do I stand the chance of losing out? Indeed I do. But then we are participating in the politics of what Augustine calls the 'earthly' city. As Wolterstorff puts it, 'We do not live in a pristine state. We all live east of Eden. We, one and all, are all mucked up, not only in our actions but in our beliefs about moral matters.'[14] And, one might add, about political matters as well.

It follows that the reasons offered in political debate and argument are governed by two factors: personal conviction, and the likelihood of the reasons that I have for holding my convictions being convincing to others, or to a sufficient number of others. If I believe that abortion is wrong because I believe that God says it is wrong, that is my conviction. And I might seek to advance my conviction by using that as a reason. Could I, in order to promote the political effectiveness of that view, devise a secular argument for it? I might. But the argument may be too abstruse or technical to be politically effective. If I judge that the majority might be in favour not of the outlawing of abortion but of something short of that – a proposal to lessen the opportunities of obtaining an abortion, say – and if that possible majority has a whole range of reasons, some of them secular, some of them 'religious', some of them overtly Christian, ought I not then to ally myself with this consensus and vote for something less than I believe the ideal to be? Perhaps I ought. So we may offer whatever reasons seem right for us to offer, and our fellow citizens ought to

---

14. Wolterstorff, in Audi and Wolterstorff, *Religion in the Public Square*, p. 164.

offer theirs, in turn.[15] Sometimes we shall be on the side of the majority, sometimes not. That's politics, and that's life.

What has all this to say to the issue of 'privatization'? Just this: that it shows us that there is not a hard and fast distinction between the 'privatization' of religion and its denial, even granted the qualifications earlier. There will be occasions when a Christian or a group of Christians may judge it to be appropriate to offer secular reasons in support of a position which they themselves see as having primarily a religious or specifically Christian justification. There will be occasions when they may judge it to be appropriate to offer 'religious' reasons for such a position; and there will be occasions when they may judge it to be appropriate to offer specifically 'Christian' reasons. Which will be appropriate depends on which is more likely to achieve the agreement of a majority for a position which moves closer to the Christian position. So, in some instances, Christianity but not religion will be 'privatized'; in some cases both; in some cases neither: privatized in the sense that an explicit religious or Christian confession is not an explicit or avowed element in the argument.

Conclusion

The subtitle of this paper is 'An Augustinian approach'. I recognize that there has been little or nothing explicit in it from Augustine. And certainly I do not think that Augustine can be made to speak directly to our situation without us falling into anachronism. For instance, Augustine, like his disciple John Calvin, was an advocate of the persecution of those whom he regarded as insufficiently 'orthodox'.[16] Nevertheless, I want to

---

15. Compare Audi's view, which is that in a liberal democracy, in debating and deciding on issues which have a coercive effect (i.e. which restrict freedom), religious people should offer only secular reasons for their views (*Religious Commitment and Secular Reason*, Part Two).

16. And Robert Markus has argued that there was a brief period in Augustine's life when, impressed by the influence of the Constantinian Settlement

claim that our main themes echo what Augustine centrally held about 'the earthly city'. First, the earthly city is 'earthly'. It is not a regenerate society, nor is it, or is it to be, based on explicitly Christian values. What motivates the inhabitants of the heavenly city is not what motivates the members of the earthly city. The earthly city is fallen, and exhibits its fallenness in an unreserved way. It will never transform itself into the new Jerusalem. Second, nevertheless Christians live in that city, not in the sense that they are an enclave within it, but they are to regard themselves as members in good standing, with the rights and privileges of membership, whatever from time to time these may be, unless they are expressly prevented from holding these rights and privileges. Third, the formation and flourishing of the celestial city is helped by the civic peace that the earthly city affords, and to which Christians contribute as best they may.

I believe that in asserting these political themes Augustine was echoing themes of the New Testament itself, and that we do well to allow our own political stance in the rather different (but not altogether different) circumstances in which we live to be governed by these themes.[17]

Bibliography

Audi, Robert (2000), *Religious Commitment and Secular Reason*, Cambridge: Cambridge University Press.

Audi, Robert and Wolterstorff, Nicholas (1997), *Religion in the Public Square: The Place of Religious Convictions in Political Debate*, London and New York: Rowman and Littlefield.

---

during the 390s, he wrote in terms of the 'christianization' of society. Such optimism was gone by 405, and in the *City of God* Augustine sought to undermine the theological foundations of his previous optimism. See Robert A. Markus, '"*Tempora Christiana*" Revisited', in Robert Dodaro and George Lawless (eds.), *St Augustine and his Critics*.

17. Thanks to David Hoffner for reading this text and correcting a number of mistakes.

Clark, J. C. D. (1985), *English Society 1688–1832*, Cambridge: Cambridge University Press.

Dodaro, Robert and Lawless, George (eds.) (2000), *St Augustine and his Critics: Essays in Honour of Gerald Bonner*, London: Routledge.

Leith, John H. (ed.) (1982), *Creeds of the Churches*, 3rd edn, Atlanta: John Knox Press.

Mill, John Stuart (1859), *On Liberty*, Oxford: World's Classics, 1912.

Milton, John (1834), *The Prose Works*, London.

Rescher, Nicholas (1993), *Pluralism: Against the Demand for Consensus*, Oxford: Clarendon Press.

6. THE CROWN RIGHTS OF KING JESUS TODAY

David McKay

All through the history of the church, the central assertion of the people of God has been that 'Jesus is Lord'. The church has proclaimed, with varying degrees of clarity and consistency, the kingly reign of the Lord Jesus Christ. Whatever the calling of God's people with reference to contemporary society may be, it will undoubtedly centre on Christ, crucified, risen and reigning.

The phrase 'the crown rights of King Jesus' has come to have particular associations with the Scottish Covenanters of the seventeenth century and their successors in the various branches of the Reformed Presbyterian Church, who still consider themselves to be 'Covenanters'. They of course have no monopoly of the doctrine of Christ's kingship, but it is in these circles that considerable attention has been given to the interrelationship between Christ's royal authority and socio-political engagement.

The nineteenth century produced a number of pastor-theologians in the Reformed Presbyterian Churches of North America and of Scotland who addressed many of the issues raised by an assertion of 'the crown rights of King Jesus'. This study will begin by setting out some fundamental principles regarding Christ's kingship as expounded by one of these authors, who is representative of their general approach. We will then move on to examine a number of doctrinal issues which need to be considered in greater depth, concluding with several areas of practical application which are particularly divisive in Christian circles, as well as beyond.

Basic principles

In order to open up a pathway into the subject of the crown rights of King Jesus, we may turn to an influential publication by Alexander McLeod (1774–1833), a Scotsman who became pastor of the Reformed Presbyterian congregation in New York. In his day, he was widely read and respected as a defender of biblical orthodoxy. The focus of our attention is McLeod's *Messiah, Governor of the Nations of the Earth*, first published in 1803 and reprinted in 1992.[1]

The text which McLeod takes as his starting point is Revelation 1:5, Jesus Christ 'the Prince of the Kings of the earth'. As McLeod indicates, the word translated 'prince' is the Greek *archōn*, often translated 'ruler' in the New Testament. Christ is a ruler and his subjects are the kings of the earth 'in their official characters'.[2] This assertion, which McLeod holds in common with other Reformed Presbyterian writers on the subject, is foundational to his view of the crown rights of King Jesus. It is over kings *as kings*, not merely in their private capacity, that Christ reigns.[3] McLeod goes on to assert:

The word for kings (basileus) is not a personal designation, nor is it confined to the chief magistrate of a monarchal or despotic

---

1. Alexander McLeod (1803), *Messiah, Governor of the Nations of the Earth* (Elmwood Park, NJ: Reformed Presbyterian Press, 1992).

2. McLeod, *Messiah*, p. 3.

3. See for example: James Willson, *Prince Messiah's Claims to Dominion over all Governments* (Albany, NY: Packard, Hoffman and White, 1832), pp. 13–17; Samuel B. Wylie, *The Two Sons of Oil; or the Faithful Witness for Magistracy and Ministry upon a Scriptural Basis* (Philadelphia, PA: Wm. S. Young, 1850), p. 19. The most extended treatment of the subject is by the Scottish

government. It would be a perversion of Scripture and of common sense to affirm that nations governed by kings were ruled by the Mediator while of other forms of government he took no notice.[4]

Two issues then occupy McLeod's attention: first a defence of his view that Christ as Mediator rules over all the nations of the earth, and second an exposition of the acts of Christ's government.

Christ as Mediator rules over all the nations of the earth

The great truths regarding Christ's gracious mediatorial work are known only through divine revelation. To establish the fact of Christ's mediatorial rule over the nations appeal can be made both to the explicit teaching of the Bible and also to inferences legitimately drawn from explicit statements. On this basis McLeod offers six lines of argument:

The character of Jesus Christ

By this McLeod means what he terms 'a moral fitness in the mediatorial person to be the Governor among the nations'.[5] Whilst intelligence and power to carry through plans to completion are requisite in such a Ruler, it is the moral character he possesses that chiefly fits Christ for the exercise of rule over the nations. He is possessed of supreme moral excellence as God. In addition, as God he has perfect knowledge of all man's needs and as man he understands human infirmities from personal experience.

The necessity of Christ's rule

As McLeod puts it, 'It is necessary that Messiah should rule the nations because otherwise the mediatorial office would be

---

Reformed Presbyterian pastor William Symington in *Messiah the Prince or, The Mediatorial Dominion of Jesus Christ*, originally published in 1839. The most accessible edition is the 1990 reprint of the 1884 American edition (Edmonton, AB: Still Waters Revival Books, 1990). See especially chapters 8 and 9.

4. McLeod, *Messiah*, pp. 3–4.

5. McLeod, *Messiah*, p. 5.

inadequate and imperfect.'[6] Here a link is made between the atonement offered by Christ at the cross and the application of that atonement in the salvation of sinners. In particular, the fulfilment of the Great Commission entails Christ's supremacy over the nations: 'Unless his authority were paramount to that of the existing governments, it would have been a usurpation inconsistent with divine perfection to have sent his ambassadors to negotiate with the inhabitants of the earth.'[7]

It is the supreme authority of Christ that ensures the effective preaching of the gospel in spite of the opposition of rulers and peoples to that message. It is an authority, as Philippians 2:8–9 demonstrates, which is a reward for his redemptive sufferings and which ensures the fulfilment of all his purposes. It is also an authority which ensures the preservation of his church in the midst of its enemies.

The promise of the Father to the Son

McLeod bases his comments on this matter first on Old Testament passages such as Psalm 2:8 and Psalm 89:19, 23, 25–27, which he sees as being fulfilled in Christ's royal reign. Although the term itself is not used by McLeod, he is working here within the framework of what is known as the Covenant of Redemption. In some varieties of Federal Theology this is the pre-temporal covenant established within the Trinity in order to provide redemption for God's elect. [8] In McLeod's words: 'The Scriptures uniformly teach that the Father has engaged to place the Mediator on the throne of the nations upon condition that he should become a substitute for sinners and make atonement for them.'[9] The repeated quotations from Psalm 2 in Acts, Hebrews and Revelation with reference to Christ are particularly significant for understanding his mediatorial reign. It is

---

6. McLeod, *Messiah*, p. 7.

7. McLeod, *Messiah*, p. 8.

8. A concise summary is provided by Louis Berkhof in *Systematic Theology* (London: Banner of Truth Trust, 1958), pp. 265–271.

9. McLeod, *Messiah*, p. 11.

noteworthy that in Psalm 2:10–12 rulers are exhorted to submit to Christ, and in Isaiah 53:12 Christ's exaltation and suffering are closely linked.

Christ's authorization to rule the kingdoms of the earth

Two biblical passages are cited as proof of the giving to Christ of a commission which authorized him to rule over all nations. The first is Daniel 7:13–14, the vision in which 'one like the Son of man' comes to 'the Ancient of days' and receives from him 'dominion, and glory, and a kingdom, that all people, nations, and languages should serve him' (AV). The one like the Son of man is the Mediator, and to him is given authority over the nations. In McLeod's view, he was proclaimed King of Kings at his ascension to the Father's right hand, but 'he actually governed in this capacity from the period in which mercy first dawned on our guilty world'.[10] An example of the latter is found in Genesis 3:8ff, where the Mediator reveals God's gracious answer to man's sin.

The second passage is Revelation 5:1–2, 5–7, where only 'the Lion of the tribe of Judah, the Root of David' is found worthy to open the sealed book of God's purposes. In the taking of the book and the opening of the seals the reign of the Messiah over all things, including the kings of the earth, is depicted.

The testimony of Christ himself

In addressing the Father, Jesus states, 'Thou hast given him power over all flesh' (John 17:2), and to his people he says, 'All things are delivered to me of my Father' (Luke 10:22). The incarnation did not entail the giving up of any of the essential perfections possessed by the eternal Son. He always possessed the *ability* to govern the nations, McLeod argues, but in his official capacity as Mediator he required the *authority* to rule, and this the Father has conferred upon him. Christ can on this basis lay claim to all authority in heaven and on earth, as he does in Matthew 28:18. He exercises unbounded authority over every creature, whether in heaven or on earth.

---

10. McLeod, *Messiah*, pp. 14–15.

The confirmation of other witnesses

A number of other witnesses are quoted to confirm the Mediator's authority to rule the nations. The witness of the Holy Spirit is drawn from some of the Scriptures he has inspired, in particular Psalm 8:6 as expounded in Hebrews 2:8 and applied to Christ. The nations and their rulers have been put under the feet of Christ. A second set of witnesses comprises the four living creatures, who testify to Christ's headship over the nations in Revelation 5:8–9, along with the twenty-four elders, who join in their song. In McLeod's view the creatures represent all faithful ministers of Christ, whilst the elders denote the saints of both Old and New Testaments. The final witnesses are the church in glory together with the angels. Their testimony is to be found in passages such as Revelation 5:11–13. McLeod concludes, 'Whatever may be the present views of rational creatures, there is a day coming when none can deny that Jesus is Lord of Lords.'[11]

The acts of Christ's government

Although McLeod recognizes that it would be impossible to list all the acts of Christ in his capacity as Ruler of the nations, he nevertheless selects a number of aspects of this royal work which in fact cover a very wide range of matters.

Christ executes God's purposes for the nations

McLeod begins with a strong assertion of the sovereign power of Christ, applying to him Paul's reference in Ephesians 1:11 to 'him who worketh all things after the counsel of his own will' (AV). Thus he says:

> The origin, progress, and dissolution of national associations and governments, and every accompanying circumstance, were fore-ordained by him . . . There is not a motion or a change in the physical or moral world he did not foresee, and to which he did not give a place in eternal arrangements.[12]

---

11. McLeod, *Messiah*, p. 22.
12. McLeod, *Messiah*, p. 23.

McLeod then applies this statement in two ways. He asserts first Christ's direction of the rise, progress and fall of nations. Whatever the proximate causes of the history of each nation, none can operate independently of the Lord. The details of national history are as subject to divine providence as are the great events of rise and fall. Even those endeavouring to bring about changes of government are subject to God, whether they succeed or fail.

The second application of this truth is for the comfort of the church. The actual execution of the divine plan is in the hands of the Mediator, and it is here that McLeod makes more specific reference to Christ. He has been given power over all mankind and all things have been given into his hands by the Father, as stated in John 17:2 and Matthew 11:27. McLeod believes that one of the purposes of the book of Revelation is to illustrate this truth and so comfort the church. Here again Christ's opening of the seals in Revelation 5 is significant. McLeod sees in Revelation a depiction of historical events from the fall of the Roman Empire to the fall of the Papacy and of the European governments supporting it. At the consummation of history, the Mediator will confer universal dominion on the saints.

Christ opens doors for the gospel

Since every unregenerate person is at enmity with God (as Rom. 8:7 indicates), the kingdoms of this world are opposed to the outworking of God's gracious plan. Governments constituted without reference to God and so without his approval receive sanction from 'the prince of the power of the air' (Eph. 2:2, AV) and are depicted as the beast rising out of the sea in Revelation 13:1-3. Christ the King, as supreme over the nations, turns all their activities to serve his purpose and ensures the entrance of the gospel among them. As Matthew 28:18ff indicates, the Mediator who claims all authority also commissions his messengers to go into all the nations, with the promise that he is always with them. The church is constantly encouraged by assurances of Christ's power to rule the nations, by which he opens a door that no-one can shut (Rev. 3:7ff). It is very important to note McLeod's emphasis on the spread of the gospel. It shows that an interest in the political application of biblical truth need not diminish a concern for evangelism and mission, although some fear that this will be the case.

Christ calls their subjects into his kingdom
This is in a sense a logical extension of the previous point. Not only has Christ the authority to send preachers into the dominions of the rulers of the nations, he also has authority 'to take those over whom they rule under his protection and enlist them under his banner'.[13] Not only does King Jesus provide for the preaching of the gospel but he also, by sending out the Holy Spirit, secures a positive response among the citizens of the nations. Although those who are converted continue to live as citizens of their respective nations, the Lord teaches them that 'there is no concern or business incident to humanity, either in an individual or collective capacity, that the principles and motives of Christianity ought not to pervade and govern'.[14] Allegiance to King Jesus transforms life in all its aspects.

As history demonstrates, even active persecution by the rulers of the nations serves, rather than frustrates, the King's saving purposes. He demonstrates the power of his grace by supporting the persecuted; persecution scatters believers and so spreads the gospel further afield; martyrs who seal their testimony with their blood are introduced into endless happiness. Nothing can halt the growth of his kingdom.

Christ instructs earthly rulers how they are to conduct themselves with respect to the church
In common with many theologians of diverse viewpoints throughout the history of the church, McLeod holds that rulers are to promote true religion and protect the true church. Although Christ's kingdom is 'not of this world' (John 18:36), the kingdoms of the world are bound to recognize its existence. In countries enjoying the light of the gospel, rulers cannot ignore the presence

---

13. McLeod, *Messiah*, p. 29.
14. McLeod, *Messiah*, p. 29.

of the church of Christ, nor can they legislate as if it did not exist. To behave thus would be to set themselves in direct rebellion against the authority of God, exercised by the Messiah. Hence the exhortation to kings in Psalm 2:10, 12: 'Kiss the Son'.

On the one hand, rulers are to remove impediments to the progress of the church, since the diffusion of Christian principles advances individual and social happiness. Coercion may never be used to make subjects Christians, but it must be used 'to suppress immorality, prophaneness [sic], and blasphemy, and to remove the monuments of idolatry from the land'.[15]

On the other hand, it is the duty of rulers to protect and support the church. How this works out in practice, says McLeod, will vary depending on circumstances, but it cannot be rejected entirely. Scripture sets out qualifications for civil rulers and commands them to succour the church. Passages cited in this regard are 2 Samuel 23:3–4, Romans 13:3–4 and Isaiah 49:23 and 60:16; Hezekiah is held up as an example of such actions (2 Kgs 18:3–4, 7).

Christ overrules the disobedience of governments and renders all national acts subservient to his own glory and the church's good
Whether or not individuals or societies want to serve the Messiah, they in fact do so: even the wrath of man praises him. By his providential working he overrules the actions of sinful men and bends them to advance the cause of his church. Christ's decrees are inevitably fulfilled. As the Scriptures put it, no weapon against Zion will prosper, since all things are under the feet of the Mediator.

Christ punishes the powers of the earth for the neglect of their duty
The fact that Christ overrules the actions of rulers so that they serve his cause does not in any way reduce the sinfulness of opposition to him. All will be called to account and kings and judges who do not submit to him will 'perish from the way', to use the language of Psalm 2:12. As McLeod says, 'Christ not only administers covenant blessings to his church; he also dispenses

---

15. McLeod, *Messiah*, p. 33.

the cup of God's wrath to the wicked.'[16] This he does in various ways, including the overthrow of tyrants in revolutions. Psalm 110:5–6 speaks of the Messiah crushing kings in the day of his wrath, whilst in Ezekiel 21:26–27 he is portrayed as removing crowns and replacing rulers. King Jesus cannot be disobeyed with impunity, and all rulers are accountable to him.

Key Doctrines

Having surveyed one influential approach to the crown rights of King Jesus, we may now turn to address a number of important doctrinal issues which the subject under consideration inevitably raises.

Christianity as world-and-life-view
We begin with an appeal for what might be termed 'big-picture thinking'. Christian contributions to contemporary political and social debates are often fragmented and disorganized, reflecting the lack of a coherent theological perspective which would provide necessary biblical strength and unity. The result is that Christians generally respond only to perceived threats, rather than formulating carefully thought-out positions on the major issues confronting society. It is no surprise that the world often regards them as entirely negative voices in the public square. The situation is exacerbated by zealous Christians who believe that their only responsibility is to preach the gospel, leaving social and political concerns to those whose theology is dubious or downright 'unsound'. The cure for such fragmentation and the resultant ineffectiveness of much Christian activity is a renewed biblical vision for the whole of life lived in obedience to King Jesus.

The position expounded by McLeod and those who share his outlook assumes that issues of politics, government and social involvement are not beyond the concern of the church or of individual Christians. Much of what they have to say is based on

---

16. McLeod, *Messiah*, pp. 36–37.

the assumption that every aspect of life is touched and is to be shaped by the royal authority of the Mediator. This is reflected, for example, in William Symington's statement that:

> [Christ's] authority extends to *associations* of every description, domestic, civil and ecclesiastical. The social principle is deeply lodged in the constitution of man, and makes its appearance in a thousand varied forms . . . Societies, like persons, are under the government of God, and subject to the divine law. Bodies-politic or corporations are to be regarded as large moral subjects. [17]

There is in this perspective a thoroughgoing rejection of any privatization of the Christian faith. Christian principles cannot be restricted in their application to private and church matters (however those are envisaged), but have relevance to every sphere of life. The task of the people of God, individually and corporately, is not only to seek the conversion of sinners, but also to train them to live in every part of life in accordance with the royal word of King Jesus. The commission of Matthew 28:19 is 'go and make disciples of all nations', and that disciple-making will have an impact on everything the disciple does, in public as well as private life.

Although these Covenanter writers do not use this terminology, implicit in their position is a belief that Christianity must be thought of as a 'world-and-life-view'. This is a perspective which has become common in Calvinistic thinking, especially in its Dutch form. Often the term 'worldview' is used. Although, as David Naugle has shown,[18] 'worldview' and its German antecedent *Weltanschauung* have a long and complex history of use in philosophy, a number of Reformed thinkers have made use of this terminology to express a crucial insight regarding the Christian faith. As a worldview, Christianity embraces every aspect of life and thus provides no ground for distinctions between the 'sacred'

---

17. Symington, *Messiah the Prince*, p. 97.
18. David K. Naugle, *Worldview: The History of a Concept*, (Grand Rapids/Cambridge: Eerdmans, 2002).

and the 'secular'. For the Christian seeking to live out his faith consistently, all of life is religious.

The development of worldview thinking of a distinctively Christian variety is associated especially with the Dutch theologian, philosopher and politician Abraham Kuyper (1837–1920), although earlier writers such as James Orr (1844–1913) did significant pioneering work in this field.[19] Using the terms 'life-system' and 'life and world view', which he preferred to other alternatives, Kuyper argued in his 1898 Stone Lectures at Princeton University that 'Calvinism is not a partial, nor was a merely temporary phenomenon, but is such an all-embracing system of principles, as, rooted in the past, is able to strengthen us in the present and to fill us with confidence for the future.'[20]

It is Kuyper's contention that every life-system or worldview must address three comprehensive, fundamental relations in which every person stands, namely 'our relation to *God*, to *man* and to the *world*'.[21] He expands this as follows:

> For our relation to *God*: an immediate fellowship of man with the Eternal, independently of priest or church. For the relation of man to *man*: the recognition in each person of human worth, which is by virtue of his creation after the Divine likeness, and therefore of the equality of all men before God and his magistrate. And for our relation to *the world*: the recognition that in the whole world the curse is restrained by grace, that the life of the world is to be honored in its independence, and that we must, in every domain, discover the treasures and develop the potencies hidden by God in nature and in human life.[22]

19. James Orr, *The Christian View of God and the World as Centring in the Incarnation*, 4th edn (Edinburgh: Andrew Elliott, 1897).

20. Abraham Kuyper, *Lectures on Calvinism*, (Grand Rapids: William B. Eerdmans, 1931), p. 19. An excellent commentary on Kuyper's lectures is *Creating a Christian Worldview* by Peter S. Heslam (Grand Rapids/Cambridge: Eerdmans; Carlisle: Paternoster Press, 1998).

21. Kuyper, *Lectures*, p. 31.

22. Kuyper, *Lectures*, p. 31.

Such relations are addressed fully in the divine revelation on which Christianity is based, a Christianity best expressed, in Kuyper's view, in historic Calvinism.

Whilst we would disagree with some of Kuyper's applications of his principles, for example in regard to racial issues, it does appear that he is correct to designate Christianity as a life-system or world-and-life-view, which embraces every aspect of life. No aspect is beyond the concern of the God who speaks in Scripture and so cannot be beyond the concern of those seeking to live faithfully for him in his world. If this is indeed the case, the 'crown rights of King Jesus' must be seen to have application beyond the private and the ecclesiastical realms. Those rights must relate to all of life, including the spheres of politics, government and social action. They cannot be restricted in any way, lest dishonour be done to the King.

The fact that the King has 'rights' implies that his subjects have 'responsibilities', and it is important to stress that Christianity is a world-*and-life*-view. It is more than an intellectual construct or a set of propositional truths, although it includes both. The Christian faith also sets out the marching orders for the King's army. His exercise of his crown rights requires a certain lifestyle to be implemented in each person's calling in the world. The King makes demands on each person's thinking *and* acting.

This issue has been addressed recently by James Sire in *Naming the Elephant*, a companion volume to his much-used handbook of worldviews, *The Universe Next Door*.[23] With the subtitle 'Worldview as a concept', the book examines crucial issues involved in defining 'worldview' and critically reconsiders Sire's own definition in his earlier writing. A significant modification which Sire now considers necessary is the inclusion of living along with thinking. He writes, for example, of 'Worldview as a Way of Life',[24] showing how people demonstrate their worldview by the way that they live.

---

23. James Sire, *Naming the Elephant* (Downers Grove: InterVarsity Press, 2004) and *The Universe Next Door*, 4th edn (Downers Grove: InterVarsity Press, 2004).

24. Sire, *Naming the Elephant*, p. 98.

Worldviews are, he says, 'ways of seeing'. In this connection he quotes the opinion of Walsh and Middleton that 'A world view is never merely a vision of life. It is always a vision *for* life.'[25] Sire writes too of 'Worldview as Master Story' and stresses that Christians *indwell* the biblical story in daily living.

The 'crown rights of King Jesus' entail a world-and-life-view which is comprehensive in its scope and demands for thinking and living. No aspect of life operates according to its own autonomous rights; no aspect of life is beyond the Christian's concern. Writing in 1947 to expose the folly of evangelical withdrawal from social engagement, Carl Henry spoke of 'the uneasy conscience of modern fundamentalism'.[26] A thoroughly biblical understanding of the King's crown rights will address that unease which still troubles many.

Ideologies and idolatries

Attempts to assert the crown rights of King Jesus in the public arena often meet with the objection that to do so is to import religion into a sphere where it has no place. The impression is given that a variety of non-religious social philosophies and political ideologies compete in the public arena for allegiance, and so references to God, to Jesus Christ, to Christianity or to the Bible are dismissed as alien intruders who have left their proper sphere. At best Christians are making a category mistake in speaking as they do; at worst they are seeking to set up a 'theocracy' (apparently one of the worst offences that can be committed in political life).

The fallacy of this common view has been exposed by a number of thinkers – theologians, philosophers, social theorists – from a variety of religious traditions. Writing in 1984, Richard John Neuhaus, at the time a Lutheran and now a Roman Catholic, spoke about 'the naked public square'. Introducing his study of the same name, he stated:

---

25. Brian J. Walsh and J. Richard Middleton, *The Transforming Vision: Shaping a Christian World View* (Downers Grove: InterVarsity Press, 1984), p. 31.
26. Carl F. H. Henry, *The Uneasy Conscience of Modern Fundamentalism*, 1947 edn (Grand Rapids/Cambridge: Eerdmans, 2003).

The naked public square is the result of a political doctrine and practice that would exclude religion and religiously grounded values from the conduct of public business. The doctrine is that America is a secular society. It finds dogmatic expression in the ideology of secularism. I will argue that the doctrine is demonstrably false and the dogma exceedingly dangerous.[27]

Neuhaus went on to say that a central claim of his book is that:

[T]he public square will not and cannot remain naked. If it is not clothed with the 'meanings' borne by religion, new 'meanings' will be imposed by virtue of the ambitions of the modern state.[28]

When attempts are being made to achieve or retain the 'nakedness' of the public square, prospects for the assertion of the crown rights of King Jesus are not promising.

Whilst Neuhaus highlights one of the greatest problems faced by those seeking to make a Christian impact on public life, we need to probe deeper in order to understand the forces that are actually at work in the public square. When the competing options that are on offer in the public square are examined more closely, it becomes apparent that they are in fact *all religious*. The claims of Christ asserted by Christians are actually no more – and no less – religious than the claims of the other voices in the square. If all 'religious' voices are silenced, not a sound will be heard in the square.

This assertion may at first appear to be counter-intuitive: are not many ideologies on offer in the public square blatantly secular? Careful analysis of the ideologies, however, such as that conducted by political scientist David Koyzis,[29] demonstrates that all ideologies are religious and, unless submitted to the Lordship of Christ,

---

27. Richard John Neuhaus, *The Naked Public Square: Religion and Democracy in America* (Grand Rapids: Eerdmans, 1984), p. vii.

28. Neuhaus, *The Naked Public Square*, p. vii.

29. David T. Koyzis, *Political Visions and Illusions* (Downers Grove: InterVarsity Press, 2003). Koyzis teaches at Redeemer College, Ancaster, Ontario.

idolatrous. The ideologies surveyed by Koyzis are Liberalism, Conservatism, Nationalism, Democracy and Socialism, the main contenders for allegiance historically and currently. Koyzis identifies five characteristics of ideologies which expose the core of their true nature:[30]

• Ideologies are inescapably religious. Koyzis argues, convincingly, that an ideology flows out of the idolatrous religious commitment of a person or a community. Idolatry is defined as putting something else in the place of God, and on that basis all other sins may be regarded as expressions of idolatry. As Paul argues in the opening chapters of Romans, sinners put something taken from the creation in the place of the Creator and accord it worship and service. An idol need not be in the form of a carved image: it may be human reason, military might, one's homeland, the nation. Even 'atheists' worship a god and serve some 'higher power', often some aspect of their own being.

In this regard Koyzis cites the work of Dutch thinker Bob Goudzwaard on the connection between ideology and idolatry. Goudzwaard argues that the religious nature of human beings can be understood in terms of 'three basic biblical rules'.[31] The first rule is that every man is serving god(s) in his life, seeking the resting place for his restless soul, to use Augustine's description. Goudzwaard mentions technology and intellect as possible gods. The second rule is that every man is transformed into an image of his god. The choice of one's god has therefore far-reaching consequences for how one lives. Paul in Romans 1:24–25 speaks of the animal behaviour of those whose gods were such creatures. Thus if reason is a man's god, he will rationalize every aspect of life. The third rule is that mankind creates and forms a

---

30. Koyzis, *Political Visions*, pp. 27–34. The full analysis is well worth careful consideration.

31. Bob Goudzwaard, *Aid for the Overdeveloped West* (Toronto: Wedge Publishing Foundation, 1978), p. 14.

structure of society in its own image. Man produces a society which reflects his own likeness and so, ultimately, the likeness of his god. Idolatry cannot be confined to some personal, privatized realm, any more than can biblical Christianity.

- If ideologies deify something within God's creation, they inevitably view this humanly made god as a source of salvation. This is the soteriological dimension of idolatry, whereby the false god promises deliverance to human beings from some fundamental evil. In political terms, that evil could be poverty, oppression, anarchy or any one of a number of societal ills. Salvation might then come from the communal ownership of the means of production, liberation from foreign domination, either military or economic, or the submission of citizens to the collective will of the State.
- Ideologies tend to locate the source of this evil somewhere within the creation. Ideologies thus establish their own antithesis between supposed good and supposed evil. Koyzis sees in this a revival of ancient Gnosticism, whereby evil was located in the material creation and salvation consisted of liberation from the created order.
- Given this defective soteriology, ideologies have a fundamentally distorted view of the world, and hence of government and politics. Because people live out their religious views, albeit more or less consistently, political life is deeply affected by idolatry. Some may see the State as the source of salvation, as in various totalitarian ideologies, whilst others may regard the State as a source of evil, as in some libertarian ideologies. Each has profound effects on public policy and on individual lives.
- In the modern ideologies goals supplant principles. Ultimately the end is seen as justifying the means, and pragmatism rules. As Koyzis points out, this means that, for example, justice ceases to be a norm governing all political action and instead becomes a goal to be achieved at some (probably distant) time.

Those who seek to assert the crown rights of King Jesus are thus entering a spiritual and religious battle, which must be recognized for what it is. Even humanism and secularism are idolatrous religions which worship the creature rather than the Creator. The true nature of the contending ideologies needs to be exposed as religious, when the cry often heard is to keep 'religion' out of the public square. It cannot be kept out.

The King and his kingdom

Discussion of the crown rights of King Jesus will dissolve into utter confusion if there is not a clear understanding of the nature of his kingship.

The first generations of Covenanters, including Commissioners to the Westminster Assembly such as Samuel Rutherford and George Gillespie, generally held the view of Christ's kingship current among Reformed theologians of their day. This view distinguished between the rule which Christ exercises as eternal Son, along with the Father and the Holy Spirit, which embraces the whole creation, and the rule which he exercises as Mediator, the God-man, which is over the church.

The views of George Gillespie, for example, emerged in the course of a pamphlet debate with Erastian divine Thomas Coleman. The latter asserted that Christ rules over all things as Mediator, and sought to deduce from this his own view of the civil magistrate's authority in church affairs. In his first contribution to the debate, entitled *A Brotherly Examination*, Gillespie stated at the outset the principle on which both writers agreed, namely 'that Christ, as he is the eternal Son of God . . . doth, with the Father and the Holy Ghost, reign and rule over all the kingdoms of the sons of men'.[32] As Mediator, the eternal Son of God made flesh, crucified and risen in triumph, Christ also exercises dominion. As God, he has power to subdue the Church's enemies, but, argued Gillespie, 'as Mediator he is only the Church's King, Head, and Governor, and hath no other Kingdom'.[33]

---

32. George Gillespie, *A Brotherly Examination of some passages of Mr Coleman's Late Sermon upon Job xi.20 as it is now printed* (London: Robert Bostock, 1645), reprinted in *The Presbyterian's Armoury* (Edinburgh: Robert Ogle and Oliver and Boyd, 1846), vol. 1, p. 11.

33. Gillespie, *A Brotherly Examination*, p. 11. For a fuller examination of these debates in the wider Reformed context, see: W. D. J. McKay, *An

Gillespie's concern was to avoid any suggestion that as Mediator Christ is king over those who are not members of his spiritual body: specifically, in the context of the debate with Coleman, over unbelieving rulers and magistrates. Thus, when he came to a text like Ephesians 2:22, which reads 'God placed all things under his feet and appointed him to be head over everything for the church', Gillespie opted for a different translation. In his view the verse should read 'him who is over all, he gave to be head to the church', implying that God gave to the church as head the Christ who was already over all things as Son of God. According to Gillespie's case, Christ is exalted above all principalities and powers and exercises dominion over them *as God* (along with the Father and the Holy Spirit), but not as Mediator. This is summed up in the heading of one of the chapters in his influential treatise *Aaron's Rod Blossoming* (1646):

> Of a twofold kingdom of Jesus Christ: a general kingdom, as he is the eternal Son of God, the head of all principalities and powers, reigning over all creatures; and a particular kingdom, as he is Mediator reigning over the church only.[34]

In using the terminology of 'two kingdoms' Gillespie shows himself to be within the broad stream of Reformation theology extending back to Luther and Calvin. Luther's doctrine of the Two Kingdoms has provoked endless controversy, not least because he formulates the distinction in various ways in his writings.[35] He speaks often of the kingdom over which Christ reigns by his word, the kingdom comprising all those who are justified by faith, the

Ecclesiastical Republic: Church Government in the Writings of George Gillespie (Carlisle/Edinburgh: Paternoster Press/Rutherford House, 1997), cpt 2.

34. George Gillespie, *Aaron's Rod Blossoming; or, the Divine Ordinance of Church Government Vindicated* (London: Richard Whitaker, 1646), reprinted in *The Presbyterian's Armoury*, vol. 2. The title is that of book 2, chapter 5.

35. A helpful consideration of Luther's views is by J. R. Stephenson, 'The Two Governments and the Two Kingdoms', *Scottish Journal of Theology*, 34.4 (1981).

kingdom over which Christ became king as a result of his death on the cross by which he conquered sin, death and Satan. In its present form this kingdom of Christ is hidden from the world. As Luther puts it, with reference to Psalm 2:8,

> This King will not change or abolish this course or order of the world. For His kingdom is not of this world. But to all kingdoms, to all commonwealths, He will bring the new Word and new teaching about Himself that all who believe in him and are baptised will have forgiveness of sins and life eternal. This is the kingdom of this King, this is His dominion, this is His imperium.[36]

As far as Christ's authority over the nations is concerned, Luther ascribes supreme authority to Christ and relates it closely to the bringing of the gospel to the Gentiles. Commenting on the same verse, he continues:

> The Lord has granted to Christ the King the rule over all nations, and so through His gospel He calls all nations to faith . . . the rule over all nations has been given to our King so that they are His possession, that is, so that through Him they are saved and receive the remission of sins and the Holy Spirit.[37]

It is characteristic of the complexities of Luther's thought, however, that he is able at other times to speak of two forms of 'government' in the world. These he terms *zwei Regimente*, but unfortunately he also refers to them as *zwei Reiche*, using the terms by which he refers to the kingdoms of Christ and Satan elsewhere. The two governments are not in opposition but are correlates which express God's authority over the *Corpus Christianum*. The two forms of government are the spiritual and the secular. As far as the spiritual government is concerned, Christ rules his people through the church by his word, exercising authority over the soul.

---

36. Martin Luther, *Works* (St Louis: Concordia; Philadelphia: Muhlenberg Press, 1955–86), vol. 12, p. 57.
37. Luther, *Works*, vol. 12, p. 58.

Secular authority, on the other hand, is wielded by the magistrate, who has authority over the body, not the soul, and who is able to use force to coerce obedience. The Christian is under both the spiritual authority of Christ and the secular authority of emperor, prince or magistrate. Although Luther considers the latter to be necessary, he regards rulers as performing God's *opus alienum* in restraining outward sin by force, and he does not succeed in relating this authority to Christ directly.

As we might expect, John Calvin also links the reign of Christ closely to the church. Thus, for example, in comments on 1 Thessalonians 1:1 Calvin states that 'we are to seek the Church only where God is Head and where Christ reigns'.[38] Indeed 'Kingdom of Christ' is, along with 'Body of Christ', frequently used by Calvin as a description of the church, as for example in *Institutes* 4.2.4, when he says that 'the church is Christ's Kingdom, and he reigns by his Word alone'.[39] Calvin stresses that the kingdom of Christ is spiritual: it is nothing else than 'the inward and spiritual renewal of the soul'.[40] Although Calvin does not speak explicitly of a mediatorial Kingship, it is significant that he juxtaposes his treatment of Christ's work as Mediator (*Institutes* 2.12–14) with that of Christ's threefold office of Prophet, Priest and King (*Institutes* 2.15). He appears to envisage that these three functions constitute Christ's mediatorial work, which he discusses entirely in relation to the salvation of the Church.

Calvin also deals with the issue of government in Book 4 of the *Institutes*. He too speaks of two forms of government, indeed of two 'kingdoms':

[T]here is a twofold government in man: one aspect is spiritual, whereby

---

38. John Calvin, *The Epistles of Paul the Apostle to the Romans and to the Thessalonians*, translated by Ross Mackenzie (Edinburgh: St Andrew Press, 1961), ad loc.

39. John Calvin, *Institutes of the Christian Religion* (1559 edn), translated by Ford Lewis Battles (Philadelphia: Westminster Press, 1960), 4.2.4.

40. John Calvin, *A Harmony of the Gospels of Matthew, Mark and Luke*, translated by A. W. Morrison (Edinburgh: St Andrew Press, 1972): comment on Luke 17:20.

the conscience is instructed in piety and in reverencing God; the second is political, whereby man is educated for the duties of humanity and citizenship that must be maintained among men. These are usually called the 'spiritual' and the 'temporal' jurisdictions . . . The one we may call the spiritual kingdom, the other, the political kingdom . . . There are in man, so to speak, two worlds, over which different kings and different laws have authority.[41]

Although Calvin stresses that civil government is totally distinct from the kingdom of Christ, which is entirely spiritual, he also recognizes on the basis of passages such as Romans 13 that civil government is instituted by God to promote peace and general well-being, to restrain and punish sin, to encourage godly living and to facilitate the work of the church. He speaks at one point of magistrates as 'vicars of God',[42] although he does not at that point relate them directly to Christ. One other reference to Christ's reign, however, is of particular interest. In expounding Psalm 2:8, which he takes to be prophetic of Christ's reign, Calvin writes:

As the eternal Word of God, Christ, it is true, has always had in his hands by right sovereign authority and majesty, and as such can receive no accessions thereto; but still he is exalted in human nature, in which he took upon him the form of a servant. This title, therefore, [i.e. 'governor over the whole world'] is not applied to him only as God, but is extended to the whole person of the Mediator.[43]

Calvin links this authority of Christ with the calling of the Gentiles to salvation, and also argues that rulers are to demonstrate their devotion to God by submission to the Son whom he has placed over all things. As Douglas Kelly comments in a useful study of Calvin's sermons on 2 Samuel, '[Calvin's] thought

41. Calvin, *Institutes*, 3.19.15.

42. Calvin, *Institutes*, 4.20.6.

43. John Calvin, *Commentary on the Book of Psalms*, translated by James Anderson (Grand Rapids: Eerdmans, 1963), ad loc.

was marked by a strong political concern throughout his entire life.'[44]

Post-Reformation Reformed dogmaticians generally deal with the kingship of Christ in connection with his threefold office. They then speak of a twofold kingship, making distinctions similar to those found in Gillespie. On the one hand, there is the *regnum Christi* in a general sense (also termed the essential, natural or universal kingdom) which, as the eternal Son of God, Christ exercises over the world along with the Father and the Holy Spirit. On the other hand, there is the *regnum personale* or *regnum oeconomicum*, defined as the kingdom of grace which accrues to Christ as the God-man. This position is well summarized by Johann Alsted in his *Theologia Scholastica Didactica* (1618):

> Christ's Kingship is twofold, essential and personal; the essential, which is
> also called natural or universal, Christ holds with a glory and majesty
> equal to the Father and the Holy Spirit; the personal, which is also called
> the donative, the economic and the dispensative, Christ administers as the
> *theanthropos* in a single mode; and it is of grace or of glory; the former is
> the Church militant, the latter the Church triumphant.[45]

The mediatorial Kingship is said to be assigned to Christ because of his propitiatory sacrifice which has purchased a people for himself. Although his power extends to his enemies, it is for the purpose of building his church, and it is over the church that his personal reign is properly said to be exercised.

It will be evident that this standard Reformed view, shared wholeheartedly by the early Covenanters, differs significantly from that of later Covenanters such as McLeod and Symington. As noted in the first section of this study, the later writers contended vigorously for the mediatorial kingship of Christ over all things, nations and rulers included. It is not the case that these writers

---

44. Douglas Kelly, 'The Political Ideas of John Calvin as Reflected in his
    Sermons on II Samuel', in *Evangel* 2.4 (Autumn 1984), p. 11.
45. Quoted in Heinrich Heppe, *Reformed Dogmatics Set out and Illustrated from the
    Sources* (Grand Rapids: Baker Book House, 1978), p. 481.

were ignorant of objections that could be raised against their position. William Symington, for example, deals with a number of objections to his views, such as the claim that the Father and the Holy Spirit are excluded from the government of all things, or that he confuses the essential and the mediatorial rule of Christ.[46] To the latter he replies:

[I]t may be remarked that there may be a formal distinction where there is a material identity. The same thing may be viewed in different aspects. Things, the same in themselves, may be viewed as under the dominion of Christ both essentially as God and officially as Mediator.[47]

It is not clear from their writings if they were aware of how significantly they differed from their Covenanter predecessors, and from much of the Reformed tradition. How and when the change of view came about requires further study. Roy Blackwood in his evaluation of Symington argues that his view of Christ's mediatorial kingship was an original contribution to Scottish theology, and sees in it a significant influence by Martin Bucer.[48] Could it be that they came to a better understanding of Christ's kingship than those who went before?

It does appear that the later Covenanters did achieve a more unified view of the person and work of Christ, especially in regard to his royal office, which is more in harmony with the New Testament teaching on the kingdom. To this material we now turn our attention. Renewed consideration of this subject on the part of Evangelical and Reformed scholars in the second half of the twentieth century has proved to be very fruitful in terms of our understanding of the nature of Christ's reign.

At the outset we must underline the importance of asserting the unity of the person of Christ, as Christian theology had traditionally done in opposition, for example, to the views of the

---

46. Symington, *Messiah the Prince*, pp. 100ff.
47. Symington, *Messiah the Prince*, p. 101.
48. Roy Blackwood, *William Symington: Churchman and Theologian* (unpublished PhD thesis, University of Edinburgh, 1963).

Nestorians. Christ is one person with two distinct natures. The natures did not become mixed nor (in response to Cyrillian and Lutheran ideas of the *communicatio idiomatum*) are the properties of one nature communicated to the other. All the works of Christ are the works of the one person, albeit each nature performs what is proper to it. Loraine Boettner sums up the orthodox view thus:

> In Scripture the attributes and powers of either nature are ascribed to the one Christ, and conversely the works and characteristics of the one Christ are ascribed to either of the natures in a way which can be explained only on the principle that these two natures were indissolubly united in a single person.[49]

We make this point not in order to suggest that Gillespie or his Reformed contemporaries are Nestorians, and we reject the imputation of Nestorianism to Calvinistic Christology, but rather to raise the question as to whether they followed consistently the implications of their doctrine, especially in relation to the reign of Christ.

The New Testament picture of the kingdom of God is of a single reign exercised by the God-man, Jesus Christ, the incarnate Son of God. In saying this, we are not forgetting the truth of the maxim *finitum non capax infiniti*, nor are we denying that each nature performs what is appropriate to it. It is significant that in the Gospel records Jesus begins his public ministry by proclaiming the coming of the kingdom of God. Thus in Mark 1:15 he says 'The time is fulfilled, and the kingdom of God is at hand; repent and believe in the gospel' (NASB). Indeed, in Jesus' ministry and teaching, culminating in his death and resurrection, the kingdom of God is actually present.

The kingdom proclaimed by Jesus is above all *theocentric*. As Herman Ridderbos in his outstanding study *The Coming of the Kingdom* puts it:

---

49. Loraine Boettner, *Studies in Theology* (Nutley, NJ: Presbyterian and
   Reformed, 1947), p. 198.

[T]he idea of the coming of the kingdom is pre-eminently the idea of the kingly self-assertion of God, of his coming to the world in order to reveal his royal majesty, power and right.[50]

Later he states:

This absolutely theocentric character of the kingdom of God in Jesus' preaching also implies that its coming consists entirely in God's own action and is perfectly dependent on his activity.[51]

The kingdom can be said to be present because the King is present. God is at work in royal power in the person of Jesus Christ. The words of Jesus imply nothing less. As he says, for example, in Luke 11:20 (NASB), 'if I cast out demons by the finger of God, then the kingdom of God has come upon you'. There is no indication that the incarnate Son, performing the work of the Mediator (cf. 1 Tim. 2:5), exercises the reign of God in only a limited sense. The bringing in of the kingdom of God is a divine-human work in the sense that the King who is present is both God and man.

The core of Jesus' message is the inbreaking of the eschatological reign of God. *Already* the powers of the coming age are at work, but *not yet* in their ultimate glorious manifestation. The final revelation of the kingdom lies in the future, when the King will say, 'Come, you who are blessed of my Father, inherit the kingdom prepared for you from the foundation of the world' (Matt. 25:34, NASB). This double 'coming' is reflected in Jesus' words in the Nazareth synagogue recorded in Luke 4:16ff., when he quotes from Isaiah 61:1–2. Significantly, he omits the words 'the day of vengeance of our God' from the quotation: *now* he proclaims 'good news' to the poor, but *not yet* 'the day of vengeance'. It is necessary to stress that present and future elements do not constitute two kingdoms, but rather two aspects of

---

50. Herman Ridderbos, *The Coming of the Kingdom* (Nutley, NJ: Presbyterian and Reformed, 1962), p. 19.
51. Ridderbos, *Coming*, pp. 23–24.

the one kingdom of God. Richard Gaffin helpfully distinguishes three stages in Jesus' royal work:

a. the period of Jesus' earthly ministry, b. the period from his exaltation to his return (the time of the church), and c. the period beyond his return.[52]

At this point it is vital to establish the extent of the kingdom proclaimed by Jesus and present in him. Of great significance is his statement to the disciples just before his ascension: 'All authority in heaven and earth has been given to me' (Matt. 28:18). The one who stands before the disciples is the one who has all *exousia*, and hence this is predicated of the God-man, the risen Christ who is also Mediator. It is he who exercises authority over all things. No distinction can be made exegetically between a reign as eternal Son and a different reign as Mediator. In Charles Hodge's words: 'As Theanthropos and as Mediator, all power in heaven and upon earth has been committed to his hands.'[53]

The implication of this fundamental truth is that the crown rights of King Jesus are universal in their extent. This is indicated, for example, by his sitting at the right hand of the Father, which involves equality with respect to glory and dominion. As the Mediator triumphant, he is invested with all the power and authority of God. It is in this context that a passage such as Ephesians 1:20–22 should be viewed. The position of supreme glory and power which Paul ascribes to Christ is clearly occupied by the God-man, following as it does a description of the resurrection. In this setting, 'all things' are put under his feet and he is described as 'head over all things for the benefit of the church' (author's translation). Similarly, in Philippians 2:9–10 the Mediator is 'superexalted' (*hyperypsōsen*) and given supremacy over all things, in heaven, on earth and under the earth.

One powerful factor that influenced writers like Gillespie and

---

52. R. B. Gaffin, article 'Kingdom of God' in *New Dictionary of Theology*, S. B. Ferguson and D. F. Wright (eds.) (Leicester/Downers Grove: InterVarsity Press, 1988), p. 368.

53. Charles Hodge, *Systematic Theology*, 1871 edn (Grand Rapids: Eerdmans, 1977), 2.600.

Rutherford in their view of Christ's two kingdoms was a desire to avoid saying that he is mediatorial King over those who are not saved. The position we have set out from the New Testament, however, resolves this apparent problem.

We note first that the term *basileia* in the New Testament is most often used in a dynamic sense to describe the 'reign' of God, the putting forth of his royal power. The spatial meaning of 'realm' is certainly present, but it is secondary. The focus of older writers on the spatial meaning, considered in terms of a body of people over whom the King reigned, led to a concentration on delineating who did and did not belong to the kingdom. The New Testament focus, however, is on the coming of the King with power to redeem and judge. It is for this reason that a text such a Mark 9:1 can speak of the kingdom 'coming with power'. It is the reign of the King that is in view.

If *basileia* is taken in this sense, then it is clear that Christ's kingdom is universal and embraces all things. Not all human beings, however, submit willingly to the reign and authority of King Jesus. It is only those who are changed by grace and who are brought to experience the redemption accomplished by Christ who willingly give allegiance to the King. As Richard Gaffin says:

> The church alone has been entrusted with 'the keys of the kingdom' (Mt. 16:18, 19), as it alone has been commissioned to preach 'the gospel of the kingdom' (Mt. 24:14). The church and only the church is made up of the citizens of the kingdom, those who by repentance and faith submit to the redemptive lordship of Christ.[54]

It is therefore the church alone that benefits in a salvific way from Christ's mediation. The kingship of Christ is manifested in the church, and the citizens of the kingdom are identical with the members of the church.[55]

---

54. R. B. Gaffin, 'Kingdom of God', p. 369.

55. See further on this issue G. Vos, *The Kingdom of God and the Church* (Nutley, NJ: Presbyterian and Reformed, 1972), chapter 9, and R. O. Zorn, *Church and Kingdom* (Philadelphia: Presbyterian and Reformed, 1962), part 1.

What of those outside the body of the church? Can Christ be said to be king over those who do not acknowledge his rule? Given the New Testament description of Christ exercising a universal dominion, it can be said that such people are under his authority and power, whether or not they recognize it or acknowledge it. Just as God exercised sovereign control over Nebuchadnezzar and Cyrus in Old Testament times, so Christ has authority even over those who refuse to recognize his rule. Their resistance does not diminish his authority in any way. His crown rights remain the same, whether or not individuals acknowledge those rights. They cannot be described as citizens of the kingdom of God, but are rather rebels who ought to be citizens and who will be answerable to the King at the last day for their rebellion. The messianic fulfilment of Psalm 2, for example, depicts the reign of God's Son triumphing over rebellious nations, and the power of King Jesus is demonstrated in the Gospel accounts of exorcisms, when the demons must instantly obey his commands.

It is legitimate to posit a distinction between the way in which Christ rules his people and the way in which he rules the rest of creation. One traditional formulation of the distinction has been that between a kingdom of grace and a kingdom of power. There is a danger that such terminology may suggest two separate kingdoms, and the ways in which Christ rules cannot be neatly separated into 'grace' and 'power'. His power is not absent from his rule over the church, where he rules by word and Spirit, since he purges and disciplines his people. Equally, his grace, albeit not 'saving grace', is not absent from his rule over the rest of creation. Nevertheless, the primary characteristic of his rule over the church is grace, whilst power is the primary characteristic of his rule over the rest of creation. If the unity of his reign is preserved, this distinction may be employed.

Christians, it has rightly been said, live 'between the times'. They are positioned between the 'already' of the arrival of the kingdom and the 'not yet' of the final consummation. This raises the question – to which we will return – as to how much transformation is to be expected in the world on this side of the *eschaton*. To what degree may we expect the crown rights of King Jesus to be acknowledged in any particular society? Even among Reformed thinkers, opinions differ widely.

The cross and the kingdom

The crown rights of King Jesus are the crown rights of a *crucified* King. The death of Christ can never be relegated to a secondary role when his royal prerogatives are being considered. Some Christian thinkers believe there is a real danger that 'Christian politics' as practised, for example, in the United States loses sight of the cross and so loses a crucial 'Christian' foundation. Historian Mark Noll, for example, warns:

> A Christian politics that forgets the cross, a Christian politics that neglects the realities of redemption, a Christian politics that assumes a godlike stance towards the world, is a Christian politics that has abandoned Christ.[56]

Noll's concern, supported by a number of historical examples, is chiefly about the attitude exhibited by Christians in the public arena. A proper focus on the cross, Noll believes, will promote a spirit of humility, rather than the arrogance that so often appears among Christian activists. He concludes his study with this challenge:

> Our politics will be a Christian politics if we follow the commanding Christ as he takes possession of the world, but it will be fully Christian politics only if we remember the road to Calvary that the Lord Jesus took to win his place of command, and never forget that the robes of the saints shine white only because they are washed in the blood of the Lamb.[57]

It is significant that Noll proposes adding some 'Lutheran leaven' to Christian political thinking. Luther himself was greatly concerned

---

56. Mark A. Noll, *Adding Cross to Crown: The Political Significance of Christ's Passion* (Washington, DC: The Centre for Public Justice; Grand Rapids: Baker Books, 1996), p. 32.

57. Noll, *Adding Cross*, p. 46.

lest a *theologia crucis* should be eclipsed by a *theologia gloriae*, and in his theses for the Heidelberg Disputation he sharply contrasted the 'theologian of glory' with the 'theologian of the cross'.[58] At the time Luther's particular targets were scholasticism and Erasmian humanism, but his abiding concern was that the cross should be the test of all sound theology. The 'theology of glory' seeks to know God on the basis of his creation. As Lohse comments, 'In such an attempt the *theologia crucis* sees the effort to arrive at God apart from sin and the divine judgment.'[59] Some would argue that contemporary efforts by Christians to engage in political and social action have more to do with a *theologia gloriae*, and are in sore need of revision in terms of a *theologia crucis*.

We may begin by acknowledging the accuracy of some of Noll's criticisms of Christian politics. There can indeed be a hardness and an arrogant spirit which dishonours Christ and which is seen by others as self-righteous smugness. Undoubtedly some in more activist roles or who have risen to public prominence are seduced by the 'political game' into using the language and methods of the world, perhaps having first given them a light Christian veneer. Power, or the prospect of power, can exercise a dangerous fascination on those who ought to know better. Part of the antidote must be a proper focus on the King who was also the Suffering Servant, the Good Shepherd who laid down his life for the sheep. The call to be a *servant* of Christ includes those who exercise some form of power, in the nation as well as in the church, and all are ultimately 'unprofitable servants' (Luke 17:10, AV).

That, however, is not the whole story. The cross of King Jesus certainly speaks of humiliation and suffering, and the citizens of the kingdom are to take up their cross and follow him (Matt. 16:24). Self-seeking and hunger for power are to be mortified. The cross, nevertheless, also speaks of *victory*. At Calvary the King conquered by dying. In fulfilment of Genesis 3:15, the

---

58. Luther, *Works*, 31.52–53. See also Bernhard Lohse, *Martin Luther's Theology: Its Historical and Systematic Development* (Edinburgh: T. & T. Clark, 1999), pp. 36–39.

59. Lohse, *Martin Luther's Theology*, p. 38.

Seed of the woman has indeed crushed the head of the serpent. His heel was injured in the process, but he overcame, and the blow dealt to the kingdom of Satan is fatal. It is in going to the cross that he prepares a place for his people (John 14:2). It is through being lifted up from the earth that he draws all men to himself (John 12:32). His final words on the cross can be translated 'It has been finished and remains finished' (John 19:30, a Greek perfect tense).

This neglected motif of victory in the biblical view of the atonement was re-emphasized by Lutheran theologian Gustaf Aulén in his 1931 publication *Christus Victor*.[60] Aulén designated this view the 'classic' view of the atonement. Rather than regarding it as *the* biblical view, it is best regarded as one vital element in a thoroughly biblical understanding of the redemptive work of King Jesus. This theme has more recently been studied from a Reformed perspective by F. S. Leahy in his popular study *The Victory of the Lamb*. He states at the outset:

> It is because of the fact that Satan was routed at the cross and robbed of his prey by means of Christ's sacrificial suffering and death that the triumph of the Redeemer is portrayed in Scripture as the victory of the Lamb.[61]

A *theologia crucis* thus entails triumph as well as suffering. The final words of the King were words of victory. The resurrection, as 1 Corinthians 15 demonstrates, seals the triumph of Christ and guarantees that he has fully accomplished the work that the Father gave him to do. It is not a licence for superficial triumphalism on the part of his people and never warrants a proud spirit, but it is an assurance that the King reigns over all things.

There is an intimate connection between Christ's atoning work and the dominion which he exercises. In Philippians 2:6–8 Paul describes the humiliation which the Saviour underwent, culminating with 'became obedient unto death – even death on a cross'.

---

60. Gustav Aulén, *Christus Victor*, 1931 edn (London: SPCK, 1970).

61. Frederick S. Leahy, *The Victory of the Lamb* (Edinburgh: Banner of Truth Trust, 2001), p. x.

The description of his subsequent exaltation in verses 9–11 significantly begins with 'therefore' (*dio*). It is because of his obedience to the point of death in redemptive suffering that he has been 'superexalted' by the Father. It is in this context that the confession 'Jesus Christ is Lord' is heard. This may be linked with statements made by Christ about his dominion and also by Paul elsewhere in his epistles. In Matthew 28:18 Christ says the 'all authority in heaven and on earth *has been given*' to him, and at that point he speaks as the crucified and risen Mediator. Similarly, in Ephesians 1:20ff., Paul speaks of Christ raised, exalted to the position of highest honour and *given* to be 'head over everything to the church'. The imagery of the book of Revelation teaches the same lesson when Christ is depicted as both the Lion and the Lamb. He reigns *because* he shed his blood as the purchase price for his church.

Alexander McLeod in his exposition of Christ's Kingship notes this connection several times. He cites, for example, Isaiah 53:12 (AV): 'Therefore will I divide him a portion with the great, and he shall divide the spoil with the strong; because he has poured out his soul unto death.' McLeod also refers to Isaiah 49:7, where he sees the Messiah in his humiliation subject to rulers. He then comments:

> He sat before them to be tried and judged, and although perfectly innocent, the Lord of life condescended to suffer the sentence of death passed by an earthly ruler. In his exalted state, he must, therefore, be ruler in the kingdoms of men, have a right to demand their submission to his authority, and take such measures as may secure the fulfilment of all his purposes respecting them.[62]

McLeod stresses, rightly, that the dominion of King Jesus is a reward for his sufferings.

We must keep in mind that redemption, as accomplished by the Mediator at the cross, has in view *restoration*. This restoration is brought about by the grace of God and by the power of the Holy

---

62. McLeod, *Messiah*, p. 9.

Spirit first of all in individuals who are saved. As Brad Frey and his co-authors put it:

> [R]estoration implies a reworking of something, not replacing it with something new. Applied to our lives, this means that God restores us by confirming that which is appropriate within us at salvation. He further develops the appropriate while eradicating the sinful and inappropriate that remains. He does not eliminate every trace of who we are and start building all over again.[63]

The Christian's relationship with God is restored in Christ. Restoration, however, embraces more than the individual. No-one in fact lives as an entirely isolated individual. All live in a complex web of social relationships. As Christians are restored, they have an impact for good on the society and culture in which King Jesus has placed them. In their diverse callings the citizens of the kingdom are to effect a measure of restoration in those aspects of life which they are able to influence, not only those traditionally considered 'spiritual'.

As we will see in considering eschatology, the continuing presence of sin right up to the return of Christ means that restoration on this side of the *eschaton* will always be incomplete. At his return, however, King Jesus will usher in the new creation described, for example, in Revelation 21. The final state of perfection will be inaugurated. As Frey says,

> This new order, it must be remembered, is not something substituted for the old; it is the transformation of the old order. The old is not annihilated – it does not cease to exist – but is changed, renewed, reborn, restored, made right and completed.[64]

Restoration and transformation, begun now and consummated at his return, are the fruit of the cross-work of King Jesus. Viewed in

---

63. Bradshaw Frey et al, *All of Life Redeemed* (Jordan Station: Paideia Press, 1983), pp. 35–36.

64. Frey et al, *All of Life Redeemed*, pp. 36–37.

this light, all the work of his servants, done to his glory, has profound and eternal significance.

A covenant perspective

The theme of 'covenant' runs all the way through the Bible, from Genesis to Revelation, and provides a significant unity amid the diversity of the sixty-six books. All of theology can be viewed from a covenantal perspective.[65] Given that many of those who first asserted the crown rights of King Jesus were 'Covenanters', it might be expected that covenantal themes may be relevant to a modern understanding of those rights. As we shall see, 'covenant' has been used in several ways by Reformed and Covenanter writers.

In John Knox's views of civil government the motif of the covenant played an important role.[66] He thought in terms first of all of a covenant between God and the people, including their rulers, a consequence of which was to be avoidance of all idolatry. This idea is found especially in *An Admonition or Warning* (1554).[67] The second kind of covenant is that between ruler and people, which laid obligations on both parties. This idea is found in Knox's *Appellation* (1558),[68] where he cites the example of the covenant made by Asa with Judah to serve God faithfully (2 Chr. 15).

The two covenants which gave rise to the name 'Covenanters' in the seventeenth century were the National Covenant of Scotland (1638) and the Solemn League and Covenant of England, Scotland and Ireland (1643). Both took the form of an engagement with God by the rulers and people, undertaking to preserve the Reformed faith and, in the case of the Solemn League, to pursue

---

65. See e.g. David McKay, *The Bond of Love* (Fearn: Mentor, 2001). A more historical overview of covenant theology is provided by Peter Golding in *Covenant Theology* (Fearn: Mentor, 2004).

66. See R. L. Greaves, *Theology and Revolution in the Scottish Reformation* (Grand Rapids: Christian University Press, 1980), chapter 6.

67. John Knox, *The Works of John Knox*, 6 vols., collected and edited by David Lang (Edinburgh: Thomas George Stevenson, 1854), vol. 3.

68. Knox, *Works*, vol. 4.

reformation beyond the borders of Scotland. The latter covenant also served to establish a political bond between the Scots and the Parliamentary cause in England which secured Scottish help in the Civil War against Charles I.

One of the greatest thinkers among the Covenanters was Samuel Rutherford, whose chief contribution to political theology was his 1644 treatise *Lex, Rex, or the Law and the Prince*.[69] Rutherford undoubtedly accepted the propriety of a covenant between the nation and God, and he was deeply involved in promoting the Covenanter cause, especially in the context of the Westminster Assembly and the Civil War ferment of the 1640s. Nevertheless, he makes no use of this theme in his study of civil government. There are, however, a number of references to a covenant between the ruler and his people, which are sufficient to show that his position is fundamentally that of Knox.

Thus, arguing as usual from the biblical record, Rutherford can write:

> [T]he people maketh a covenant at David's inauguration, that David shall have so much power, to wit, power to be a father, not power to be a tyrant, — power to fight for the people, not power to waste and destroy them.[70]

Although he does not explicitly state here that a covenant is made with the king in every case, the use he makes of David as a paradigm indicates that he believes this to be the case. The covenant envisaged is evidently designed to set out the powers and obligations of both ruler and people.

In another place Rutherford speaks generally, not with specific reference to Israel, in these terms: 'when their fathers made a covenant with the first elected king'.[71] He seems there to

---

69. Samuel Rutherford, *Lex, Rex, or the Law and the Prince* (London: John Field, 1644), reprinted in *The Presbyterian's Armoury*. All quotations are from this edition.

70. Rutherford, *Lex, Rex*, Q.9, p. 38.

71. Rutherford, *Lex, Rex*, Q.8, p. 31.

regard such a covenant as a general feature and principle of civil government. In answer to Bishop John Maxwell, Rutherford asserts the principle which was to be used frequently in the Covenanter tradition, that a covenant lawfully made 'tyeth the children'.[72] Unless the covenant be broken by the king, the succeeding generation may not set aside the bond or their election of the king. Thus we see the principle of the 'descending obligation' of the covenant between rulers and subjects. Rutherford also points out, however, that future changes of ruler are not impossible: 'it cannot deprive them of their lawful liberty naturally inherent in them to choose the fittest man to be king'.[73]

Although it might seem that the terms of the covenant deal only with limitations on the king's powers, Rutherford recognizes obligations resting on the people too. When they enter into such a compact, which Rutherford regards as based on natural law and also on the institution of God,[74] they resign certain rights to the ruler, such as the power of punishing offenders. Rutherford also considers the breaking of the covenant by the people to be not only a violation of faith, but also an act of disobedience to the ruler.[75] As he shows at length elsewhere, however, he does not believe that the people in covenant with their ruler have so resigned their power of government that they cannot resume it if necessary.[76] This principle was of course very significant in the context of the Civil War.

The use of covenantal categories in political thought is also to be found in Rutherford's German contemporary, Johannes Althusius. In his *Politica Methodice Digesta* (3rd edition, 1614),[77] Althusius works out in some detail a 'consociational' view of

---

72. Rutherford, *Lex, Rex*, Q.8, p. 31.

73. Rutherford, *Lex, Rex*, Q.8, p. 31.

74. Rutherford, *Lex, Rex*, Q.7, p. 25.

75. Rutherford, *Lex, Rex*, Q.7, p. 26.

76. A brief summary is provided by W. D. J. McKay in 'Samuel Rutherford on Civil Government' in *Reformed Theological Journal*, November 1988.

77. An abbreviated translation is provided by F. S. Carney, *The Politics of Johannes Althusius* (Boston: Beacon Press, 1964).

government and society which gives particular prominence to federal structures and stresses the complex interrelationships which characterize any society. For Althusius the covenant plays a significant role in the constitution of organized social life. As he puts it:

> The people first associated themselves in a certain body with definite laws, and established for itself the necessary and useful rights of this association. Then, because the people itself cannot manage the administration of these rights, it entrusted their administration to ministers and rectors elected by it. In so doing, the people transferred to them the authority and power necessary for the performance of this assignment, equipped them with the sword for this purpose, and put itself under their care and rule.[78]

It is interesting that some modern political scientists, such as Thomas Hueglin, believe that in this Calvinist tradition are to be found principles of great relevance in contemporary multicultural and multinational politics.[79]

Later Covenanter writers, however, concentrated their attention on the covenant between God and the nation. This is reflected in the various 'renewals' of the Solemn League and Covenant held by Covenanters from time to time. One took place, for example, at Auchensaugh in Scotland in July 1712, and included the National Covenant. A number of books and pamphlets produced by Covenanters on both sides of the Atlantic expounded the meaning of 'social covenanting' and defended the view that the historic British covenants were binding on the signatory nations in perpetuity.[80] At times there has been some recognition of weakness in

---

78. Carney, *Politics*, p. 88 (= *Politica* xviii.10).

79. Thomas O. Hueglin, *Early Modern Concepts for a Late Modern World: Althusius on Community and Federalism* (Waterloo: Wilfred Laurier University Press, 1999).

80. See for example James M. Willson, *Social Religious Covenanting* (Philadelphia: William S. Young, 1856); John Cunningham, *The Ordinance of Covenanting* (Glasgow: William Marshall, n.d.).

the original covenants, not least in their combining religious and political commitments. Alexander Shields, a Covenanter minister in the late seventeenth century, speaking with hindsight, believed that separate documents – a religious covenant and a political treaty – would have been more desirable. It is also a fact that the Solemn League and Covenant, which contains a profession of faith in Christ, was on occasion enforced on pain of civil penalties. In more recent times a measure of diversity has become evident in Covenanter circles, with some maintaining the binding obligation of the letter of the historic covenants and others arguing that it is the principles embodied in the documents which continue to bind, rather than a particular historical expression of them.

It is undeniable that rulers have a responsibility to acknowledge the supremacy of Christ, as Psalm 2:10–12 indicates. Such acknowledgment could not be confined to 'private life', however defined. No Christian ruler could live in private by one set of principles and conduct his public duties by another. Despite what some politicians wish to claim, private and public cannot be divorced. If, by the grace of God working in a weighty way, the majority of citizens and rulers were to acknowledge the Kingship of Christ, the biblical pattern of covenanting would seem to be an appropriate mode of expressing that acknowledgment in an official way. None would be compelled to make a commitment that they could not honestly make, but in a democratic system a minority must live within a framework of values they do not share, as Christians must currently live within a secular humanist public philosophy.

The Holy Spirit

What role does the Holy Spirit play in relation to the crown rights of King Jesus? First it must be stressed that genuine acknowledgment of the supremacy of Christ is the fruit of the regenerating work of the Holy Spirit. Paul states that 'no-one can say, "Jesus is Lord," except by the Holy Spirit' (1 Cor. 12:3). As noted previously, it is only those born again of the Spirit who can be considered citizens of Christ's kingdom. Only at the last day will the confession 'Jesus Christ is Lord' be made by the unregenerate, and that unwillingly, as they bear the weight of God's wrath (Phil. 2:11). Only by the regenerating work of the Spirit would King Jesus be given his rightful place in national life.

To assert that the crown rights of King Jesus should be recognized in every area of life is not to claim that people will be made Christians by legislation or political programmes. Proponents of this position are sometimes accused of making such a claim, but actual examples are very difficult to find. Those most committed to traditional Covenanter views, for example, also assert the necessity of preaching the gospel for the salvation of sinners and the necessity of the work of the Spirit to transform individuals and societies. Arguments about 'making Christians by legislation' address a straw man.

From the Scriptures it is clear, however, that God in his sovereign wisdom can and does overrule the actions of national leaders in fulfilment of his purposes. Thus pagan Cyrus is termed by God 'my shepherd' (Isa. 44:28), one who 'will accomplish all that I please'. The general principle is stated in Proverbs 21:1:

> The King's heart is in the hand of the LORD;
> he directs it like a watercourse wherever he pleases.

The same is true with regard to the citizens of any nation. Thus God can and does act to influence actions and attitudes in the public arena so that the work of Christ's kingdom is advanced, without the individuals concerned necessarily being saved. There may at times be a tolerance of, or even sympathy for, Christian principles in a society where few are actually Christians. In such circumstances the work of God's people is facilitated. Something of this is reflected in Paul's exhortation that prayers are to be offered 'for kings and all those in authority, that we may live peaceful and quiet lives in all godliness and holiness' (1 Tim. 2:2). In the light of what has been said earlier about Christianity as a 'world-and-life-view', such godliness and holiness cannot be thought of as confined to the private sphere.

This work of God in a society may be described in terms of 'common grace', the operation of God through the Holy Spirit which restrains the expression of man's sinful nature without leading to the salvation of the sinner. Louis Berkhof defines it thus:

Those general operations of the Holy Spirit whereby He, without renewing the heart, exercises such a moral influence on man through His general or special revelation, that sin is restrained, order is maintained in social life, and civil righteousness is promoted.[81]

This work may be termed 'grace' in that God does not owe such goodness to any sinner, and whatever is given is by his gracious will. The extent of such common grace may be debated, and theologians like Abraham Kuyper have thought of it as being quite extensive,[82] nevertheless it is a valuable restraint on sin's expression and does facilitate the advancement of the reign of Christ. The guilt of sinners is not mitigated, but a society where, for example, the unborn are not murdered in the womb is surely more pleasing to King Jesus than a society where they are.

Eschatology

How does eschatology relate to an assertion of the crown rights of King Jesus? Many of the Covenanters who wrote about the Kingship of Christ were postmillennial in outlook. They expected that before the return of Christ the vast majority of the world's population would acknowledge his authority, thus leading to an earthly millennium of godliness and peace. This is reflected in the *Testimony* of the Reformed Presbyterian Church of Scotland, published in 1842. In chapter 16 of the doctrinal part of the document we read:

> We believe that a period approaches, in which the kingdom of Christ shall triumph over all opposition, and have a universal diffusion, influence and prosperity. The Romish antichrist shall be destroyed . . .

---

81. Berkhof, *Systematic Theology*, p. 436.
82. Selections from Kuyper's writings on common grace are available in *Abraham Kuyper: A Centennial Reader*, ed. James D. Bratt (Grand Rapids/Cambridge: Eerdmans; Carlisle: Paternoster Press, 1998), pp. 165–201. Kuyper clearly asserts the necessity of saving grace in regard to redemption in *Particular Grace: A Defense of God's Sovereignty in Salvation* (Grandville: Reformed Free Publishing Association, 2001).

The Jews shall be converted to Christianity, and added to the church. The greater fullness of the Gentiles shall be brought in . . . There is reason to believe, that the truth shall be felt in its illuminating, regenerating and sanctifying efficacy, by the greater number of those who profess it. Knowledge, love, holiness and peace shall extensively prevail, under the copious effusions of the Holy Spirit . . . The social institutions of men shall be erected and administered under the influence of scriptural principle.[83]

It is, no doubt, a stirring vision which stimulated many Covenanters to hold fast to their position. Is it necessary, however, to hold to this postmillennial eschatology, such as today is found for example among theonomists, in order to assert the crown rights of King Jesus?

It does not appear to us that it is necessary. There are eschatological views which do seem to suggest that Christians can expect to make little impact on the world and so they should engage solely in evangelism as they await the return of the Lord. Another option, however, is the amillennial view, which in recent years has come to have significant influence in Reformed circles. We need not set out in detail here a view which has been ably expounded and defended by, among others, A. A. Hoekema and Kim Riddlebarger.[84] Suffice it to say that there is nothing in an amillennial eschatology which precludes an assertion of the crown rights of King Jesus.

The amillennialist asserts that the kingdom has come in the person and work of the Lord Jesus Christ. The powers of the age to come have broken into the present age. By the power of the Holy Spirit sinners are being saved and, by God's grace, become salt and light in the world. The number who willingly acknowledge the kingship of Christ is growing until the full number of the elect

83. *Testimony of the Reformed Presbyterian Church of Scotland* (Glasgow: John Keith, 1842), pp. 348–349.

84. A. A. Hoekema, *The Bible and the Future* (Exeter: Paternoster Press, 1979); Kim Riddlebarger, *A Case for Amillennialism* (Grand Rapids: Baker Books; Leicester: Inter-Varsity Press, 2003).

is brought in and Christ returns in glory. At the same time, as various texts foretell, evil too is becoming worse, and the distinction between the kingdom of Satan and the kingdom of Christ is becoming clearer. A passage such as 2 Timothy 3:1ff. seems to indicate that this is to be expected, and it is a significant objection to a postmillennial eschatology. At God's appointed time, King Jesus will return, all will acknowledge his authority, the unsaved will be condemned and the citizens of the kingdom will enter into the joys of the new creation (Rev. 21:1ff.). Passages such as Isaiah 65:17–25 and Isaiah 66:22–23, which postmillennialists expect to be fulfilled in a future period before the return of Christ, may be regarded by amillennialists as descriptions of the new creation, foreshadowed in the present spiritual blessedness of the church.

Amillennialists and postmillennialists both seek the recognition of the crown rights of King Jesus. Where they differ is on the degree to which such recognition will precede the return of the King. Working for such recognition neither requires nor precludes either eschatology.

Questions and applications

In conclusion, a number of issues may be addressed briefly, to stimulate discussion rather than provide extended consideration.

Plurality and pluralism

It has become commonplace to speak of Western European nations as 'pluralist'. The term in fact has a variety of meanings; in this context it indicates the presence of a variety of religions and philosophies vying for allegiance in the public arena. The development of such pluralism, after a period of broadly Christian hegemony, has been a characteristic of late modern Western culture.

Pluralism of this kind is lauded by many as a desirable state of affairs, and thus what might be termed 'plurality' (as a statement of fact) becomes 'plural*ism*' as a goal to be pursued. As a social philosophy, pluralism argues that all viewpoints are to be treated equally in the public arena: government should not favour any one of them in legislation or social policy. Often it is coupled with a relativistic view of the truth value of all viewpoints. How does pluralism coexist with an assertion of the crown rights of King Jesus? Some Christians, spiritual descendants often of Abraham Kuyper, argue that government ought to pursue such an even-handed policy, although they do not in any sense relinquish the truth claims of Christianity.[85] The danger posed by this approach, however, is that the assertion of Christ's authority easily becomes muted, and too often governments which profess to pursue neutrality towards all views in practice pursue a secular humanist agenda.

Those who seek a full-orbed assertion of the crown rights of King Jesus must of course accept the pluralist nature of contemporary society. They must accept *de facto* 'plurality'; they cannot, however, accept *de jure* 'pluralism' as a social philosophy. Within whatever democratic structures exist, they must seek to advance the cause of Christ's kingdom, always acknowledging the truth of Zechariah 4:6: ' "Not by might nor by power, but by my Spirit," says the LORD Almighty.' They will preach the gospel and act as salt and light in their respective callings, including in government, if that is the King's will. Wherever they find themselves, they will act on Christian principles in both private and public life. The present reality may be pluralism, but their prayers and aspirations will be for public recognition of the prerogatives of King Jesus. Progress may be limited, at times apparently non-existent, but they know that work done for the glory of the King honours him and is never futile. At times they may make tactical alliances with others who do not share their views, but their strategic goal is the submission of all to the rule of Christ. Like any other group in society, they will have to compete in the marketplace of ideas and win by persuasion, not force.

---

85. See: Gordon J. Spykman, 'The Principled Pluralist Position', in Gary Scott Smith (ed.), *God and Politics: Four Views on the Reformation of Civil Government* (Phillipsburg: Presbyterian and Reformed, 1989).

Government and religion

In formulating and defending their Presbyterianism, Covenanters like Rutherford and Gillespie stressed strongly that there are two separate jurisdictions established by God, the ecclesiastical and the civil, neither of which is to encroach on the sphere of the other. They did not believe that the recognition of King Jesus entailed any 'theocratic' domination of the State by the church, whilst, on the other hand, the Covenanters were engaged in a prolonged struggle against the attempts of the king to manipulate the church to serve his own ends. They knew how important it was to restrain the two jurisdictions to their proper spheres, both subject to the supreme divine authority that created them. Asserting the crown rights of King Jesus does not in principle entail a confusion of church and State.

That civil government has a duty to promote the interests of true religion, however, was a view held in common by the Covenanters and the majority of their contemporaries, of whatever theological tradition. It was inconceivable to most people that rulers could or should be indifferent to religion. In dealing with the tasks carried out by civil government, Calvin states that it is concerned with more than ensuring that men 'breathe, eat, drink and are kept warm'. He continues:

> [I]t . . . prevents idolatry, sacrilege against God's name, blasphemies against his truth, and other public offences against religion from arising and spreading among the people; it prevents the public peace from being disturbed; it provides that each man may keep his property safe and sound; that men may carry on blameless intercourse among themselves; that honesty and modesty may be preserved among men. In short, it provides that a public manifestation of religion may exist among Christians, and that humility be maintained among men.[86]

In a similar vein, the Westminster Confession of Faith says of the civil magistrate:

> [H]e hath authority, and it is his duty, to take order, that unity and

---

86. Calvin, *Institutes* 4.20.3.

peace be preserved in the church, that the truth of God be kept pure
and entire, that all blasphemies and heresies be suppressed, all
corruptions and abuses in worship and discipline prevented or
reformed, and all the ordinances of God duly settled, administered
and observed. (18.3)

How in practice such a mandate could be carried out without encroaching on the sphere of the church presents many
difficulties. In the context of contemporary 'pluralistic societies'
the complexities multiply exponentially. At the most basic level, it
has to be recognized that only in a nation which had Christian
leaders and a substantial proportion of the population converted
could such a programme even be envisaged. It may be agreed that
civil rulers should maintain the conditions in society which allow
the work of the church to advance, but to go further raises many
questions. Very quickly the line between civil and ecclesiastical
jurisdictions becomes blurred. Samuel Rutherford, for example,
believed that the civil magistrate had the duty of ensuring orthodox preaching in churches and of calling ministers to account for
failure in this regard.[87] He also argued that civil rulers should add
civil penalties to church censures, having tested the church's
decision by Scripture:

> [T]he magistrate [is] obliged to follow, ratifie, and with his civil sanction
> to confirme the sound constitutions of the Church: But conditionally,
> not absolutely and blindely, but in so far as they agree with the Word
> of God.[88]

It is interesting that in adopting the Confession of Faith in 1647
the General Assembly of the Church of Scotland qualified
the Confession's ascription to the civil magistrate (in 18.3) of
an authority to convene church synods. Even among those in

---

87. Samuel Rutherford, *The Divine Right of Church-Government and
    Excommunication* (London: John Field, 1646), cpt 24, Q.20, pp. 544ff.
88. Rutherford, *Divine Right*, cpt 24, Q.22, p. 579.

fundamental agreement, demarcation lines between civil and ecclesiastical jurisdictions were difficult to draw.

Differences also arise in regard to the establishment of a particular church. Ought the civil power to recognize and materially support one out of the available selection of Christian churches? Both positive and negative answers have been given by equally Reformed writers. John McDonald, a Reformed Presbyterian elder, wrote a lengthy treatise entitled *Civil Church Establishment*, in which he sought to show that 'the Church of Christ is independent of States and Parliaments, self-sustaining, and bound to provide for the support of those who minister to her in holy things'.[89] On the other hand, the duty of civil rulers to afford material support to the Christian church is defended by Free Church of Scotland minister Neil Macleod in an essay on 'Church and State' contributed to a symposium on that denomination's principles.[90]

It must be kept in mind that to Rutherford and his contemporaries the concept of different Christian 'denominations' existing side by side was inconceivable. In their view there would be in the nation one legally recognized expression of Christianity, Reformed in doctrine and Presbyterian in polity. 'Liberty of conscience' did not extend to the expression of opinions beyond the bounds of that church's confession of faith. Rutherford, for example, defends this at great length in his 1649 treatise *A Free Disputation against pretended Liberty of Conscience*.[91] Other than Judaism, no other religion had to be considered. In the contemporary pluralist culture any who assert that the supremacy of King Jesus requires that only expressions of Christian truth should be permitted in the public arena can expect a very hostile reception.

---

89. John McDonald, *Civil Church Establishment* (Glasgow: Aird and Coghill, and John Menzies, 1902), Prefatory Note.

90. Neil A. Macleod, 'Church and State', in Donald Macleod (ed.), *Hold Fast Your Confession*, (Edinburgh: Knox Press, 1978).

91. Samuel Rutherford, *A Free Disputation against Pretended Liberty of Conscience* (London: Andrew Crook, 1649).

Law and rights

An assertion of the crown rights of King Jesus provides a solid foundation for law as well as government. The King has expressed his will in the written word of God provided by the work of the Holy Spirit. The Scriptures provide God-breathed instruction not only for personal life but also for public life. In the Old Testament the Mosaic law provided detailed guidance for many areas of Israel's national life, and this, as completed in the New Testament revelation, continues to express the will of King Jesus.

How the Old Testament law should function today has occasioned spirited debate. Those in the 'Reconstructionist' or 'Theonomic' movement have argued that the 'standing judicial laws' of the Old Testament continue to be binding on all nations. In other words, the civil laws of Israel should still be the laws of every nation. On the basis of Matthew 5:17–19, Greg Bahnsen has argued for 'The Abiding Validity of the Law in Exhaustive Detail'.[92]

On the other hand, the majority of the Reformed tradition, going back to Calvin himself, has taken the view that the *principles* embodied in the Old Testament law are to be expressed in contemporary terms in each particular society. This view is reflected in the statement of the Westminster Confession of Faith (19.4):

> To [the people of Israel] also, as a body politick, he gave sundry judicial laws, which expired together with the state of that people, not obliging any other now, further than the general equity thereof may require.

Sinclair Ferguson, among others, has argued at length against a theonomic interpretation of this section of the Confession.[93] Detailed work by Vern Poythress has cast serious doubt on

---

92. Greg L. Bahnsen, *Theonomy in Christian Ethics*, 2nd edn (Phillipsburg: Presbyterian and Reformed, 1984), title of chapter 2, p. 39.

93. Sinclair B. Ferguson, 'An Assembly of Theonomists? The Teaching of the Westminster Assembly of Divines on the Law of God', in William S. Barker and W. Robert Godfrey (eds.), *Theonomy: A Reformed Critique* (Grand Rapids: Academie Books, 1990).

Bahnsen's exegesis of Matthew 5:17, regarding Jesus' 'fulfilling' the law.[94] This option of re-applying principles is in some ways more difficult, but divergence among theonomists suggests that their method is not without significant difficulties either.

Both options, however, direct attention back to the word of God, the word of King Jesus, as a vital source of guidance for rulers which is to a great extent ignored or derided by contemporary leaders.

The Scriptures also provide fundamental guidance in the area of human rights, an area which increasingly is on the agenda of everyone in public life, not least of political leaders. Great emphasis is laid on human rights, and at present in Northern Ireland the Human Rights Commission is consciously seeking to develop a 'rights culture' and has produced a draft Bill of Rights for the Province, beyond the legislation in force in the rest of the United Kingdom. In such documents, however, no basis is provided for the establishment of 'rights', or indeed for deciding between rival claims. Although those engaged in the pursuit of various rights are often deaf to Christian voices, the assertion of the crown rights of King Jesus provides such a basis. The supremacy of Christ, the dignity of man as God's image-bearer and the reality of fallen human nature are essential foundation principles. Without them, 'human rights' degenerates into a free-for-all in which the loudest and most insistent voices triumph.

Conclusion

The vision for the recognition of the crown rights of King Jesus is one that should stir the heart of every servant of this King. There are of course many questions still to be answered: exegetical questions about the meaning of particular biblical texts; practical questions about the application of the principles in a society characterized by cultural and religious diversity which earlier

---

94. Vern S. Poythress, *The Shadow of Christ in the Law of Moses* (Phillipsburg: Presbyterian and Reformed, 1991), Appendix C.

generations could scarcely have imagined. Often Christians will differ on the best route even to goals on which they are agreed, and just to mention some of these goals today will draw accusations of bigotry or incitement to religious hatred. Many people, Christians included, are discouraged or frightened by historical examples of Christians wielding political power. Great wisdom and grace will be needed to promote the realization of the vision. We are, however, people of hope and of prayer. We do not know what God may do in the future by the mighty working of his Spirit, and where in the world he works may come as a complete surprise to us. Mistakes will be made by the servants of the King, but a start needs to be made if a disintegrating culture is to be brought back from the brink of disaster. 'So why do you say nothing about bringing the king back?' (2 Sam. 19:10).

7. WHAT HAS JERUSALEM TO DO WITH WESTMINSTER?

Stephen Clark

It was Alistair Campbell, one-time Press Secretary to Tony Blair, who famously said, 'We don't do God.' It was a politically adroit manoeuvre, intended to forestall any probing questions from political journalists about the Prime Minister's faith. 'What has Jerusalem to do with Westminster (or Brussels, or Capitol Hill, and so on)?' is the question which lay behind Mr Campbell's statement.

What *does* Jerusalem have to do with Westminster? The answer of the secularized State (and, presumably, that of Mr Campbell) is, 'Nothing at all.' The implications of this answer become increasingly clear, almost on a daily basis, in the approach sanctioned by Western governments and parliaments to issues connected with the beginning and end of life, sexuality, and 'alternative models of the family'. The rise of Islamic terrorism, complete with suicide bombers in the cities of western Europe and the USA, understandably confirms many people in the rightness of their belief that politics and religion must be kept apart. On the other hand, a growing body of perceptive Christian thinkers has drawn attention to the fact that secularism is not 'neutral' but is itself an ideology, and an extremely intolerant one at that. Furthermore, many of the values which secularism has taken for granted grew out of the Judaeo-Christian tradition and were the result of its influence upon national institutions. Remove that influence and the values may well not long survive. Therefore it is time, say some, for Jerusalem's voice once again to be heard in Westminster.

The earlier chapters were originally presented as papers at a study conference which was called to explore the relationship of the Christian and of the church to political life. In this final chapter I shall seek to identify some of the key issues which have been raised, as well as some matters which have not been touched upon. In addition I shall try to draw attention to areas where further consideration and exploration are necessary.

Biblical theology and the relationship between the two testaments

A question which has to be addressed early on concerns the nature of the relationship between the Old Testament and the New. It is impossible to consider in any adequate way to what extent the nation of Israel and its laws may be a paradigm for other societies today until one has explored this relationship.

While Gordon Wenham is surely right to criticize the 'developmental' approach to Old Testament study which has characterized theological liberalism and to emphasize the importance of reading the Bible as it stands, rather than seeking to 'go behind the text', it is important to emphasize that the Bible itself refers to the fact that revelation is 'progressive', in that God's revelation of himself kept in step with the unfolding of his redemptive plan. In this respect Exodus 6:2–5 are crucially important verses. As Alec Motyer has so helpfully pointed out, the Lord is *not* saying in verse 3 that the patriarchs had not heard the divine name of Yahweh; rather, he is emphasizing the fact that *the significance* of that name and something of the fullness of its meaning will be made known to Moses and the Israelites in the Exodus-Sinai event in a way in which they had not been made known to the patriarchs.[1]

Indeed, Genesis itself traces the development of God's promise: first we learn that the seed of the woman will crush the serpent's head; then that God's redemptive purpose will be accomplished through the line of Seth; and this is then further narrowed down to the line of Abraham, then of Isaac, and then of Jacob. This is surely *progressive revelation*. The revelation is progressive not because Israel's religious consciousness was developing, but rather because the divine author of Holy Scripture was gradually revealing his purposes, as the events which form redemptive history unfolded in time and space. This is a fundamental principle of biblical theology and is a necessary entailment of the fact that the living God both acted and spoke in his world, a world which exists in space and time.

It is helpful to place the question of the relationship between the two testaments in this wider context of the nature of progressive revelation and of biblical theology. Indeed, this is how the New Testament itself approaches this matter. In John 1:17 we read: 'the law was given through Moses; grace and truth came through Jesus Christ.' Even those with only a cursory knowledge of the Old Testament will realize that the 'giving of the law through Moses' involved the giving of fuller revelation than had hitherto been the case. The inner logic of Paul's argument in Galatians 3:15 – 4:7 depends upon the fact that the Mosaic revelation came after the revelation given to Abraham and that it served a very specific purpose. And the coming of grace and truth by Jesus Christ inevitably means that there is even greater revelation through him; for, when John refers to truth in verse 17, he does not mean to contrast it with what is false, but rather with what was partial and incomplete.[2] As Don Carson has pointed out, the passage in which this verse is located is soaked in language found in Exodus 34: the glory of God which Moses

---

1. J. A. Motyer, *The Revelation of the Divine Name* (London: Tyndale Press, 1959).

2. J. Murray, *Principles of Conduct* (Grand Rapids: Eerdmans, 1957), p. 123.

desired to see is to be found in its fullness in the person of Jesus Christ.[3] John's Gospel then works out what have sometimes been referred to as 'the replacement motifs', where Old Testament institutions find their climactic fulfilment in Jesus himself. Thus, he is the glory who tabernacled with men (1:14); he is the temple (2:19–22; 4:19–26); he is the true bread or manna (6:25–65); and so on.

This emphasis on Jesus fulfilling the Old Testament is part of the substructure of New Testament teaching, which, like a stratum of rock which pushes through the surface at repeated intervals, is to be seen in many New Testament passages. Jesus himself spells it out in Matthew 11:13, and it was central to his understanding of the Old Testament (Luke 24:25–27; John 5:39). It is a fundamental postulate of Paul's message that Jesus is the fulfilment of the Old Testament Scriptures: Romans 1:2 and 3:21 are but two verses from a plethora of material which demonstrates this fact. Perhaps in no New Testament book is this expressed more clearly than in the letter to the Hebrews. This letter is dominated by the emphasis that what has come with Christ is both 'new' and 'better' than what the people of God had hitherto experienced. The opening two verses inform us that the same God who had spoken at many different times and in various ways in the past has 'in these last days . . . spoken to us by his Son'. Revelation reaches a climax in the person of God's Son and in the witness which is borne to him (2:1–4). The verses just cited clearly indicate that greater light has come with God's Son and, therefore, even greater responsibility rests upon hearers of God's message through him than that which was borne by the hearers of Moses (cf. 12:25–26).

This does not entail a dispensationalist approach to the Old Testament, still less the approach of Marcion. What it surely means is that we must take seriously the fact that there will be elements both of continuity and of discontinuity between the Old Testament Scriptures and those of the New Testament.

---

3. D. A. Carson, *The Gospel According to John* (Leicester: Inter-Varsity Press, 1991), pp. 127–130.

Don Carson has drawn attention to the fact that the whole of the Old Testament, law as well as prophets, has a predictive role (Matt. 11:12–13).[4] While the Old Testament – and the whole of the Old Testament – remains God's word for us and is profitable in every way for us (Rom. 15:4; 1 Cor. 10:11; 2 Tim. 3:15–17), the fact that it finds its fulfilment in Jesus means that much of it will apply to us somewhat differently from the way in which it applied to the covenant community of the Old Testament period. Since Jesus Christ is the eschatological fulfilment of the Old Testament, this cannot but affect the way in which we apply it today.

The New Testament treatment of Old Testament material

The *use* of Old Testament material clearly lies at the heart of some of the differences amongst God's people concerning the nature of the authority of the State and the relationship of the individual Christian and of the church to the State. What has been said in the previous section is clearly relevant at this point. David Field's chapter on Samuel Rutherford's *Lex, Rex*, amply demonstrates that Rutherford drew very heavily upon Old Testament material to support the case which he presented. It may be thought, however, that Rutherford, for all of the intensity of his devotion to the person of Jesus Christ, did not work through with sufficient clarity, rigour and thoroughness the effect which the coming of Christ had upon the application of certain Old Testament material to political matters. How does the New Testament treat these things and how does it view the Old Testament's teaching upon political matters? To be specific, is it sound interpretation to take Old Testament passages concerning the relationship of the king with Old Testament Israel, and then Judah, and deduce principles from that material to guide us in political thinking today? These are questions to which we must later return.

---

4. D. A. Carson (ed.), *From Sabbath to Lord's Day* (Grand Rapids: Zondervan, 1982), p. 77.

The status of the Mosaic law

This issue follows on quite naturally from the previous points. It surfaced repeatedly at the conference during discussion of the papers. If agreement can be reached on this question, it might well lead to greater unanimity of conviction, if not total agreement, on some of the vexed questions concerning the relationship of the Christian and of the church to the State. The subject is indeed complex and has generated a vast literature, both popular and scholarly. Although the brief observations which are made here inevitably run the risk of gross over-simplification, there is value in identifying the main approaches which have characterized evangelical treatments of the place of the Mosaic law.

The Westminster Confession gives classic expression to the 'threefold division': ceremonial law, moral law and civil law.[5] The ceremonial law ('the types and shadows') was fulfilled by Christ and no longer applies to us. The moral law, summarized in the Ten Commandments, continues to bind all people today. It remains a rule of life, even though those who have faith in Christ have been delivered from its punishment and penalty and are free, therefore, from its curse. Since Israel was a nation state, as well as being the people of God, the civil law is no longer normative as to its detailed requirements, though the equity of its principles is still valid.

The last few decades have witnessed the rise of what has been known, perhaps rather unfortunately, as *theonomy*. The writings of Greg Bahnsen and Rousas Rushdoony were particularly influential in the promotion of this general hermeneutical approach to the Old Testament.[6] The common denominator amongst theonomists is the belief that the Old Testament 'civil law' continues to apply today. In the realm of practical affairs this hermeneutic gives rise to what is known as *reconstructionism*. Those who espouse this view

5. *The Confession of Faith of the Assembly of Divines at Westminster* (1646), ch. 19.
6. G. Bahnsen, *Theonomy in Christian Ethics* (Nutley, NJ: Presbyterian and Reformed, 1977); R. J. Rushdoony, *The Institutes of Biblical Law* (Nutley, NJ: Craig Press, 1973).

believe, with varying degrees of intensity, that Christians should seek to 'reconstruct' society by the application of the Old Testament civil law.

At the opposite end of the theological spectrum is what may broadly be classified as a *dispensational* approach to the Mosaic law. There are many who, while not necessarily buying into this overall theology, are prepared to say that the Mosaic law no longer applies today, and that specific Mosaic commandments are to bind the conscience only where they are reaffirmed by New Testament writers.

In more recent years a 'paradigmatic approach' has gained in popularity. This view (which is particularly associated with the name of Chris Wright and some of the details of which are worked out and applied in the chapter by Gordon Wenham) sees Old Testament Israel and the laws which God gave to her as being something of a paradigm for societies today.

Another understanding of the relationship of the Mosaic law to the New Testament is that which may be called *eschatological fulfilment*. This approach sees the whole of the Old Testament as pointing forward to Christ. The Mosaic law, as well as the prophets, 'prophesied' until John the Baptist (Matt. 11:13). Jesus 'fulfilled' the Law and the Prophets (Matt. 5:17).[7] This general hermeneutical approach may be applied in a number of different ways: it is possible within this framework to arrive at conclusions which are virtually identical with those of the Westminster Confession or, alternatively, with those which are more congruent with a dispensational approach. It is also possible to arrive at a somewhat distinctive position, which is more nuanced in its perception of the nature of the relationship of the New Testament to the Old.

Old Testament history and human sinfulness

From Genesis 3 onwards until the glorious vision of chapters 21 and 22 of Revelation, human sinfulness is a brute fact the reality

---

7. D. A. Carson, *John*, p. 77.

of which permeates the whole of the Bible. It is an essential element to the background and context in which all discussion of the Bible and political matters must take place. The Old Testament is, no doubt, many things; but whatever else it may be, it is certainly a record of the appalling sinfulness and failure of the human race. Man is placed as God's vicegerent in a perfect environment to rule over the earth (Gen. 1:28). As such, and having come directly from the hand of God, Adam is God's son (Luke 3:38). He rebels against God, with catastrophic consequences for himself and for the world (Gen. 3:7–24). The 'creation mandate' is renewed in modified form after the flood in a 'cleansed world' (Gen. 9:1–3), but shortly afterwards Noah gets drunk and Ham disgraces himself (Gen. 9:18–23). This does not bode well for the future. God's choice falls on Abram and, eventually, in fulfilment of God's word to Abram (Gen. 15:12–16), Moses is sent to lead the descendants of Abraham, Isaac and Jacob out of Egypt, and, after the great exodus, Moses is given God's law for God's people. However, even before Moses has returned from the mountain, the people descend into great idolatry (Exod. 32:1–10) and it quickly becomes clear that they need far more than excellent laws; they need Moses to 'stand in the gap' to intercede for them (Exod. 32:11–14, 31–32). Eventually they settle in the promised land. This is surely intended to be evocative and reminiscent of Eden. Here again is God's son (Hos. 11:1) in an ideal environment, with laws which were intended to be the envy of the surrounding nations. But by the period covered in the book of Judges things are in a very sorry state indeed. The biggest threat to Israel comes not from the surrounding nations but from the spiritual and moral corruption which is within the nation itself: a number of times towards the end of the book we hear the refrain, 'In those days Israel had no king' (18:1; 19:1; 21:25a), and at the very end of the book we learn that the absence of a king meant that 'everyone did as he saw fit' (21:25b). The purpose of these words is twofold: first, to emphasize that Israel, like Adam, was failing to live under the kingly reign of the Lord; second, to prepare the ground for the historical books, with their emphasis upon kingship within Israel.

The first king, King Saul, proves to be very disappointing and something of a 'false start'. But with David we have a man after

God's own heart and our expectations are raised. Yet even David has feet of clay. There is his sordid adultery with Bathsheba and, though forgiven and restored to fellowship with God, he never seems to be quite the same man again: witness his failure of judgment in dealing with Amnon and Absalom. The building of the temple during Solomon's reign is a high point in the history of Israel, yet Solomon goes seriously astray: his taking of many foreign wives and the attendant idolatry make for very sad reading indeed. The point of all this is that the king represents the nation and, as the one to rule God's people, is also called God's son (2 Sam. 7:14; Ps. 2:7). The subsequent history of the Davidic dynasty is largely one of failure, and even those kings who followed the Lord had their blemishes. Eventually the nation is taken into exile and the Davidic dynasty seems to be lost in the sands of time.

What all of this proclaims so clearly is that sin is endemic to the human race: if even the chosen people, with God's laws written for them and God's son as their king, can still sink to indescribable depths of idolatry and depravity, what hope is there for anyone else? If the leaders are corrupt, then what can one expect of the people? This surely is the import of Romans 3:19–20. After a catena of Old Testament quotations where the sins of people within Israel are catalogued, Paul writes, 'Now we know that whatever the law says, it says to those who are under the law, so that every mouth may be silenced and the whole world held accountable to God.' The words 'under the law' might be better translated 'in the law'. Similar words are used in Romans 2:12, where they can only refer to those who possess the written revelation of God's word. The point of what Paul is saying in Romans 3:19–20, therefore, is this: the fact that God's word can catalogue in such devastating detail the sins of those who possess the law must mean that the whole world is guilty before him. If Israel is so bad, what can be said of the rest of the world?

There is an important deduction to draw from this. Possession of good laws, even of God's own law, cannot guarantee righteousness. Righteousness indeed exalts a nation, but that is not the same as saying that possession of righteous laws makes a person righteous (Rom. 2:13). Indeed, in Romans chapter 7 Paul demonstrates how the coming of God's law can even stir up sin (cf. 5:20a).

A second deduction is that people can degenerate very quickly from a certain standard of morality. The decline of Israel during the days of the judges and, later on, in the days of her kings is the Old Testament's way of preaching the doctrines of original sin and total depravity. This is a fact which must always be borne in mind by legislators; even – I might say, especially – Christian legislators. And this being the case, Christian *agitators* or lobbyists must bear this in mind and not expect more from their politicians and legislators than they can deliver. This, surely, is the force of our Lord's words in Matthew 19:8: 'Moses permitted you to divorce your wives because your hearts were hard. But it was not this way from the beginning.' The presence of sin was something which Moses had to take into account. If this was so in the theocracy, how much more may it need to be true in other kinds of society! The propensity to sin in a society may be such that not only will prohibitory laws fail to achieve their purpose, they may even be productive of greater evil. Faced with such a situation, legislators may *regulate* or *control* certain evil practices, rather than categorically forbid them. A number of examples may help to illustrate and clarify this point.

There was a period in English law when certain gaming contracts were illegal.[8] Since 1960 this has no longer been the case.[9] Illegal gambling was productive of so many other evils that gambling was eventually decriminalized. Although no longer criminal, many gaming contracts are unlawful, in that they are unenforceable through the courts, and gambling is today a heavily regulated activity. Prostitution, 'the oldest profession in the world', is another example of an evil which is no longer a criminal activity, but a contract to engage in sexual relations with a prostitute is unlawful, and much activity connected with prostitution continues to be criminal. One of the reasons for the introduction of the Divorce Reform Act 1969 was that the law was being brought into

---

8. The Gaming Act 1738, s. 2; the Gaming Acts 1739 and 1744 made illegal certain games which depended upon chance and all games played with dice, except backgammon.

9. Betting and Gaming Act 1960, schedule 6.

disrepute through connivance: a couple who wished to be divorced would arrange for one of them to spend a night in a hotel room with a person of the opposite sex in order that the other spouse could then petition for a divorce on the grounds of adultery. This was making something of a farce of the existing divorce law and was one of the reasons for the 'no fault' divorce which the 1969 Act introduced.

Christians, of all people, should take the reality of human sinfulness with great seriousness and realize that this cannot but have implications for the legislators in a given society. But recognition of this fact gives rise to a very important question: how far should such a principle be extended? This is a question which merits sustained and profound consideration.

The promised Messiah

If the Old Testament graphically portrays humanity's plight, it no less clearly points to the coming Deliverer. As Judah's kings are seen to be failing, the prospect of a very different king shines through all the more brightly and clearly. The 'Immanuel' section of Isaiah (chs. 7 – 12) both prophesies doom on the Davidic dynasty and looks forward to a descendant of David who will be very different indeed. This promised Messiah will be both son of David and 'Mighty God' (9:6–7). As Davidic king, He will be God's son. But as God himself, new content will be poured into this title: hence in John's Gospel especially we learn that Jesus has always been God's Son and that this Sonship entails full equality with God. Here, then, is Israel's hope, but also the hope of the nations. What Israel failed so signally to be (the light to the nations), the Messiah will be: he will bring righteousness to the nations and his kingdom will extend throughout the whole world (Isa 9:7; 11:4, 10; 42:1; cf. Dan. 2:44).

It is quite clear from the Old Testament's account of the coming messianic kingdom that as the King will be gloriously different from Judah's other kings, so his kingdom will also be different. Although Daniel emphasizes, as do many other biblical passages, that it is God who raises up rulers and gives to them their power (e.g. 5:18), it also teaches that God will set up a kingdom which is uniquely his, in the establishment of which men and women will play no part (2:44–45). (Note the emphasis in verse 45 that the rock will be cut out of a mountain 'but not by human hands'.) The reign of God on earth, through his promised king, is a recurrent theme in the prophetic literature of the Old Testament. It looks back to the failure of Adam to fulfil his role as God's vicegerent; to the failure of Israel to represent the Lord and be a light to the nations; and to the failure of Israel's kings, as the representatives of the nation, to execute the Lord's reign amongst his people. It looks forward, therefore, to the Messiah, who will triumph and succeed where Adam, Israel and her kings – and, therefore, by implication, all of us – have so miserably failed. The roots of the New Testament emphases upon Christ as the last Adam, as the true Israel and as the Davidic King are found, therefore, in the Old Testament literature (Rom. 5:12–19; 1 Cor. 15:20–22, 44–49; Matt. 2:15; John 15:1–8; Rom. 1:3–4, etc.).

The kingdom of God and the kingdoms of men

Volumes have been written on the meaning of this enigmatic phrase. For our present purposes we need simply to note that the kingdom centres upon the person and work of the King himself, the Lord Jesus Christ (Matt.3:1–3 [cf. Isa. 40:1–11]; Matt. 12:28; Luke 17:20–21 [where the last clause can be translated, 'the kingdom of God is among you']). He is the one who inaugurates this kingdom. Entrance into kingdom membership, and citizenship of the kingdom, are also dependent upon God's activity, namely the activity of the Holy Spirit in giving new birth (John 3:1–8). Here is a radically new kingdom which is inhabited by radically new people. The 'kingdom manifesto' makes it quite clear that these new people live a radically new life (Matt. 5:1–20; 6:25–34; 7:21–23).

Although the kingdom *has* come (Christ has inaugurated it) and *is coming* (as people are born again and enter into it), it is also *yet to come* (Matt. 13:47–50; 25:1, 31–36; Rev. 11:15). The question for the Christian is how he is to relate to the kingdoms of this world during this present age. The Christian belongs to God's kingdom (Col. 1:13), but is also a citizen on earth (Acts 16:37). Paul makes it quite clear in Colossians 1:13 that entrance into the kingdom of God's dear Son means that we have been delivered out from the kingdom of darkness. This is not the same, however, as saying, that the Christian has been delivered out of every earthly kingdom. How are the citizens of God's kingdom to function as the citizens of earthly kingdoms?

Christ is reigning at present (1 Cor. 15:25), but, as the verse just cited makes clear, there are enemies of Christ still within his world. Indeed, though Christ reigns, Satan can still be referred to as 'the god of this age' (2 Cor. 4:4). The Great Commission, as recorded by Matthew, brings together these two strands of biblical teaching: all authority in heaven and upon earth has indeed been given to Christ, but the fact that people need to be made disciples means that not all are disciples at present, and this implies that not all bow to the authority of Jesus. It is this which gives rise to the tensions which the Christian and the church may experience with respect to various institutions upon earth.

It is essential to grasp that it is only as people are born of God's Spirit that they may enter into God's kingdom. It is theological confusion to believe that unregenerate men and women can display 'kingdom behaviour' or give practical expression to 'kingdom values'. The New Testament calls to holiness repeatedly base the *ethical imperatives* on *ontological indicatives*. It would be tedious to list all the examples, but the following may suffice: 1 Corinthians 6:19–20; Ephesians 4:1–2, 17–28; Colossians 3:1–14. One may go further: talk of God's people 'redeeming' politics or culture, or anything else for that matter, is a theological category error. These are, after all, aspects of creation and the created order. As Paul spells out so eloquently in Romans 8:18–25, creation will remain in its bondage to decay until the sons of God will be revealed. God's people have received 'the firstfruits of the Spirit'. These guarantee the full harvest, but they must not be confused with that full harvest. As such, the people of God are 'a kind of firstfruits of all that [God] created' (Jas 1:18). In their engagement with culture and politics, Christian people do so as those who are a firstfruits of what the new heavens and new earth will be. But this does not mean that they are 'redeeming' culture and politics. The Christian farmer does his work as unto the Lord and does so as a kind of firstfruits of the new heavens and the new earth. But he does not, and cannot, remove the curse from the earth, a curse which will be removed only when the creation will be delivered from its bondage to corruption when the sons of God will be revealed (Rom. 8:18–25; cf. 1 John 3:2–3).

The people of God today are no longer to be identified with a particular nation living in a particular land. This is surely a significant difference between God's people in the Old Testament period and God's people in 'these last days'. It is those who have faith in Jesus Christ who now constitute the true Israel (Matt. 21:43–44; Rom. 11:17–24; Gal. 6:16; Eph. 2:11–22). This means that care is needed in treating Israel as a paradigm for other nations. While one may well see that underlying the laws which were given to Israel are principles which express God's character and concern for people and which may, therefore, be beneficially applied to societies today, the fact remains that the New Testament treats Israel and the distinctiveness which she should have displayed during the Old Testament period as a paradigm, *not* for nation states today but, rather, for the church. It is the disciples of Jesus who are the salt of the earth and the light of the world. It is Peter, in his first letter, who particularly picks up the theme of the distinctiveness of Israel and applies it to Christians today. He describes Christians as 'a chosen people, a royal priesthood, a holy nation, a people belonging to God, that you may declare the praises of him who called you out of darkness into his wonderful light' (2:9). This, of course, is language which is used of Israel when the Lord espoused her to himself after taking her out of Egypt (Exod. 19:6; Deut. 4:20; 10:15). Christians are the true Diaspora (1. Pet. 1:1) and their relationship to the world about them is similar to that of the people of Judah during the exile (1:1; 2:11). It is this fact, that the church is the Israel of God, which enables Paul to 'transpose' the language of *execution* from the Old Testament nation of Israel and apply it to *excommunication* in the New Testament church (1 Cor. 5:13; cf. Deut. 17:7).

The practical implications of all this are considerable indeed. The Old Testament treatment of idolatry is *not* a paradigm for society to do the same today; rather, it enshrines those principles by which the people of God must order their lives. In 1 Corinthians chapters 8 – 10 Paul applies God's truth to the problem of idolatry *within* the church. His concern at this point is not with those outside (cf. 1 Cor. 5:12–13). This does not mean, however, that he was not concerned with the idolatry that was found in the world; quite the contrary! He was stirred to the depths of his being by the idolatry which he saw in Athens (Acts 17:16). But his response to that idolatry – namely, reasoning with all who would listen to him about Jesus and the resurrection, and calling upon people to repent (vv. 17–18, 22–31) – was grounded in his conviction that only the gospel could remove idolatry from people's lives. This surely is the whole thrust of what he says in Romans 1:14–32. Putting together what Paul writes to the Corinthians with what he said and did in Athens and what he wrote to the Romans, we arrive at the following position: the church is to be the church and must deal with idolatry in its ranks; but the world needs to be delivered from idolatry and this is achieved by the sword of God's word – by gospel proclamation – not by the State wielding the sword. The Old Testament execution of the prophets of Baal during the time of Elijah is not a pattern for the way in which the Lord's people are today to approach the problem of idolatry and false religion within society at large (Luke 9:51–55).

Luke brings out this emphasis very clearly in his Gospel and in Acts. Attention has frequently been drawn to the heavily 'Jewish atmosphere' of the first two chapters of Luke's Gospel. Zechariah speaks of the God of Israel coming to redeem his people by Mary's son (1:68–69) and of the salvation from their enemies (v. 71) which his people – the descendants of Abraham (v. 73) – would experience. Towards the end of the book it becomes clear that even amongst the disciples the belief was cherished that Jesus would redeem Israel, as a nation, from her enemies (24:21). Indeed, it is quite clear that the sadness of Cleopas and his fellow disciple was the result of their hopes having been shattered by the failure of the Jewish leaders and by the crucifixion of Jesus (vv. 20–21). Given that we already know from Zechariah's prophecy that Jesus will redeem Israel, it becomes clear, in Jesus' words to the Emmaus road disciples, that it was precisely by his death and resurrection that this redemption was accomplished (24:25–27). The point, of course, is that the *nature* of this redemption was radically different from that expected by these two disciples. And if its nature was different, so would be its *consequences*. This is the whole point of the way in which Luke records the Great Commission. Having explained to the disciples that Christ had to suffer and rise from the dead (24:45–46), Jesus immediately goes on to say that repentance and forgiveness is to be preached to all nations, beginning at Jerusalem. It is by gospel proclamation, not by political activity, that Christ's redemption will be brought to bear upon people's lives. And this redemption is not confined to the nation of Israel.

This emphasis then becomes programmatic in Acts. In chapter 1 verse 6 it is clear that the disciples are still thinking in terms of Israel being restored to her former glory. Jesus responds by telling them that they are to be his witnesses in Jerusalem, Judea, Samaria, and the ends of the earth (v. 8). The power to be such witnesses will come from the Holy Spirit. This is clearly reminiscent of the Great Commission in Luke. The very last verse of Acts, which has Paul in Rome (cf. 1:8: 'the ends of the earth'), 'preach[ing] the kingdom of God and [teaching] about the Lord Jesus Christ', demonstrates that *this* is the way in which the kingdom has been restored to Israel. This, of course, is all of a piece with a major strand of New Testament teaching, which sees the kingdom being taken from the Jewish leaders to be given to another, a fruitful, nation (Matt. 21:43), and which interprets the rebuilding of the Davidic dynasty in terms of Messiah's rule over those – both Gentiles and the 'remnant' of Israel – who trust in him (Acts 15:16–18). This is how the New Testament writers can refer to the church as being the 'Israel of God'.

I shall seek to draw out the practical implications of all this towards the end of this chapter.

Relationship of God's people to the State

Two questions need to be considered: first, how should Christians behave with respect to the state; and, in the second place, may Christians be active in political life? We shall consider each in turn.

The first question is neatly answered by Jesus' words that one is to render to Caesar what is Caesar's, and to God what is God's. F. F. Bruce has helpfully put these words and the question which they answered into their proper historical context and has shown that lying behind the question is the teaching of Judas the Galilean: that the payment of taxes to Caesar would be incompatible with Israel's theocratic ideals, because the Romans were pagans.[10] Bruce demonstrates convincingly that this was a novel doctrine and he points to passages where Old Testament prophets taught that foreign domination was to be viewed as a judgment of Yahweh upon his people and, as such, had to be endured until he would lift it. Withholding tribute would, therefore, be rebellion against Yahweh. This was true of Zedekiah's withholding of tribute from Nebuchadnezzar; Jeremiah chapter 27 is a crucial part of Scripture with respect to this issue. As Bruce points out, this is consistent with the implication of Malachi 1:8.

Jesus' teaching on the payment of taxes to Caesar is to be understood, therefore, against this Old Testament prophetic background. Jesus reasserted the older doctrine, one which was fully consonant with certain Old Testament strands of teaching. The significance of this can hardly be overstated. Rome had subjugated the theocratic people. Whatever liberties God's ancient people enjoyed under this regime, it was nevertheless the case that the Roman religions would have been viewed by the Jews as idolatrous. Yet Jesus did not proclaim revolt against Rome.

This teaching is picked up by Paul in Romans 13:1–7. It is essential to a proper understanding of this passage to realize that Paul is referring to the powers which actually were in place at the time of his writing, not to some ideal government. Paul was not writing a treatise for kings and rulers, setting out their God-given role and duties and the limits of their powers, but rather telling

---

10. In E. Bammel and C. F. D. Moule (eds.), *Jesus and the Politics of His Day* (Cambridge: Cambridge University Press, 1984 [pbk edn 1985]), pp. 249–263.

Christians in Rome how they were to relate to those in actual political authority. Tom Wright has shown that this passage is fully in line with the following Old Testament passages: Isaiah 10:5–11; 44:28 – 45:5; 46:11; Jeremiah 27:6–11; 29:4–9; Daniel 1:2; 2:21, 37–49.[11]

The objection may be raised that this essentially positive view of government has to be balanced with what we find in Revelation, where Rome is pictured as a beast, a demonic power which makes idolatrous and blasphemous claims for itself and blasphemous demands upon others. Can a Christian possibly view such a government in the way that Romans chapter 13 verses 1–7 tells us to do? Is not the situation envisaged in Romans unrecognizable by the time we come to Revelation, and, for that reason, is not a different response required?

The answer to these questions is, of course, far from merely theoretical. For many Christians in different parts of the world these are urgently relevant and important questions. For all the complexity of the issues involved, the answer is still supplied by Jesus' words found in Matthew 22:21. One is to give to Caesar only what is Caesar's; one is not to give him what belongs to God. How this works out in practice is illustrated for us in Daniel. It can too easily be forgotten that in Daniel not only is the coming Roman Empire pictured as a monstrous beast (7:7), but so were those empires in which Daniel served (7:4–5). Nebuchadnezzar made idolatrous and blasphemous claims for himself and blasphemous demands of the people (3:1–6; 4:30), and Darius essentially claimed for himself what rightly belonged to God (6:7). What is surely significant is that Daniel and his three friends served under these kings *and* were faithful in their service to God. When the kings commanded what was sinful or forbade what God commanded, they obeyed God, disobeyed their rulers, and were prepared to face the consequences (3:16–18; 6:10). They did not, however, attempt to overthrow or remove the kings from their position.

---

11. In L. E. Keck et al. (eds.), *The New Interpreter's Bible*, vol. 10 (Nashville: Abingdon Press, 2002), pp. 715–723.

It needs to be borne in mind that both the temple and the land had been taken from God's people by Nebuchadnezzar. These were things which 'belonged to God', not to Caesar. Yet in spite of what was to the people of God an act of unspeakable sacrilege, Daniel and his friends submitted to the regime in obedience to the word of the Lord through Jeremiah. I shall seek to draw out the practical implications of this towards the end of this chapter.

Daniel and his friends were, of course, not only living under particular political regimes; they were also involved in some form of political office themselves. Both Joseph and Daniel served under rulers who did not belong to God's covenant people. In the New Testament Erastus held what appears to have been a significant position in the local government of the city of Corinth (Rom. 16:23).[12] Since political power has been ordained by God (Rom. 13:1), it is clearly legitimate for Christians not only to be involved in political life, but also to occupy political office. This does not mean, of course, that the Christian is to try to create a 'Christian state', any more than the chief executive of a car-manufacturing company who also happens to be a Christian is to seek to make it a 'Christian company'. This is such an important point that it needs to be unpacked in more detail.

First, it is essential that one does not identify the kingdom of God with any particular nation state. Some of the British Puritans, as well as those who settled in the New World, made this mistake, as did some of the Dutch Reformed Christians in South Africa. This type of case of mistaken identity has been productive of numerous ills. The invasion of Iraq is a good example of the damage which can result from failure to distinguish between God's kingdom and a particular nation. I am not concerned to discuss the merits or otherwise of that invasion and whether or not it was justifiable in terms of public international law. Rather, I wish to draw attention to the fact that, if people identify the interests of the USA with those of God's kingdom and confuse the two, as

---

12. On the precise position which Erastus held, see J. D. G. Dunn, *Romans 9–16*, Word Biblical Commentary, vol. 38B (Dallas: Word Incorporated, 1988; Word UK edn: Milton Keynes, 1991), p. 911.

some American Christians undoubtedly do, then it is hardly surprising if many of the Middle Eastern peoples are deeply prejudiced against the Christian message. I think of an Arab Christian, based in the Middle East, who is involved in evangelism, church planting and church support. His knowledge of the whole of that region is both extensive and intensive. He has commented on the fact that the invasion of Iraq has made gospel work much harder in the Middle East, even when done by people from the region. They are viewed as 'pro-Western' and as betraying their people. This does not, I repeat, settle the question as to whether the invasion was justifiable or not; it is simply to acknowledge that if people cannot tell the difference between Uncle Sam and God's kingdom, then damage is bound to be done to the cause of Christ. The thrust of Steve Wilmshurst's chapter warns against this danger, and David Smith has some salutary things to say concerning the danger of God's kingdom being identified with the prevailing culture of any particular nation.

Second, there is a 'bare minimum' which every Christian should be concerned for. It is laid down in 1 Timothy 2:2. Paul has told Timothy that requests, prayers, intercession and thanksgiving are to be made for all men (v. 1). He then specifies that this is to be done for kings and all those in authority (v. 2). The purpose of such praying is 'that we may live peaceful and quiet lives in all godliness and holiness' (v. 2). The thrust of the verse is that God's people may be able to get on with living a dignified Christian life. The next few verses make it quite clear that these conditions are conducive to the spread of the gospel, and this pleases God because he wants all people to be saved. Since there is only one God and only one Mediator between God and men, the man Christ Jesus, it is essential that men and women hear this gospel and are taught the truth as it is in Jesus (vv. 3–7).

These verses, therefore, bring together a number of important themes. There is a strong note of religious exclusivism sounded here: there is only one God, and only one way to God (v. 5). This is true for all people (v. 6: 'ransom for all men'; v. 7: 'a teacher of the true faith to the Gentiles'). At the same time there is a strongly inclusivist note: although there is only one way, it is open to all people. But there is an absence of any emphasis in these verses upon *political* exclusivism: Paul is not for one moment suggesting that the church should pray for the equivalent of 'special favoured nation status' for itself. He does not say that prayer should be offered that rulers stamp out false religion or that external godliness be enforced by those in authority. His concern is much more modest: that God's people might be able to live their lives in peace and quiet in all godliness and holiness. If this is a 'bottom-line' matter for Christian prayers, then it is, surely, a bottom-line matter for Christian politicians. Daniel's friends were willing to be thrown into the fiery furnace for not bowing down to Nebuchadnezzar's image; there is no suggestion that they would protest about others worshipping the image or that they would be prepared to be thrown into the fire for such a protest.

It is instructive to compare what Paul says in 1 Timothy 2:2 with what he writes in Romans 13:3–4. At the time that he writes Romans he can say:

> rulers hold no terror for those who do right, but for those who do wrong . . . do what is right and he will commend you . . . But if you do wrong, be afraid, for he does not bear the sword for nothing. He is God's servant, an agent of wrath to bring punishment on the wrongdoer.

As we have already observed, Paul was not describing some ideal of government but the actual Roman authorities. Clearly, therefore, when he speaks of doing 'right' and doing 'wrong', he is speaking *relatively*, not absolutely. The reason for saying this is that we know that many things were permitted within the Roman Empire which would certainly have been categorized by Paul as sinful. In chapter 1, for example, he refers to idolatry, homosexuality and lesbianism, as well as a host of other sins (vv. 21–27). Yet he still acknowledges the legitimacy of the governing authorities and even refers to them as God's servants to commend those who do right and punish those who do wrong. It would seem, therefore, that Paul acknowledged the legitimacy of a government which permitted idolatry and many of the evils which flow from idolatry. Indeed, given Jesus' words concerning the payment of taxes to Caesar, it would seem that he acknowledged the legitimacy of such a government.

—

Putting together Romans 13:1–7 with 1 Timothy 2:2, it would appear that for Paul a government is fulfilling its God-given purpose when it regulates affairs between men and women in such a way that people, Christians included, are permitted to live their lives in peace and quiet. The maintenance of the public order which is essential to living one's life in peace and quiet (what would today be called 'the enjoyment of personal freedom') is evidently one of the chief purposes of government. Luke, concerned to emphasize that Christianity is not subversive of the state, records that it was not Christians who caused the riot in Ephesus but the worshippers of Artemis–Diana. The city clerk carried out his task well by restoring order to a city in uproar (Acts 19:23–41). The idolatry in Ephesus had been challenged *not* by the Roman authorities forbidding it but, rather, by Paul's preaching of Christ.

Christian politicians, legislators and the law

What has been said in the previous section can place the Christian politician in something of a dilemma. What is he to do when certain matters traditionally concerned with 'private morality' come up for consideration? Does he simply opt for the 'bottom line', or should he seek for legislation which will outlaw certain immoral practices? It is impossible to deal adequately with the complex range of issues which lie behind this question in a chapter of this length. The question merits a book which is devoted to the issues underlying it.[13] The following are merely suggestions and pointers as to the way in which this question should be approached.

First, there is need to establish what is the *rationale* for outlawing an immoral act. In the seventeenth century, the New England states of Massachusetts, Connecticut and New Haven made

---

13. I hope by the end of October 2005 to have completed the manuscript for a book exploring these issues as they touch upon issues at the very beginning and at the very end of life, and as they affect issues of public policy with respect to sexual behaviour.

adultery a capital offence, although it seems that the punishment was only carried out three times.[14] 'For the most part they sentenced offenders to fines, whippings, brandings, the wearing of a letter 'A' and symbolical executions in the form of standing on the gallows with a rope about the neck.'[15] Adultery *is* sinful. Furthermore, it can devastate the lives of a number of families and have profound psychological effects upon the children. These are the innocent victims of a marriage breakdown, often when they are at their most vulnerable age. So should it be a crime? If so, what punishment should it carry? If it should not be outlawed, are there other sinful actions which should be outlawed? If the answer is 'Yes', on what basis does one distinguish one immoral action or sinful act from another? What is the distinguishing element which, in the one case, leads one to say, 'This should be a crime', and, in the other case, 'This should not be a crime'?

The importance of these questions can be illustrated in the following way. For some time there has been an increasing body of opinion that euthanasia should be legalized. Most Christians are implacably opposed to such a move, the bottom line being not the risks which may result from greedy family members wanting to get their hands on the inheritance but, rather, the fact that it is a breach of God's law. When the question is put, however, as to whether fornication and adultery should be made crimes, there is often ambivalence on the part of those Christians who are against the legalizing of euthanasia. But if the rationale for keeping euthanasia as a crime is that it breaches God's law, would not consistency demand that adultery and fornication also be made crimes? If not, then the rationale for keeping euthanasia as a crime cannot be simply that it breaches God's law. Or might it be the case that we learn to accept the status quo but are uneasy with any further erosion of the law of God in public life? In other words, because neither fornication nor adultery have been crimes in the lifetime of most Christians in the West, the possibility of these acts being

14. E. S. Morgan, *The Puritan Family: Religion and Domestic Relations in Seventeenth-Century New England* (New York: Harper and Row, 1966), p. 41.

15. Morgan, *The Puritan Family*, p. 41.

outlawed is not seriously entertained, except amongst theonomists. On the other hand, because euthanasia has always been a crime, it is felt that the sanctity of life will be seriously imperilled if this were to be legalized. But has not the sanctity of sex been imperilled by adultery and fornication? So why should these not be made crimes?

I put these questions in this deliberately provocative way in order to try to help to focus the issues. There is need for more thought and work to be given to these questions. The liberal has a ready-made answer: only those things which interfere with the freedom and choice of other agents should be made crimes. Freedom of the individual is trumps every time. However much one might disagree with this position, it is both rational and coherent. But, in the strict sense of the words, it is both irrational and incoherent to say that euthanasia should remain a crime because it is contrary to God's law but that fornication and adultery should not be made crimes.

Before moving on from this, there is value in pointing out that the classic liberal or libertarian approach, which was advocated by political philosophers like John Stuart Mill and legal theorists such as H. L. A. Hart, is today at risk of collapse. There are two pressure points where classic liberalism or libertarianism is vulnerable. The first arises from the fact that libertarianism arose in a context where many regarded it as axiomatic that freedom was a good thing. But there are numerous groups in the world who believe that there are values much higher than freedom, values for which it is worth sacrificing freedom. Faced with such a challenge, libertarianism can be defended only if its advocates argue for the *morality* of protecting freedom: for the morality of outlawing only those acts which impinge upon the freedom of others. But this means that libertarianism, in the final analysis, becomes a highly moralistic position: it can be defended only by recourse to one overarching ethical principle, namely, the moral goodness of freedom. The effect of this, therefore, is to expose the claim of libertarians – namely, that their position is not moralistic – as being entirely empty.

The second pressure point results from the rise to prominence of the animal rights lobby and from developments in medical technology as they touch upon the unborn child. Both of these developments give rise to the question: *whose* liberty is to be protected? The idea that libertarianism could avoid hard questions concerning the ontological status of entities by simply appealing to the principle of liberty is seen to be as vacuous as the claim that it could short-circuit hard moral questions.

The first of these two challenges to classic libertarianism provides an opportunity for Christians working in the area of public policy to raise fairly fundamental questions concerning the legitimate foundations of law. The Christian sees the basis for the State as rooted in a transcendent God, who has laid down that human affairs need to be regulated by law and government. But what basis does the libertarian have for his belief in law and government? Since in the present climate the Christian has the opportunity to demonstrate in the public forum that he has an adequate *basis* for law and government and to question what possible basis *the secularist* can have for these things, how important it is that the Christian has thought through carefully what should be the *content* of the laws which should be enacted!

The second point to note is that it is possible to say that there is a difference between the situation where a sinful act is not yet a crime and one says that the status quo should be maintained and the action not be outlawed, and saying that a sinful act which is already a crime should be legalized. There is an element of what might be called 'Christian pragmatism' in arguing in this way. There are certain historic 'moral landmarks' which may well be the result of the Christian influence in previous generations. These landmarks are part of the Christian heritage with which some nations have been privileged. This being the case, one should be vigilant in preventing these landmarks from being removed. In other words, while 1 Timothy 2:2 provides 'the bottom line', Christian influence in a society may well have been such that public opinion has been affected and this has had effects upon the legislation which has been passed. But the legislation in turn helps to 'solidify' that public opinion.[16] This being the case, no Christian

---

16. On the relationship between law and public opinion, reference should be made to A. V. Dicey, *Lectures on the Relation between Law and Public Opinion in England during the Nineteenth Century* (London: New Brunswick), 1981.

should lightly fritter away that heritage in the way that Esau so lightly let go of his birthright.

Where some of the landmarks have been removed or dismantled, it may well be impossible for them to be erected again unless and until there is such a powerful movement of God's Spirit that the whole outlook of a nation is affected. But this being the case, it may be all the more important to ensure that one preserves as much as possible of what remains of that Christian heritage. It would not be too difficult to show that over the last thirty to forty years laws which were the result of Christian influence have been removed as a result of articulate and vociferous minorities campaigning for change without Christians realizing what was happening. The change in the law has then affected public opinion, and this is making it all the more difficult to preserve what remains of Christian influence on the statute book. This being so, Christians are frequently these days put on the back foot and are perceived to be reactionary, negative and conservative, always reacting to the agenda of those who are 'progressive'.

What this means, of course, is that there is no simple blueprint for the Christian who is involved in political life. Account has to be taken of the context in which the Christian finds himself or herself. A Christian politician in the UK or in the USA is in an entirely different context from that of a Christian politician in France. The revocation of the Edict of Nantes, with its catastrophic effect upon the Huguenots; the secularizing influences of the French Enlightenment; the discontinuity brought about by the French Revolution: all of this has made France a very different country from the UK. Again, the position of Christians in a democracy is inevitably different from that of Christians living under a totalitarian regime. Similarly, a Christian MP in a parliamentary democracy will have different opportunities from those of a Christian who belongs to a government which is not democratically elected. In other words, it is possible to argue that were Daniel or Paul living in a country which had had the benefit of Christian influence and which was governed under a system of parliamentary democracy, they might well be setting higher goals for what one should expect from the legislature and the government than 'the bottom line' found in 1 Timothy 2:2. As Gordon Wenham points out, the 'floor' of acceptable behaviour, below which behaviour becomes un-acceptable, is much lower in Britain today than that which would have been tolerated in ancient Israel. A strong case can be made for saying that in circumstances such as these, the Christian should seek to raise the 'floor' by arguing for the kinds of 'creational realities' to which Gordon Wenham refers, the kinds of realities referred to in the first nine chapters of Genesis. Since God's standards are good for mankind, it is possible to argue for some of these things, even amongst those who dismiss the Bible, on the basis of their benefit to human life. In the public arena, in a society where a kind of utilitarianism holds sway, the Christian may argue for the social utility of certain measures. This approach can be extended, in measure, to the Ten Commandments; at least to some of them. One does not have to accept the paradigmatic hermeneutic of Old Testament law to argue in such a way.

This leads on to a third point. Where Christians gain in influence and are heavily represented in a parliamentary democracy, they may aim higher than 'the bottom line'. The danger which must then be avoided is that of seeking to 'Christianize' society. This was attempted in England in the decade following the execution of Charles I in 1649. The long-term consequences were pretty disastrous. The restoration of the monarchy in 1660 and the Act of Uniformity in 1662 triggered one of the most spiritually bankrupt and morally decadent periods in English public life from the time of the Reformation to the present day. Christian behaviour can be practised only by Christian people, and Christian people become such by regeneration. Acts of Parliament can never effect what requires nothing less than an act of God. It is bad theology to attempt to 'Christianize' society. It is also pastorally wrong-headed and practically harmful. It is pastorally wrong-headed because people may well resent what is being attempted, and this, in turn, hardens them and alienates them yet more against the Christian gospel. It is practically harmful because, should the situation change – as it did in England in 1660 – the resentment which has been created may well boil over into hostile action against the church (as it most certainly did in 1662).

Thomas Chalmers, the great Scottish Christian leader who led 'the Disruption' from the Church of Scotland in the 1840s, well understood this. Chalmers was a convinced evangelical, who was opposed to Roman Catholicism. Nevertheless he supported the cause of Catholic emancipation. He reasoned as follows: 'Give the Catholics of Ireland their emancipation, give them a seat in the Parliament of their country; give them a free and equal participation in the politics of the realm; give them a place at the right hand of majesty and a voice in his counsels; and give me the circulation of the Bible, and with this mighty engine I will overthrow the tyranny of Antichrist, and establish the fair and original form of Christianity on its ruins.'[17] If for 'Catholics' one substitutes the word 'Muslims', and if instead of 'emancipation' one puts the word 'participation', it will become immediately apparent that Chalmers' general approach has as much to say in twenty-first-century Britain as it did in the nineteenth century.

What has just been said needs, however, to be qualified. It is one thing for a state to allow people the liberty to practise their religion: if the Christian is granted this liberty, then denying the same right to others is bound to be perceived by them as a case of Christians simply wanting to have their own way. But it is another matter altogether to tolerate a religion with an agenda to seek to subvert the state. It is perverse to allow people to use the freedoms which a country gives them to destroy those freedoms for other people.

A fourth consideration, which must never be forgotten, is that while the 'bottom line' is as laid down in 1 Timothy 2:2, behaviour which is above that bottom line may be so reprehensible that a society which practises and institutionally approves it is heading for ruin. Leviticus chapter 18, for example, refers to a whole range of sexual sins. Verses 24–28 state that it was for these very sins that God punished the inhabitants of Canaan and that the land 'vomited' them out. Here we are in the realm of sinful activities some of which were practised and approved throughout the Roman Empire. Although neither Jesus nor Paul taught that Rome had thereby lost its legitimacy to govern and rule, the society would have been healthier if these activities were, at the very least,

---

17. A. R. Vidler, *The Church in an Age of Revolution* (Harmondsworth: Penguin, 1974), p. 58.

discouraged. In this connection it may be possible for the Christian to make common cause with all kinds of people to argue in the public arena for the wisdom of forbidding such behaviour.

The 'symbiosis' of church and society

Before turning to some areas of practical application, attention needs to be drawn to the way in which the state of the church can impact upon society and vice versa. When the church falls under God's chastening hand, this may well have implications for the wider society. When the Lord sent the storm because of Jonah's disobedience, all the sailors on the ship, not to mention all the other boats which may have been in the vicinity, were caught up in the same storm. On the other hand, because of God's good hand upon Paul, all who sailed with him were graciously protected by God's hand (Acts 27:24). Sometimes the Lord will chasten his people by allowing things to spiral out of control in society and to impact adversely upon the people of God. This is surely what happened at the time of the exile and is referred to in Habakkuk and Jeremiah. By the same token, therefore, when God is richly blessing his Church, the world around may well share in blessings and benefits. This is surely part of the explanation for the different results which were achieved by the Clapham Sect as compared with what happened at the time of the Restoration. In the former case, huge swathes of the nation had been influenced by the eighteenth-century evangelical awakening. There were benefits to society at large which resulted from that work of God. By contrast, the societies for the reformation of manners, which preceded that period of revival, could not boast the same successes. The reverse is also true: judgments on nations may well have implications for the people of God within those nations.

It is, of course, important to point out that this world is always 'mixed': blessings and judgments mingle together and, for the church, even chastening is a mercy, albeit a severe mercy. This means that in *some* areas of public life part of the Christian heritage of a nation may be being dismantled, while in other areas things are being erected which are very much in line with Christian teaching.

Recent years have seen, for example, a greater concern on the part of many first-world governments for dealing with third-world poverty, while greater protection has been given to people suffering from disabilities. There has also been a wholesome concern for the welfare of children, even though the pendulum has undoubtedly swung too far in the direction of a 'child-centred' society. This last point notwithstanding, these developments are positive and wholesome. The fact that they have taken place at the very time when other parts of the Christian heritage have been dismantled simply underlines the fact that the world is 'mixed'. Similarly, even when Christian influence in the past led to very good laws being enacted, it cannot be denied that all was not sweetness and light: the world was just as 'mixed' then as now.

One of the implications of what has been said in the previous two paragraphs is the underlining of a point to which reference has been made earlier: namely, that one has to seek to understand one's context. 'Understanding the times' is crucially important in this whole area of life. If such understanding is harnessed to an ability to present a coherent and unified approach to matters of public policy which can be applied to a given context, there will be greater likelihood of Christians moving from the back foot onto the front foot. Where positive initiatives are taken in areas where society can see the benefits, there is a greater chance of society not dismissing the Christian voice as narrowly bigoted when it is heard in the public arena arguing for the retention of the Christian heritage.

Practical considerations

The first thing to say is that a lot of political activity is not *directly* concerned with religious or moral issues. Secondly, the political parties are really quite broad coalitions, which identify themselves around a number of areas of agreement. A certain amount of compromise is inevitable within any party. This means that a candidate must identify himself or herself with the party manifesto. It is important for Christians who elect an MP who happens to be a Christian to realize this. In the third place, an MP or a local councillor must represent *all* his constituents. Let us imagine that an MP represents an area which has had a very high unemployment rate. Homes are being repossessed and people are moving from the area in search of work. A property developer is keen to develop an industrial estate and, in conjunction with that, is intent on developing a large out-of-town shopping complex that will both serve the local population and draw in shoppers from outlying districts. Both of these developments will be a shot in the arm for local employment and for the local economy. Public development funding is available to help with such a project, but there are other, competing projects in a different part of the country. Each region needs to put forward the case to have the development in its area, and the support of the local MP and local councillors is crucial in this. Now, it will be a feature of the shopping complex that it will be open for most of a Sunday, while the biggest employer on the industrial site will be a brewery. The MP is a man who regards the Lord's Day as sacred and who has been very concerned at the aggressive advertising and marketing of the brewery which will be on the site.

If the MP is less than enthusiastic about these developments because of his own convictions, and the public funding goes elsewhere, it might be thought that he has failed to do his best to deal with one of the major social problems in his constituency. He will not get re-elected next time, or may even be deselected by his party. On the other hand, if he does a good job and the development goes ahead, local Christians who voted for him may feel that he has sacrificed his principles and betrayed the Christian portion of the electorate. A politician's lot is not a happy one.

There will also be many areas where there is no specifically *Christian* answer to a problem. Is a registered system of title to land superior to an unregistered system? What does the Bible say? Which is more Christian, an income tax or a purchase tax? Some might argue for the latter because thereby saving is encouraged and irresponsible spending discouraged, and incentives are given to the workforce. On the other hand, some Christians would say that an income tax has more in common with the Old Testament tithe and is fairer in that purchase taxes are more likely to hit the poorer people. Or what about inheritance tax? Given that the Scripture warns of the dangers which a large inheritance can give, might this be an argument for not raising thresholds of inheritance tax? On the other hand, given that the Scriptures commend the laying up by parents for their children, and given the difficulty many young people have in buying a property, might this not suggest that thresholds should be raised? Could there conceivably be a Christian political party with the specifically Christian answer to this question? Surely not! In fact, might the way in which different Christians approach these issues have as much to do with their own socio-economic status and background as with the interpretation and application of passages of Scripture?

The Christian will want to do good to all people, especially those of the household of faith (Gal. 6:10). While all Christians will have this same goal, the *ways and means* of achieving that goal may well vary from Christian to Christian, just as they will from party to party. Two Christians may both be committed to the ideal of full employment. One may feel that for the State artificially to assist in this realm will, in the long haul, not only damage the economy but also – for that very reason – damage employment prospects. The other Christian may feel that unemployment is such a terrible thing that a government is justified in putting taxpayers' money into employment schemes. The difference between the two Christians has as much to do with ways and means as it does with goals. Politics is full of ways-and-means issues.

While some may well question Gordon Wenham's emphasis on vegetarianism, every Christian would surely agree with his plea that animals be farmed in a humane way and without cruelty. But this could mean that the price of meat would rocket, the gap between rich and poorer grow greater with respect to standards of living, and farmers be faced with insolvency. A Christian MP in a rural constituency who ignored the plight of the farmers might thereby be ousted at an election and get a name for having greater concern for animals than for people, and greater concern for animals than for the farmers and for those who would be unable to afford to buy meat. He might be replaced at the next election by a much more hard-nosed individual who has no scruples as to the way in which farm animals are treated. The Christian MP, mindful that politics is the art of the possible, may well have to bide his time and seek incremental changes.

Is it the job of Government to provide a health service? Some Christians would answer in the negative, while others would be uncomprehending at such a response. And what of the common European currency? Is there a 'Christian' position on this? Given that as a matter of fact there is probably as much diversity of opinion amongst Christians as others over these issues; given that these kinds of issues – the NHS, the economy, relationships with Europe – are major electoral matters; and given that British political life is organized on the basis of the party system: given these things, is it not obvious that a Christian who wants to 'speak for Jesus' in the public forum but who is clueless about these kinds of issues is not the sort of person who will be an effective politician? What this means is that there cannot be a 'single issue' approach to political matters.

Another area where Christians may adopt unworkable positions is with respect to punishment, especially capital punishment. In recent years many convictions for murder have been overturned by the Court of Appeal (Criminal Division) as being unsafe. Were capital punishment to be reintroduced, it is not beyond the realm of possibility that jurors who would convict someone indicted for murder where the punishment would be imprisonment might well hesitate to convict where a conviction would mean sending someone to their death. The result could be that some who should be convicted would be acquitted. Would this be a desirable state of affairs? Surely not! A Christian MP who believes in capital punishment for murder might well, therefore, oppose the reintroduction of capital punishment for this reason.

The Hebrew word for 'wisdom' can carry a range of meanings. It is clear from the Wisdom Literature of the Old Testament that it is sometimes used in the sense of 'skill'. Ruling and governing involve 'skill'. Being a Christian does not necessarily make one a more wise, in the sense of 'skilled', politician than a non-Christian, any more than being a Christian automatically makes one a more skilled car mechanic, accountant or lawyer.

The foregoing examples surely demonstrate that politics is indeed the art of the possible and that compromise is essential in a parliamentary democracy. But is not Jesus king? And do not principles come before pragmatism? Of course Jesus is king and of course principles come first. But it is possible to believe that his kingship, while requiring that all bow to him as Lord, does not mean that every Christian politician must, in his or her every public utterance, insist that every other politician accept the crown rights of King Jesus. It may, rather, mean that, just as Daniel could serve under Nebuchadnezzar, and Erastus could hold a senior public position in the city of Corinth (Rom. 16:23b), so Christian politicians should seek to make the best of the situation in which they find themselves, ever seizing every opportunity to speak for the Lord, even as Daniel did in his situation (Dan. 4:27).

Conclusion

'We don't do God,' said Alistair Campbell. Had Daniel had a press secretary, it would have been absurd to have made such a statement: everyone knew that Daniel 'did God' (Dan. 6:5). The personal integrity and piety of Daniel were such that everyone knew that his whole life was bound up with faithfulness to his God. Perhaps his greatest achievements were those which were wrought on his knees, as he pleaded before God for his people (Dan. 9). Certainly, in a 'can do' age, where the church often mistakes performance for power, there is an urgent need for God's people to be seeking him in prayer for his rich blessing upon his church, for his mercy to be shown to his people and to the nations. We desperately need to learn the importance of that which characterized Paul's ministry:

> The weapons we fight with are not the weapons of the world. On the contrary, they have divine power to demolish strongholds. We demolish arguments and every pretension that sets itself up against the knowledge of God, and we take captive every thought to make it obedient to Christ.
> (2 Corinthians 10:4–5)

It is when the church of Christ has lived in the light of this teaching that she has seen the greatest advances, the kingdom of God has been extended in the world, and the welfare of the city has been promoted. Westminster can only benefit when Jerusalem becomes a praise in the earth.

© Stephen Clark, 2005